Early Postmodernism

a boundary 2 book

Paul A. Bové, Editor

Early Postmodernism

Foundational Essays

Duke University Press   Durham and London

1995

© 1995 Duke University Press

All rights reserved

Printed in the United States of America on acid-free paper ∞

Designed by Cherie Holma Westmoreland

Typeset in Trump Mediaeval with Futura display by Tseng Information Systems, Inc.

Library of Congress Cataloging-in-Publication Data appear on the last printed page of this book.

These essays originally were published in the following issues of *boundary 2:* William V. Spanos, "The Detective and the Boundary: Some Notes on the Postmodern Literary Imagination," 1, 1 (Fall 1972): 147–168. David Antin, "Modernism and Postmodernism: Approaching the Present in American Poetry," 1, 1 (Fall 1972): 98–133. Ihab Hassan, "The New Gnosticism: Speculations on an Aspect of the Postmodern Mind," 1, 3 (Spring 1973): 547–570. Charles Altieri, "From Symbolist Thought to Immanence: The Ground of Postmodern American Poetics," 1, 3 (Spring 1973): 605–642. Catharine R. Stimpson, "Charles Olson: Preliminary Images," 2, 1 & 2 (Fall 1973/Winter 1974): 151–172. Harold Bloom, "The Dialectics of Literary Tradition," 2, 3 (Spring 1974): 528–538. Hélène Cixous, "At Circe's, or, The Self-Opener," 3, 2 (Winter 1975): 387–397. Barry Alpert, "Post-Modern Oral Poetry: Buckminster Fuller, John Cage, and David Antin," 3, 3 (Spring 1975): 665–682. Joseph N. Riddel, "From Heidegger to Derrida to Chance: Doubling and (Poetic) Language," 4, 2 (Winter 1976): 571–592. Gerald Gillespie, "Scientific Discourse and Postmodernity: Francis Bacon and the Empirical Birth of 'Revision,'" 7, 2 (Winter 1979): 119–148. Cornel West, "Nietzsche's Prefiguration of Postmodern American Philosophy," 9, 3/10, 1 (Spring/Fall 1981): 241–270.

Contents

Paul A. Bové
Preface 1

William V. Spanos
The Detective and the Boundary Some Notes on
the Postmodern Literary Imagination 17

David Antin
Modernism and Postmodernism
Approaching the Present in American Poetry 40

Ihab Hassan
The New Gnosticism Speculations on an Aspect
of the Postmodern Mind 77

Charles Altieri
From Symbolist Thought to Immanence
The Ground of Postmodern American Poetics 100

Catharine R. Stimpson
Charles Olson Preliminary Images 140

Harold Bloom
The Dialectics of Literary Tradition 163

Hélène Cixous
At Circe's, or, The Self-Opener 175

Barry Alpert
Postmodern Oral Poetry Buckminster Fuller, John Cage,
and David Antin 188

Joseph N. Riddel
From Heidegger to Derrida to Chance
Doubling and (Poetic) Language 207

Gerald Gillespie
Scientific Discourse and Postmodernity Francis Bacon and
the Empirical Birth of "Revision" 232

Cornel West
**Nietzsche's Prefiguration of Postmodern
American Philosophy** 265

Index 291

Preface
Literary Postmodernism

Although the final history of postmodernism has yet to be written, critics generally agree that the movement first began in architecture, or, at least, that the term first began to appear in architectural work and theory to describe the new movements represented by, among others, the reborn Philip Johnson, Michael Graves, John Portman, James Stirling, and Robert Venturi. Culminating in the magisterial work of Fredric Jameson, critics have developed this architectural usage into an extensive and complex narrative of postmodernism as the cultural manifestation, as the "logic," of "late-capital." Jameson has also provided us with carefully discriminated analyses of many schools of thought about postmodernism, linking these schools to various ideological attitudes and positions within postmodernism itself. Postmodernism is like other cultural moments in the history of capital: various political elements within the postmodern develop multiple discourses to represent their claims upon newly emerging forms of economic organization, labor distribution, and technical means of production. Jameson's achievement consists, in part at least, in mapping these contests, in reading them to discover their systemic consistencies and the differences in their relations, the "logics" according to which they organize themselves. He also strives to include or master them within a Marxist thought that analytically reveals the major productive elements as well as the crises, the fault lines, of the moment, especially as these can be highlighted in the conflicting interpretations of postmodernism.

The literary academy has offered some of the important competing theories but, more important, it has itself been greatly changed by and within postmodernism—although I think it would be an exaggeration to say the academy has significantly contributed to the major economic and social transformations that make up the postmodern. In postmodernism, the university finds itself in very different relations to other major institutions than it had been for many years prior to the effective changes which often pass under the term "postmodern." One marker of this new set of relations is the pronounced decline in the importance of literature within the language and literature departments in American universities, especially perhaps, at the so-called leading institutions. Many distinguished scholar-critics of a number of different generations now recognize that literature, taken as a privileged canon of Euro-American texts, has lost its focal position in English Studies, but, having been initially displaced by theory from the most prominent place in advanced curricula, literature retreats from prominence even more as the literary academy moves into the areas of research and teaching broadly designated in the United States as "literacy and/or cultural studies."

There is some irony to the fact that Jameson, whose own original formation in literary studies so emphatically enables the development of theory and the discourses of postmodernism, helped, in so doing, to enable as well a set of practices and modes of work that have moved attention away from literature as even a source for habits of thought about language systems, other media, and cultural practices. (There is nothing that upsets specialized media scholars more than lit. crit. types who try to "interpret" movies and TV.) It is now not unheard of for new Ph.D.s to emerge from advanced and distinguished departments of language and literature with virtually no competence of any special sort in literature—defined by period, author, genre—or in literary criticism or the history of literary criticism. Unless one expands the notion of literature to include newly recognized objects of cultural analysis, such as cookbooks and Bugs Bunny cartoons, the term itself no longer usefully designates the proper area of study, especially among younger scholars or those in or approaching middle age, who have led the movements into theory, literacy, and cultural studies.

Justified opposition to the once standard exclusive curriculm of Euro-American writing extends into an opposition to literary study itself. Having been expelled from its privileged position by those sympathetic to the political needs of closely studying the workings of mass culture and marginal groups and their productions, the careful study of literature now often appears—and is sometimes derided as—mere "cultural conservatism," as a reactionary effort to reestablish literature's old ideological privilege and academic position, an enterprise hopelessly outdated by the general disregard a nonliterate culture has for verbal complexity and "high" aesthetic accomplishment. These changes do not and have not prevented a number of colleagues and departments from continuing to work in traditional areas and in traditional ways; the Reagan years were a time of significant neoconservative reaction among professors who denounced avant-garde "scams" while carrying on, sometimes profitably, an intellectual agenda suitable to those then holding state power. It is not uncommon, even today, to hear colleagues lament the fact that students do not take "straight" literature courses—the ambiguity of "straight" is marvelously unexplored—and, indeed, to regret other colleagues' refusal to take seriously—except as a reason to rejoice— students' desertion of literature. Of course, even this story should be given more nuance; there are, after all, distinctions to be made between, on the one hand, the normal practice of canonical literary instruction against which most colleagues protest, and, on the other hand, the sadly neglected efforts of colleagues whose originality lies precisely in trying to extend the literary critical project into terms important to analysis of the emerging world order. Undeniably there are students who do not make literature the subject of their work because they will not find employment or professional success; of course, this is merely the opposite side of a coin that for too long made impossible the serious study of anything other than "literature."

Critics and historians need to make symptomatic analyses of these changes; they might find, among other things, that in a global economy where national cultures are no longer economic or political prerequisites for capital's intensification, rationalization, and expansion, states and transnational corporations will no longer fund universities to produce or sustain those cultures and their literatures—at least not in the old ways. The fact that effective transnational cultures have emerged, over and against previously dominant national cultures, means, of course, that alternative cultures will increasingly have to be looked for in localities and regions not fully saturated by the emerging global cultures. There is no reason to assume that these cultures are literate, and there is every reason to assume that their aim is not the production of national identity. In this new set of relations and political needs, national literary study can and will have little (especially financial) basis.

Jameson's great work on postmodernism, which must remain for now the touchstone of all thinking in the area, comes rather late in the academic movement toward the study of this topic. The mere fact that Jameson can categorize and analyze the relations within the discourses of postmodernism indicates his powerful belatedness; it allows him to embrace and transcend the given terms. His efforts rest on the most comprehensive grasp of Marxism among living American critics; they emerge equally, however, from serious engagement with literature and the literary. Similarly, the essays in this volume, all chosen from the first decade of *boundary 2*, when it was edited by William V. Spanos and, from 1972 to 1977, coedited by the Canadian novelist, Robert Kroetsch— these essays, although forcefully inflected by theory, predominately reside in the literary and find in literature the very categories that make possible and demand the thinking of "the postmodern." This volume illuminates how reconsidering the literary, bringing literature into new relations with theory and history, developed from a perhaps too-often merely intuitive sense that "something had changed," that the modern was now "over." There was a sense that it had been replaced by a "postmodern" that appeared in newer literary writing and in elements of past literature that, after the postmoderns, could now be read to develop elements that modernist ideology and historical critical practice had either excluded or occluded.

Early critical essays on "postmodern literature," or essays that, drawing on literary phenomena, attempted to theorize the "postmodern," were in an important way both modernist and belated. Unlike most recent criticism, that is, from the mid-1980s and continuing through our time, the writings of critics like William V. Spanos, Charles Altieri, David Antin, Joseph Riddell, Ihab Hassan, Catharine Stimpson, and so on often derived their own critical practice from literature contemporary to those critics themselves. In this, they are perhaps better classified, adapting Alan Wilde's thinking about the novel, as "late modernists." Murray Krieger once called the defining critics of High Modernism "the new apologists for poetry" precisely because they saw their collective task as winning legitimacy and an audience for the new and difficult modern poets from whose works these critics drew scholarly, ideological, and sometimes religious inspiration. Postmodern critics, by contrast, have less often drawn upon their literary contemporaries and, indeed, have often derided the traditional prominence assigned to literature by modern and late modern scholars.

In the early 1970s, though, critics like those represented in this volume set out to revise the modernist conceptions of literature and literary tradition often under the sign of certain roughly contemporary writers who were taken as "postmodern" and so privileged to offer guidance in seeing how the present world and the world of (Western) writing had changed. Also, the early postmodern critics were determined to follow the aesthetic, historical, and political experiments of their models in an effort to reimagine the tradition, often discovering forgotten works, defining "classics" in new and utterly "absurd" terms—we should recall the importance of the theater of the absurd and of the existentialists, especially of Sartre in this context—and narrating the stories of literary geneses and transformations in terms much different from those found in, for example, Wellek, Warren, Auerbach, or Trilling.

It seems to me now that the actual historical location of these early postmodern critics is the 1950s. I say this not to join in the debate over when the term first appeared or when the "structures" we now recognize as postmodern first emerged. I mean, rather, to suggest that these critics found their intellectual, imaginative, and political resources in the works of that time. And I say this with an awareness that certain of these "post-war" figures, such as Beckett, William Carlos Williams, and Sartre, had produced important work before and during the war, indeed, as in the case of Beckett's *Watt*, Sartre's *Nausea*, or Williams's *Paterson*, work that is very important to these early postmodern critics. But this body of work influenced the generation of American scholar-critics who, for the most part, received their work in the context of the fifties and the writings produced then that showed marks of influence; one thinks of Robbe-Grillet, Kerouac, and Charles Olson. Such claims fly in the face of established opinion and certain apparent facts, above all the relationship between the first literary critical discussions of postmodern writing and of the Vietnam War, the counterculture, and the civil rights and women's movements. It is nonetheless worth suggesting that early postmodern critics, such as Spanos, Riddel, Antin, and Altieri, for all their profound differences, found the literary exempla, the visionary critical problems of their work in postwar writers such as Beckett and William Carlos Williams and his (and Pound's) progeny among American poets. Of course, as we see in Spanos's work in particular, the events of the sixties compelled a rethinking of literary and critical culture in a way that gave new prominence to fifties writers who had not had academic status (at Columbia University, as late as 1978, I was told by a distinguished senior colleague with close connections to Modernism that Beckett was not a "major figure" and a "senior seminar" could not be dedicated to his work) and also demanded a revision of the major practices, theories, and institutional structures of a literary academy largely formed in the critical shadow and interests of Modernism. For some time, in other words, the academy's discussion of the postmodern teetered between two models: contemporary literature, particularly the "open forms" of post-Williams poetry and the broken narratives of Beckett and the "new novels" (figures like Charles Olson, John Barth, Robbe-Grillet, and Thomas Pynchon come to mind), and contemporary theory, particularly structuralism, poststructuralism, and "European Marxism" (Lévi-Strauss, Derrida, Foucault, Althusser, and Raymond Williams are examples). Despite the efforts of certain influential critical figures, such as Altieri and Marjorie Perloff, to keep the focus on the literary, or of Harold Bloom to adapt a theory of literature from a gnosis of poetry and psychoanalysis, or of Joseph Riddel to adapt deconstructive notions of "literariness" to the reading of American poetry, gradually the emphasis on theory won the day, and the special originary focus on literature gave way to what we now see is, in the United States, a merger of postmodern studies and cultural studies with a strong vocational element of "composition" or "literacy studies."

Spanos makes the Eliotic argument that the failure of the Modernist consensus within the literary academy is a sort of fall into time, into history. Spanos is not alone, of course, in his emphasis on the fact that the various postwar schools of criticism—American Studies, New Criticism, literary history, myth criticism, and so on—were all versions of a larger "ahistorical" or even "antihistorical" paradigm that we now identify with the national, imperial problems manifest in Cold War efforts at containment. Not only did the critics who saw this "fall" turn to recent writing for a way of grasping its fundamental elements or, if you will, the hidden failures of the Modernist consensus, but importantly their students thought of literature as an aspect of cultural comprehension, value production, and societal reimagining. To put it briefly, in their own late modernism these critics and their students were not yet illiterate. Illiteracy, as I understand it in this context, involves life in a society that does not assign literature an important—let alone primary—role in the formation of language, consciousness, representation, culture, or political relations. In this context I exclude from the notion, "literature," all those mass-market products studied and sold as forms of popular culture. The matter could be put another way. Illiteracy arrives with new orders of relation among language, market, state, and knowledge. One could speak of the end of the artisanal-liberal model of individual style, of proprietary authorship marketed by highly individualized "houses" such as Scribners, and of its replacement with machine-produced montage that makes an ironic success of certain of the great antimodernist elements admired by early thinkers of postmodernism: surface rather than depth, gaiety rather than gravity, difference rather than universality, and so on.

If early conceptions of postmodernism were still strongly inflected as "literary," there were strong philosophical as well as political tones as well.[1] Given that these essays, reprinted from *boundary 2* when it was still subtitled *a journal of postmodern literature*, embody a rather unique moment in recent intellectual history, it is worth stressing that we do not see in them a coalescence but rather an intersection of these tones and inflections. Significantly, to think about postmodernism or to think in a postmodern style—and these essays attempt to do both—did not necessarily mean to adapt any one given political or philosophical, that is, theoretical position. It is somewhat surprising to look back at these materials and see that the editors so little attempted to limit the political range of thinking about the postmodern. Ihab Hassan, for example, gives us here a strong instance of what has become known as a fairly conservative, paradoxically "status quo" critical vision of the postmodern. Altieri, drawing heavily upon then recent poetic achievements of a certain sort—let us say the school of Williams and not Stevens—attempts to regenerate a model of meaning-production that we now see begins his career-long effort to understand and defend a humanistic vision at odds with both the antihumanism of much recent criticism and the "dehumanized" culture of post-Fordist American society. David Antin, with Spanos's explicit support, developed the American tradition of Whitmanic orality in specific opposition to theoretical emphases upon the priority of writing over speech, a priority asserted strongly by Barthes, Foucault, Derrida, and others. These positions, different from each other, differ as well from the radical "destruction" begun then by Spanos and carried out relentlessly by him since that time.[2] Oddly, despite the pluralism of this editorial project, a project designed it now seems to give space to and to foment thinking about the postmodern from all angles—oddly, there is little early serious thought about or representation of the conditional facts of the women's movement or the civil rights movement—or the writings of women and minorities. It is very significant, though, that important women scholars—clearly understood as feminists—would contribute to the general debate about the postmodern carried out in these pages. Catharine Stimpson, perhaps not then as well known as a politically astute feminist as now, nonetheless found *boundary 2* a congenial place for her work—as early as the second volume of the new journal's then not secure existence. It is, nonetheless, clear that the actual importance of women's struggles had not yet been fully taken into writing about postmodernism—either as a condition for thinking it or as a mode of thought that could and would add immensely to the understanding of the phenomena called "postmodern."[3]

When feminist critical thinking asserts itself in the mid-1970s, its appearance marks the end of the original effort to think postmodernism as literary. But even at that time, women's involvement in this early thinking of postmodernism had a complex genealogy. Cixous, for example, makes her first appearance in this context not as a "French feminist" and feminist writer, but as a revisionist critic of Joyce, as herself, in other words, an explicit heir of the Moderns. Cixous, we recall, wrote a massive and influential study of Joyce as the thesis for her *doctorat d'état*, a text translated into English as *The Exile of James Joyce*. In their role as critics rethinking Modernism—a defining gesture of early postmodern efforts, the gesture of rethinking the canon—women such as Stimpson and Cixous (who later come to be known precisely as "feminists") share in the early effort to make sense of postmodern literature and culture. It is worth noting this fact not only because it reminds us of the fact that feminist thinking came belatedly into postmodernism as a self-conscious and programmatic project—despite the fact that women's struggles were central to the casting aside of masculist Modernism. It also recalls how complex were the original literary critical inflections of "postmodern" and how flexible and expansive those inflections could be. Moreover, it reminds us that the work done under the term was highly fragmented, which beneficially permitted new if belated efforts to succeed.

By claiming that the early postmodern literary critics are better named "late moderns," I mean, in part, that they hoped, futilely and despite this fragmentation, to make the term "postmodern" reach as widely as the term "modern" which it was meant to displace. Indeed, there are still traces of such an effort in the way younger critics, after Jameson's work, choose to draw as many different aspects of current academic criticism as possible under the "postmodern" umbrella. This ambition has led to numerous efforts to think through the gesture as, for example, when we try to understand if the "post" in "postmodernism" is the same as the "post" in "postcolonialism," and so on. There is, though, I think a difference between the early postmodern critics' efforts and more recent scholars expansion of the term. Largely the difference can be caught in a contrast between Spanos and Jameson.

Each of these critics extends the term, "postmodern," to global proportions, but each in a very different way—and this despite certain common sources, such as their crucial formative interests in Sartre and modern fiction. Spanos's early thinking about the postmodern, greatly influenced by the existentialists, Sartre, and the absurdists, extends the term through the discourse of Heideggerean ontology to circumscribe not only the entirety of then-contemporary culture; but the ontological emphasis obliged a historical revisionism as well.[4] Spanos, for example, could adapt the term to reconsider older literatures (allowing the claims that Homer and Shakespeare and Melville are postmodern) as well as contemporary literatures of different national linguistic origin without needing to concede that particular differences of context or tradition constrained the applicability of the concept or, to put it another way, the unsuitability of the instance as an example of the larger postmodern.

Jameson, who also emerges from literary criticism and shares with Spanos and others of their generation an extended critical engagement with Sartre, develops his version of the concept "horizontally," if you will. Jameson reads postmodernism as the cultural logic of late capital and as an effort to embrace the globe within a nonhistorical historicism, within markets homogenized by instantaneity and simultaneity; it is of the essence that this postmodernism attempts to encompass and represent itself as successfully embracing all the phenomena of the cultural world, even those elements of resistance or alterity that the market sooner rather than later sucks into its own system of signification and distribution or, we might claim, produces as one of its own effects.

The character of these different totalizing gestures—Jameson and Spanos—recalls those concrete universals, verbal icons, and liberal imaginations so powerfully materialized and exercised by the New Critics and their (sometimes antagonistic) contemporaries. Ignoring the differences between the earlier and later critics or among all of them would be foolish if one tried for a serious history of this period.[5] Taking up their evident similarities, however, we see that the academic critical— we can no longer call it the literary profession—has changed fundamentally: it has fragmented to the point where the very idea that its work might be carried out under some nearly all-encompassing rubric seems absurd. (I say this because the unity provided by the phrase "cultural studies" is only apparent.) This fragmentation has its corollaries in the oft-spoken of breakdown in subjectivity and dislocation in the economy. It has critical support from many theories, especially those developed against totalization of an empirical or dialectical, that is, Hegelian sort. Most important, however, and this differentiates it from the fragmentation present in early writings about the postmodern, it has its primary relation to the capital formations of a global economy intent upon marketing not primarily by nation-state or region, but by "niches" that exist as targets of advertising, distribution, and life-style.[6] These niches exist as a result of capital's new distribution of wealth, work, and unemployment in class elements spread around the global and not contained exclusively or even primarily within national or regional economies.[7] It no longer makes sense to speak of a "labor aristocracy": any such aristocracy would have to be seen to stand in relation to certain modes of production globally constructed and distributed and not within national labor markets. It would be fruitful to study the speed and autonomy of finance in relation to nation-states in an effort to understand the reality that provokes this newer form of intellectual fragmentation and to differentiate it from the earlier fragmentation the first postmodern critics called a "crisis." Earlier efforts to link phenomena within the broadest categories of conceptual reach, to discover either dialectical or ontological unities and struggles within unity, have given way to projects carried out as if there were, in fact, no linkages among the apparently isolated elements of postmodern life—identities, subject positions, ethnicities, unemployment, sexualities, the end of thinking, and so on. New relations of power, markets, global semioses, and technological instantaneities of value shatter the efficacy of old. More important, perhaps, they make difficult the emergence of needed new thinking that might make lucid the existing relations that produce or encourage forces that try to naturalize postmodern capitalist globality.

The early efforts to produce a theory and interpretation of postmodernism resulted in several classical essays, some of which are collected here, and began a series of distinguished career trajectories that reveal a great deal about the academy and recent intellectual history. Reading them again might offer us as many new resources as reasons for objection. They embody an enormous innovative and analytic energy even though they do not sufficiently reflect the importance of the women's and civil rights' movements nor the writings of nonwhite males. As late as 1980, for example, Cornel West could adduce a discussion of philosophical vacuity to the circumstances of postmodernism, and even though we can see in this essay traces of his important philosophical-critical work of the 1980s, we see no more than the slightest prefigurations of his less scholarly, more overtly public and journalistic writing of the 1990s. Taken together, these essays, like West's and Stimpson's, bring feminism and civil rights into the context of postmodernism, or like Gillespie's essay, they bring postmodernism to bear primarily on the effort to test historical sciences; these essays inaugurate the last critical movement that did not make central either the politics of identity or the central fact of resistance. Yet they represent and reflect upon certain immediate historical political crises, the consequences of which are still with us. Spanos's often reprinted essay on the "detective and the boundary" emerges from the crises of Vietnam and Watergate; it shows the way in applying literary critical method to nonliterary texts, especially well exemplified in his later reading of the Pentagon Papers. Taken together these essays reveal that literary education not only enabled powerful intellectual responses to crises induced by political efforts to coerce unity but also built strong links at precisely those times when the emergence of new waves of resistance—to war, to segregation, to masculism—afforded some optimism to those engaged in efforts to understand and to change the existing war-machine. In other words, these essays remain important as historical documents marking the origins of much that is now valued in criticism, in recalling to mind the genealogical relation between today's nonliterate criticism and modernist literary acculturation, and in provoking thought about the resources for opposition still present in being literate as well as the gap or lack that might result from cutting criticism off from literate projects. Of course, there is little critics can do to restore traditional literacy to mainstream electronic cultures; yet the literate traditions, now precisely relegated to the few in a way not seen since the days of Irish monks in the so-called Dark Ages, still contain reserves available for thought. The populist turn away from literature and the academic turn that dissolves the reserves in the acids of current bureaucratic and political invective both impoverish the mind and society. The decision, for example, to circumscribe literature within the (porous) confines of the "New Historicism"—the paradigmatic academic equivalent to the faux historicism of postmodern architecture—instances the mistaken effort to forget the past and ironically the critical origins of intellectual analyses and polemics in the often justly condemned Eurocentrism of canonical work. The point is not a hard one to make or to grasp. These early essays on postmodernism, texts that have been formative in the discussion of the entire concept, depend upon an education in literature, emerge from a study of literature as a marker—a very early marker, a leading indicator—of the transformations in society, economy, and culture. The literariness of these essays and their authors, the transitional nature of this late-sixties, early-seventies moment, a moment when rebellious students looked to poetry, when Malcolm X drew transformative power from learning to read in a traditional role for literature and prisoners—this must not be forgotten in current populism that opposes fundamentalism to progressive resistance.

We might put the matter another way: these early critics, late moderns though they may be, comprehensively affirmed their existence;

they were active thinkers trying to assert and establish their own values in the face of established academic failure and immense crises of literacy. In this they were and are tragic and postmodern—but not yet gay. Such Nietzscheanism is important because it recalls a tradition of concern about resistance as a category of thought and being; from Lucretius to Spinoza to Nietzsche "resistance" is unworthy of those who affirm life. Indeed, the critical reading of all human action that takes directions other than those of the so-called dominant are themselves too easily assumed and transvalued into "resistance"—a move that negates their force as alternatives to the deadliness of the "cultural logic of late capital." Naming all these gestures—whether of literature, music, religion, sexual practice—as forms of "resistance" changes them into reactions, a transformation postmodern critics should realize they perform with the same or similar ease as market researchers and other more immediate and effective agents of capital.

Despite the efforts of many critic-teachers to subsume them within new solutions resting upon the supposedly more advanced positions of identity, subject position, and postliterariness, the various crises registered by the critics whose work is sampled in this volume of foundational essays still exist. The crises are now harder to see and, of course, newer ones have come into focus. The early postmodern critics, adapting the modern critics of modernism such as Nietzsche and Marx, drawing upon the complex skills of decoding, of lucid apperception made possible—but not necessary—by reading, simplified the problems but were always aware of what used to be called complicity and worried endlessly about the need to avoid "co-optation." Such concepts are now too crude especially when deployed negatively by such popularizers as Gerald Graff. Spanos, following Heidegger, and Altieri, following Williams, serve as examples of one critical virtue lost upon many: these critics, in the name of "generosity" or "letting-be," recognized the violence professors can and often do especially in those cases where they desire to make others do work in the name of their own vision, in service of their own agendas. R. P. Blackmur, himself the greatest of late modern critics, thematized this concern as humility and humiliation. The intellect must always be humble and critical work, properly carried out, should endlessly humiliate that intellect, calling it back to the necessity of its own humility.[8] In the face of something clearly emerging but equally clearly unknown these critics practiced humility. Afraid to harm by too close an embrace they created and, for the most part, preserved their creations by not allowing them the violence of their visions, of their own role as the servants of the concept. They restrained their gestures from the violence of certainty—Keats's "negative capability," we recall, was a slogan for these writers—because they knew the emergent to be beyond their reach and felt it should always be kept beyond the perspicacity of the university. This is a lesson rooted in their literariness. If some of these critics sometimes went on to become combative, to engage in struggle, and to forget the fact of humility and forgot how to learn the lessons of humiliation, their original writing at least offers an example of thought not common in an age of virtue, polemic, and populism.

Notes

1. It would be worth exploring if and how Modernism's critical, aesthetic attachments to plastic form might have prepared the way for literary criticism's easy adaptation of the architectural term, "postmodern."

2. Spanos devoted considerable energy to rethinking orality but he did so in service of his larger project of "destruction" in which "speech," understood as *Rede* rendered a sense of Heidegger that Spanos believed Derrida's deconstruction, and especially that of Derrida's American followers, such as Jonathan Culler, often neglected. It was apparent even then that Spanos was mostly concerned with an "existential" element in the Heidegger of *Being and Time* that was not central, as such, to the American deconstructive project.

3. The first of *boundary 2*'s successful "special issues" devoted to "feminism" appeared in 1984 and, under the guest editorship of Verena Conley, gave considerable attention to French theoretical feminism. Even at that time, however, it was the literary as well as theoretical production of Hélène Cixous that was central to the volume, much more so, for example, than Derrida's emerging discourse of "woman."

4. One cannot over emphasize the importance of Sartre to Spanos's thinking about postmodernism and Heidegger. Spanos seems to have come to Heidegger through a reading of Sartre and the theater of the absurd. In fact, the Sartre that influenced Spanos was *Being and Nothingness* and *Nausea*. Spanos, whose earlier work was in seventeenth-century and modern poetry—a classic modern critical formation—had been focused on the problems of immanence from his dissertation on sacramental time and verse drama. His first forays into what we would now recognize as postmodernism were a long critical essay on New Criticism as an irresponsibly atemporal practice and modernist ideology and an equally substantial piece attempting to derive nonmodernist, that is, nonplastic or "absurd" temporal structures from the plays of Ionesco, Genet, Beckett and others caught under Martin Esslin's slogan, "theater of

the absurd." See Spanos, "Modern Literary Criticism and the Spatialization of Time: An Existential Critique," *JAAC* 29 (1970): 87–104; and, "Modern Drama and the Aristotelian Tradition: The Forma Imperatives of Absurd Time," *Contemporary Literature* 12 (1971): 345–72. It is worth emphasizing that these essays prepare the ground as well as reveal many of the sources not only for the often cited and reprinted essay collected here, "The Detective and the Boundary," but that they deal with literary and philosophical materials that, with the exception of Kierkegaard, are no longer prominent in Spanos's writing.

5. It is certainly worth adding here that the concept of postmodern has been haunted by the problems associated with periodization. Spanos's work, for instance, along with that of Riddel and others influenced by Derrida and Paul de Man, crucially resisted "periodizing" as a process of reification, of spatialization, and of dehistoricization. This sometimes led critics into the anomalous position of having to claim a privilege for their own contemporaneity as "different" from what preceded— hence the "post-"—while denying the very concept that would traditionally allow them to defend the unity of their own time and their apperception of the phenomena that appeared and called to them within it. Spanos and Riddel, to take only two prominent examples, developed their critical positions within the idea that their own situation, which they refused to limit, enabled rereadings of older literatures. In the late 1970s, *boundary* 2 published two special issues devoted to rereading the canon from postmodern perspectives. The editorial point of view within that project was complex: aware of the ironic belatedness of declaring oneself to be "post," the editors adapted a pragmatic position to rethink the past in light of the present, making as self-conscious and as purposive as possible an historically common and normative practice of reinterpretation. Jameson is, of course, the most important defender of the critical practice of periodization and his notions are less troubled. He adopts a realistic attitude toward the question and designates a period as a unique set of interrelations among means of production and relations of production as they can be said to change significantly enough to acquire something like historical identity and even agency. The influence of this thinking is perhaps most easily seen in *Periodizing the Sixties*, a volume produced by the *Social Text* collective, a group with long-standing relations to Jameson's work. Of course, periodization underlies entirely the "horizontal" form of Jameson's thinking about the postmodern whereas for Spanos, the resistance to periodization allows "postmodernism" to function as a set of hermeneutic devices to reconsider literatures and cultures in ways judged critically important to the present. In these terms, the resistance to periodization has something in common with Nietzsche's idea of doing philosophy with a hammer—a notion not unfamiliar to Spanos and Riddel but less welcome to Altieri, Antin, and Gillespie.

6. It is worth pointing out that the value of geography is different in late capital from classical modernism. Contrast, for example, not only the literary representations of the city as these are transformed by and within globalism, but contrast as well intellectual projects such as Lewis Mumford's *The City in History* (New York: Harcourt Brace Jovanovich, 1961) and the work of the so-called postmodern geographers such as David Harvey. See as well the differences between Edward W. Said's monumental discussion of geography as an element of imperialism in *Culture and Imperialism* (Knopf, 1993) and William Gibson's critical remarks on urban culture (see, for example, "Told in the Prescient Tense," *Sunday Times* (of London), Octo-

ber 3, 1993, sec. 9, pp. 4ff.) It is worth offering as an example of novelists' sense of the globality of this formation, Catherine Lim's novel of Singapore, *The Serpent's Tooth* (Singapore: Times Books International, 1982).

7. Indeed, we should emphasize the importance of "worklessness" to all recent theories of economic and political criticism in literary and cultural studies. Wlad Godzich has begun an important critique along these lines in his talk, "Value Without Work," a paper presented in Valencia, Spain, summer, 1994.

8. We should recall Michel Foucault's implicating of Gilles Deleuze's similar thought in *Difference and Repetition*. Foucault insists Deleuze tells us that thought is of more importance than intelligence because the latter, having "vanquished stupidity," takes up residence in the "scholar" who cannot think and so cannot "confront stupidity." See Foucault, "Theatrum Philosophicum," *Language, Counter-Memory, Practice*, ed. Donald F. Bouchard, trans. Donald F. Bouchard and Sherry Simon (Ithaca: Cornell University Press, 1977), originally published in 1970. See Deleuze, *Difference and Repetition*, trans. Paul Patton (New York: Columbia University Press, 1994), esp. pp. 150–53.

William V. Spanos

The Detective and the Boundary

Some Notes on the Postmodern Literary Imagination

. . . All the plays that have
ever been written, from ancient
    Greece to the present day,
    have never really been anything
            but thrillers.
    Drama's always been realistic
and there's always been a
        detective about. Every
    play's an investigation brought
to a successful conclusion.
        There's a riddle, and it's
    solved in the final scene.
                        Sometimes
    earlier. Might as well give the
    game away at the
                    start.
Ionesco: Choubert,
Victims of Duty

"Elementary, my dear Watson. . . ."
Conan Doyle: Sherlock Holmes,
passim

And any explanation will satisfy:
We only ask to be reassured
About the noises in the cellar
And the window that should not have
    been open.
Why do we all behave as if the door
    might suddenly open, the
    curtain be drawn,
The cellar make some dreadful
    disclosure, the roof disappear,
And we should cease to be sure of
    what is real or unreal?
Hold tight, hold tight, we must insist
    that the world is what we have
    always taken it to be. . . .
Eliot: Chorus, *The Family Reunion*

Dread strikes us dumb.
Heidegger, "What is Metaphysics?"

Nilb, mun, mud.
Beckett: Watt, *Watt*

I

The literary revolution called Modernism that took place at the end of the nineteenth century in reaction against the European middle-class ethos and reached its apogee in the work of such writers as Marcel Proust, Stéphane Mallarmé, W. B. Yeats, Ezra Pound, James Joyce, T. S. Eliot, and Virginia Woolf—and in the New Criticism—was, ideologically, a revolt against the Western humanistic tradition and, aesthetically, against the "Aristotelian" tradition. The modern movement continues to the present to be characterized by its "anti-Westernism" and its "anti-Aristotelianism." But about the time of World War II, which witnessed—especially in the context of the Resistance—the emergence of existentialism not merely as a philosophy but as a mode of consciousness, the "anti-Aristotelianism" of the modern movement underwent a metamorphosis so profound that it has become necessary, I submit, to differentiate between an early or symbolist modernism and a later "postmodernism."

Broadly speaking, the anti-Westernism of the symbolists was above all an aesthetic reaction against the humanistic principle of utility, the imperative that man's role vis-à-vis the material world was to control or, more accurately, to manipulate Nature (the word "manipulate" will assume a different significance for the existential imagination) in behalf of the material well-being of man. Analogously, the anti-Aristotelianism of the symbolists constituted a rejection of "prose" in favor of "poetry" or, as Henri Bergson observes in *Time and Free Will*, a rejection of language that solidifies "our conscious states" for the purposes of social action in favor of a language that achieves an autonomous and something like autotelic status. On the level of *mimesis*, symbolist anti-Aristotelianism constituted a rejection of the primacy of linear and temporal plot in favor of the simultaneity of "spatial form." I will return to this all too brief definition of symbolist modernism. What I wish to suggest at the outset is that, unlike the early modern imagination—indeed, in partial reaction against its refusal of historicity—the postmodern imagination, agonized as it has been by the on-going boundary situation which is contemporary history, is an existential imagination. Its anti-Aristotelianism—its refusal to fulfill causally oriented expectations, to create fictions (and in extreme cases, sentences) with beginnings, middles, and ends—has its source, not so much in an aesthetic as in an existential critique of the traditional Western view of man in the world, especially as it has been formulated by positivistic science and disseminated by the vested interests of the modern—technological—City. It is not, in other words, the ugliness, the busyness, the noisiness of a world organized on the principle of utility that has called forth postmodern anti-Aristotelianism; it is rather, though the two are not mutually exclusive, the anthropomorphic objectification of a world in which God is dead or has withdrawn.

At the heart of the existential critique of positivistic humanism—indeed, at the heart of all existential philosophies as such—is the well known but too often misunderstood concept of dread (*Angst*) or, rather, the distinction between dread and fear (*Furcht*). According to Heidegger, for example, who, it should be remembered, derived his fundamental categories from Søren Kierkegaard, dread differs radically from fear. "We are always afraid of this or that definite thing which threatens us in this or that definite way." Fear, in other words, has an object which, as Tillich puts it with Kierkegaard and Heidegger clearly in mind, "can be faced, analyzed, attacked, endured." That is, fear has no ontological status because, having an object that can, as it were, *be taken hold of*, one is certain that it can be dealt with: eliminated or neutralized or even used. (This obsessive need to take hold of nothing, it is worth observing, reminds us of Keats's implicit criticism of the kind of writer who, because he does not have negative capability, reaches irritably "after fact or reason.")

Dread, on the other hand, has no thing or nothing as its object. This "indefiniteness of *what* we dread is not just lack of definition: it represents the essential impossibility of defining the 'what.' " It is, in other words, an existential and ontological (as opposed to existentiell and ontic) structure of reality:

> In dread, as we say, "one feels something uncanny [*unheimlich*]." What is this "something" [*es*] and this "one"? We are unable to say what gives "one" that uncanny feeling. "One" just feels it generally [*im Ganzen*]. All things, and we with them, sink into a sort of indifference. But not in the sense that everything disappears; rather, in the very act of drawing away from us everything turns towards us. This withdrawal of what-is-in-totality, which crowds round us *in dread*, this is what oppresses us. There is nothing [as there is in fear] to hold on to. The only thing that remains and overwhelms us whilst what-is slips away, is this "nothing."

What is crucial to perceive in Heidegger's phenomenological example is that dread generates a withdrawal of the world as web of definite or defined objects ("what-is-in-totality") and discloses itself in its primordial ontological state, which is oppressive not only because it "crowds round us"—invades, as it were, our formerly secure world—but also because it provides us—like the chorus in the epigraph from Eliot's *The Family Reunion*—with "nothing to hold on to." Following Kierkegaard, whose existentialism exfoliates from his assertion that "Nothing begets dread," Heidegger concludes: "Dread reveals Nothing." Put in the way suggested by his reference to the feeling of uncanniness (*Unheimlichkeit*), dread discloses Dasein's (human being's) not-at-homeness in the world.

Seen in the light of the existential distinction between dread and fear, the Western perspective—by which I specifically mean the rational or rather the positivistic structure of consciousness that views spatial and temporal phenomena in the world as "problems" to be "solved"—constitutes a self-deceptive effort to find objects for dread in order to *domesticate*—to at-home—the threatening realm of Nothingness, the not-at-home, into which Dasein is thrown (*geworfen*). It is, in other words, a rigidified, evasive anthropomorphism which obsessively attempts by coercion to fix and stabilize the elusive flux of existence from the vantage point of a final rational cause. By means of this coercive transformation, the positivistic structure of consciousness is able not only to *man*ipulate, to lay hands on, the irrational world (including man, of course) for the purpose of achieving what one early spokesman for this perspective referred to as "humane empire" over nature "for the benefit of man's estate." More basically, according to the existentialists, it can also *justify* the absurdity of human existence: it allows man, that is, to perceive the immediate, uncertain, problematic, and thus dreadful psychic or historical present of Dasein as a necessary part of a linear design, as a causal link between the past and/or future determined from a rational end. The one thing needful to fill the gaps between apparent discontinuities in both the internal and external worlds (i.e., memory and history) or, another way of putting it, to apprehend and to exploit this comforting linear design behind the absurd and dislocating, or, better, *dis-lodging* appearances, is a careful, "objective" observer of the uniformity among diverse phenomena, that is, the positivistic scientist or, what is the same thing, the behaviorist psychoanalyst.

According to the implications of existential philosophy, then, the problem-solution perspective of the "straightforward" Western man of action, as Dostoevsky's denizen of the underground calls the exponents of the Crystal Palace, has its ground in more than merely a belief in the susceptibility of nature to rational explanation. It is based, rather on a monolithic certainty that immediate psychic or historical experience is part of a comforting, even exciting and suspenseful well-made cosmic drama or novel—more particularly, a detective story (the French term is *policière*) in the manner of Poe's *The Murders in the Rue Morgue* or Conan Doyle's *The Hound of the Baskervilles*. For just as the form of the detective story has its source in the comforting certainty that an acute "eye," private or otherwise, can solve the crime with resounding finality by inferring causal relationships between clues which point to it (they are "leads," suggesting the primacy of rigid linear narrative sequence), so the "form" of the well-made positivistic universe is grounded in the equally comforting certainty that the scientist and/or psychoanalyst can solve the immediate problem by the inductive method, a process involving the inference of relationships between discontinuous "facts" that point to or lead straight to an explanation of the "mystery," the "crime" of contingent existence. " 'This is most important,' said [Holmes in *The Hound of the Baskervilles*]. . . . 'It fills up a gap which I had been unable to bridge in this most complex affair.' "

Far from being arbitrary, this way of defining the structure of consciousness into which modern Western man has coerced his humanistic inheritance from the Renaissance is, as we shall see, amply justified, especially by the evidence of his popular arts and public-political life. Though, on the whole, scientists and psychologists no longer are inclined to view existence in this rigidly positivistic and deterministic way, it is nevertheless this structure of consciousness, which assumes the universe, the "book of nature," to be a well-made cosmic drama, that determines the questions and thus the expectations and answers—in language and in action—of the "silent majority," *das Man* of the modern technological City and of the political executors of its will.

II

As the profound influence of certain kinds of literature on existential philosophy suggests, the impulse of the Western writer to refuse to fulfill causal expectations, to refuse to provide "solutions" for the "crime" of existence, historically precedes the existential critique of Westernism. We discover it in, say, Euripides' *Orestes*, Shakespeare's problem plays, the tragi-comedies of the Jacobeans, Wycherley's *The Plain Dealer*, Dickens's *Edwin Drood*, and more recently in Tolstoy's *The Death of Ivan Ilych*, Dostoevsky's *Notes from Underground*, Alfred Jarry's *Ubu Roi*, Kafka's *The Trial*, Pirandello's *Six Characters in Search of an Author*, and even in T. S. Eliot's *Sweeney Agonistes*. (These are works, it is worth observing, the radical temporality of which does not yield readily to the spatial methodology of the New Criticism, which has its source in the iconic art of symbolist modernism.) In *Notes from Underground*, for example, Dostoevsky as editor "concludes" this anti-novel: "The 'notes' of this paradoxalist do not end here. However, he could not resist and continued them. But it also seems to me that we may stop here." Fully conscious of the psychological need of the "straightforward" Gentleman of the hyper-Westernized St. Petersburg—the "most intentional city in the whole world"—Dostoevsky refuses to transform the discordant experience of this terrible voice into a "sublime and beautiful," that is, "straightforward" and distancing *story*. So also in *Six Characters in Search of an Author*. Seeking relief from the agony of their ambiguous relationships, the characters express their need to give artistic shape to the "infinite absurdities" of their lives. But when the Director (I want to emphasize the coercive implications of the word)—who hates their authorless, that is, inconclusive drama ("it seems to me you are trying to imitate the manner of a certain author whom I heartily detest")—tries to make a well-made play, a melodrama in the manner of Eugène Scribe or Alexander Dumas *fils* of their dreadful experience ("What we've got to do is to combine and group up all the facts in one simultaneous close-knit action"), they refuse to be coerced into that comforting but fraudulent "arrangement." Similarly in *Sweeney Agonistes*, just as Sweeney will not allow his anxious listeners to package the terrible "anti-Aristotelian" murder story he tells them ("Well here again that don't apply / But I've gotta use words when I talk to you"), so Eliot in his great antidetective play will not allow his audience of middle class fugitives to fulfill their positivistically conditioned need to experience the explanatory and cathartic conclusion. Rather, like Dostoevsky, he ends the play inconclusively with the dreadful knocking at the door.

But in each of these earlier works, one has the feeling that the writer has only reluctantly resisted the conventional ending. It is actually the unconscious pressure of the powerfully felt content—the recognition and acknowledgment of contingency, or what I prefer to call the ontological invasion—that has driven him into undermining the traditional Aristotelian dramatic or fictional form. The existential diagnosis and critique of the humanistic tradition had not yet emerged to suggest the formal implications of metaphysical disintegration. Only after the existentialist philosophers revealed that the perception of the universe as a well-made fiction, obsessive to the Western consciousness, is in reality a self-deceptive effort to evade the anxiety of contingent existence by objectifying and taking hold of "it," did it become clear to the modern writer that the ending-as-solution is the literary agency of this evasive objectification. And it is the discovery of the "anti-formal" imperatives of absurd time for fiction and drama and poetry (though poetry, which in our time means lyric poetry, as Sartre has said in *What is Literature?*, tends by its natural amenability to spatialization to be nonhistorical) that constitutes the most dynamic thrust of the contemporary Western literary imagination and differentiates the new from symbolist modernism.

Taking their lead from the existentialists, the postmodern absurdists—writers like the Sartre of *Nausea* and *No Exit*, the Beckett of *Watt* and the Molloy trilogy as well as *Waiting for Godot, Endgame,* and *Krapp's Last Tape* (the titles should not be overlooked), Ionesco, Genet, Pinter, Frisch, Sarraute, Pynchon, etc.—thus view the well-made play or novel (*la pièce bien faite*), the post-Shakespearian allotrope of the Aristotelian form, as the inevitable analogue of the well-made positivistic universe delineated by the post-Renaissance humanistic structure of consciousness. More specifically, they view the rigid deterministic plot of the well-made fiction, like that of its metaphysical counterpart, as having its source in bad faith. I mean (to appropriate the metaphor Heidegger uses to remind us of the archetypal flight of the Apollonian Orestes from the *Erinyes*) the self-deceptive effort of the "fallen 'they' " (*das verfallene "Man"*) "to flee in the face of death" and the ominous absurd by finding objects for the dread of Nothing, that is, *by imposing coercively a distancing and tranquillizing ending or telos from the beginning on the invading contingencies of existence.* What Roquentin says in Sartre's *Nausea* about *l'aventure* (which is the aesthetic equivalent of the Bouville merchants' arrogant positivism—their certain "right to exist") in distinguishing it from *la vie* is precisely what the postmodern absurdists seem to imply in their "de-composed" drama and fiction about the modern humanistic structure of consciousness and its metaphysical and aesthetic paradigms:

everything changes when you tell about life [*raconte la vie:* Sartre seems to be pointing here to the relationship between the mathematical associations of the etymology and the concept of story or well-made plot and, ultimately, the recounting of existence from the vantage point of the end]; it's a change no one notices: . . . Things happen one way and we tell about them in the opposite sense. You seem to start at the beginning: "It was a fine autumn evening in 1922. I was a notary clerk in Marommes." And in reality you have started at the end. It was there, invisible and present, it is the one which gives to words the pomp and value of a beginning. "I was out walking, I had left the town without realizing it, I was thinking about my money troubles." This sentence, taken simply for what it is, means that the man was absorbed, morose, a hundred leagues from adventure, exactly in the mood to let things happen without noticing them. But the end is there, transforming everything. For us, the man is already the hero of the story. His moroseness, his money troubles are much more precious than ours, they are all gilded by the light of future passions. And the story goes on in the reverse: instants have stopped piling themselves in a lighthearted way one on top of the other [as in life], they are snapped up by the end of the story which draws them and each one of them in turn, draws out the preceding instant: "It was night, the street was deserted." *The phrase is cast out negligently, it seems superfluous* [*superflue:* an equivalent of *de trop*, Sartre's term for the condition of man in the primordial realm of existence which is prior to essence]; *but we do not let ourselves be caught and put it aside: this is a piece of information whose value we shall subsequently appreciate.* And we feel that the hero has lived all the details of this night like annunciations, promises, or even that he lives only those that were promises, blind and deaf to all that did not herald adventure. . . .

I wanted the moments of my life to follow and order themselves like those of a life remembered. You might as well try and catch time by the tail. (My emphasis).

In short, the postmodern absurdists interpret this obsession for what Roland Barthes, perhaps with Sartre in mind, calls the fiction of "the preterite mode," for the rigidly causal plot of the well-made work of the humanistic tradition, as catering to and thus further hardening the expectation of—and aggravating the need for—the rational solution generated by the scientific analysis of man-in-the-world. As the reference to the technique of the detective story in the passage from *Nausea* suggests, these expectations demand the kind of fiction and drama that achieves its absolute fulfillment in the utterly formularized clockwork certainties of plot in the innumerable detective drama series—*Perry Mason, The FBI, Hawaii 5-0, Mannix, Mission Impossible,* etc.—which use up, or rather, "kill," prime television time. Ultimately they also demand the kind of social and political organization that finds its fulfillment in the imposed certainties of the well-made world of the totalitarian state, where investigation or inquisition on behalf of the achievement of a total, that is, preordained or teleologically determined structure—a "final solution"—is the defining activity. It is, therefore, no accident that the paradigmatic archetype of the postmodern literary imagination is the antidetective story (and its antipsychoanalytical analogue), the formal purpose of which is to evoke the impulse to "detect" and/or to psycho-analyze in order to violently frustrate it by refusing to solve the crime (or find the cause of the neurosis). I am referring, for example, to works like Kafka's *The Trial,* T. S. Eliot's *Sweeney Agonistes* (subtitled significantly *Fragments of an Aristophanic Melodrama*), Graham Greene's *Brighton Rock,* Arthur Koestler's *Arrival and Departure,* Beckett's *Watt* and *Molloy* (especially the Moran section), Ionesco's *Victims of Duty,* Robbe-Grillet's *The Erasers,* and Nathalie Sarraute's *Portrait of a Man Unknown* (which Sartre, in his characteristically seminal way, refers to as an "anti-novel that reads like a detective story" and goes on to characterize as "a parody on the novel of 'quest' into which the author has introduced a sort of impassioned amateur detective" who "doesn't find anything . . . and gives up the investigation as a result of a meta-morphosis; just as though Agatha Christie's detective, on the verge of unmasking the villain, had himself suddenly turned criminal").

In *Victims of Duty,* for example, the Detective, like Sherlock Holmes, is certain in the beginning that "everything hangs together, everything can be comprehended in time" and thus "keeps moving forward . . . one step at a time, tracking down the extraordinary": "Mallot, with a t at the end, or Mallod with a d." Holmes, of course, eventually gets his man (though the foregone certainty, especially of the monstrous evilness of the criminal, should not obscure the grimness of the metaphor that characterizes Conan Doyle's fictional and real universe): "This chance of the picture has supplied us with one of our most obvious missing links. We have him, Watson, we have him, and I dare swear that before tomorrow he will be fluttering in our net as helpless as one of his own butterflies. A pin, a cork, and a card, and we add him to the Baker Street collection!" But the Detective in the process of Ionesco's play cannot make Choubert "catch hold of" the elusive Mallot. Despite his brutal efforts to "plug the gaps [of his wayward memory]" by stuffing food down his throat, what he "finds" is only the bottomless hole of Choubert's being: that is, Nothing. And so, instead of ending with "A Retrospective" that ties everything together (clarifies the mystery) as in *The Hound of the Baskervilles, Victims of Duty* "ends" in verbal, formal and, analogously, ontological disintegration. The disturbing mystery still survives the brutal coercion.

What I am suggesting is that it was the recognition of the ultimately "totalitarian" implications of the Western structure of consciousness —of the expanding analogy that encompasses art, politics, and metaphysics in the name of the security of rational order—that compelled the postmodern imagination to undertake the deliberate and systematic subversion of plot—the beginning, middle, and end structure—which has enjoyed virtually unchallenged supremacy in the Western literary imagination ever since Aristotle or, at any rate, since the Renaissance interpreters of Aristotle claimed it to be the most important of the constitutive elements of literature. In the familiar language of Aristotle's *Poetics*, then, the postmodern strategy of de-composition exists to generate rather than to purge pity and terror; to disintegrate, to atomize rather than to create a community. In the more immediate language of existentialism, it exists to generate anxiety or dread: to dislodge the tranquilized individual from the "at-home of publicness," from the domesticated, the scientifically charted and organized familiarity of the totalized world, to make him experience what Roquentin sees from the top of a hill overlooking the not so "solid, bourgeois city," Bouville:

They come out of their offices after their day of work, they look at the houses and the squares with satisfaction, they think it is *their* city, a good, solid, bourgeois city. They aren't afraid, they feel at home. . . . They have proof, a hundred times a day, that everything happens mechanically, that the world obeys fixed, unchangeable laws. In a vacuum all bodies fall at the same rate of speed, the public park is closed at 4 p.m. in winter, at 6 p.m. in summer, lead melts at 335 degrees centigrade. . . . And all this time, great, vague nature has slipped into their city, it has infiltrated everywhere, in their house, in their office, in themselves. It doesn't move, it stays quietly and they are full of it inside, they breathe it, and they don't see it, they imagine it to be outside, twenty miles from the city. I *see* it, I *see* this nature. . . . I know that its obedience is idleness, I know it has no laws: what they take for constancy is only habit and it can change tomorrow.

What if something were to happen? What if something suddenly started throbbing? Then they would notice it was there and they'd think their hearts were going to burst. Then what good would their dykes, bulwarks, power houses, furnaces and pile drivers be to them?

This aesthetic of de-composition is not, as is too often protested, a purely negative one. For the *depaysment*—the ejection from one's "homeland"—as Ionesco calls it after Heidegger, which is effected by the carefully articulated discontinuities of absurdist literary form, reveals the *Urgrund*, the primordial not-at-home, where dread, as Kierkegaard and Heidegger and Sartre and Tillich tell us, becomes not just the agency of despair but also and simultaneously of hope, that is, of freedom and infinite possibility:

[If] a man were a beast or an angel [Kierkegaard, echoing Pascal, writes in *The Concept of Dread*], he would not be able to be in dread. Since he is a synthesis he can be in dread, and the greater the dread, the greater the man. And no Grand Inquisitor has in readiness such terrible tortures as has dread, and no spy knows how to attack more artfully the man he suspects, choosing the instant when he is weakest, nor knows how to lay traps where he will be caught and ensnared as dread knows how, and no sharpwitted judge knows how to interrogate, to examine the accused, as dread does, which never lets him escape, neither by diversion nor by noise, neither at work nor at play, neither by day nor by night.

Dread is the possibility of freedom. Only this dread is by the aid of faith absolutely educative, *laying bare as it does all finite aims and discovering all their deceptions.* . . .

He who is educated by dread is educated by possibility, and only the man who is educated by possibility is educated in accordance with his infinity. (My emphasis.)

Thus on the psychological level too this dislodgement not only undermines the confident positivistic structure of consciousness that really demands answers it already has (i.e., the expectation of *catharsis*). It also compels the new self to ask, like Orestes or Job—the Job who, against the certain advice of his comforters, the advocates of the Law, "spoke of God that which is right"—the ultimate, the authentically humanizing questions: *die Seinfragen*, as Heidegger puts it. To evoke the buried metaphor I have hinted at in the passage from *The Concept of Dread*, the postmodern antiliterature of the absurd exists to strip its audience of positivized fugitives of their protective garments of rational explanation and leave them standing naked and unaccommodated—poor, bare, forked animals—before the encroaching Nothingness. Here, to add another dimension to the metaphor, in the precincts of their last evasions, in the realm of silence, where the language that objectifies (clothes), whether the syntax of plot or of sentence, as Sweeney says, "don't apply" (is seen to be mere noise), they must choose authentically (*eigentlich:* in the context of the naked my-ownness of death and Nothingness) whether to capitulate to Nothingness, to endure it (this is what Tillich calls the courage to be in the face of despair), to affirm the Somethingness of Nothingness "by virtue of the absurd," or to risk letting Being be. It is this metaphor of divestment and silence, which finds its most forceful premodern expression in such works as *King Lear, Fear and Trembling, Crime and Punishment,* and *The Death of Ivan Ilych,* that gives postmodern antinovels and antiplays like Sartre's *Nausea* and *No Exit,* Ionesco's *Victims of Duty,* Tardieu's *The Keyhole (La Serrure),* Beckett's *Watt* and *Molloy,* Genet's *The Maids,* Pinter's *The Homecoming,* and Sarraute's *Tropisms* their special ambience.

III

We have seen during the twentieth century the gradual emergence of an articulate minority point of view—especially in the arts—that interprets Western technological civilization as a progress not toward the Utopian *polis* idealized by the Greeks, but toward a rationally mass-produced City which, like the St. Petersburg of Dostoevsky's and Tolstoy's novels, is a microcosm of universal madness. This point of view involves a growing recognition of one of the most significant paradoxes of modern life: that in the pursuit of order the positivistic structure of consciousness, having gone beyond the point of equilibrium, generates radical imbalances in nature which are inversely proportional to the intensity with which it is coerced. However, it has not been able to call the arrogant anthropomorphic Western mind and its well-made universe into serious question.

As I have suggested, this is largely because the affirmative formal strategy of symbolist modernism was one of religio-aesthetic withdrawal from existential time into the eternal simultaneity of essential art. The symbolist movement, that is, tried to deconstruct language, to drive it out of its traditional temporal orbit—established by the humanistic commitment to *kinesis* and utility and given its overwhelming socio-literary authority, as Marshall McLuhan has shown, by the invention of the printing press—in order to achieve iconic or, more inclusively, spatial values. Its purpose was to undermine its utilitarian function in order to disintegrate the reader's linear-temporal orientation and to make him *see* synchronically—as one sees a painting or a circular mythological paradigm—what the temporal words express. In other words, its purpose was to *reveal* (in the etymological sense of "unveil") the whole and by so doing raise the reader above the messiness or, as Yeats calls the realm of existence in "Phases of the Moon," "that raving tide," into a higher and more permanent reality.

This impulse to transcend the historicity of the human condition in the "allatonceness" (the term is McLuhan's) of the spatialized work of symbolist literary art is brought into remarkably sharp focus when one perceives the similarity between the poetic implicit in W. B. Yeats's "Sailing to Byzantium" with Stephen Dedalus's aesthetic of *stasis* in *Portrait of the Artist as a Young Man*, which has often been taken, especially by the New Critics, as a theoretical definition of modern symbolist literary form:

You see I use the word *arrest*. I mean that the tragic emotion is static. Or rather the dramatic emotion is. The feelings excited by improper art are kinetic, desire and loathing. Desire urges us to possess, to go to something; loathing urges us to abandon, to go from something. These are kinetic emotions. The arts which excite them, pornographical or didactic, are therefore improper arts. The esthetic emotion (I use the general term) is therefore static. The mind is arrested and raised above desire and loathing.

> O sages standing in God's holy fire
> As in the gold mosaic of a wall,
> Come from the holy fire, perne in a gyre,
> And be the singing-masters of my soul.
> Consume my heart away; sick with desire
> And fastened to a dying animal
> It knows not what it is; and gather me
> Into the artifice of eternity.
>
> Once out of nature I shall never take
> My bodily form from any natural thing,
> But such a form as Grecian goldsmiths make

Of hammered gold and gold enamelling
To keep a drowsy Emperor awake;
Or set upon a golden bough to sing
To lords and ladies of Byzantium
Of what is past, or passing, or to come.

For Stephen, growing up has been a terrible process of discovering the paradox that the City—for Plato, for Virgil, for Augustine, for Justinian, for Dante, for Plethon, for Campanella, the image of beauty, of order, of repose—has become in the modern world the space of radical ugliness and disorder. To put it in Heidegger's terms, it has been a process of discovering that the at-home of the modern world has in fact become the realm of the not-at-home. This process, that is, has been one of *dislocation*. Thus for Stephen the ugliness and disorder, the "squalor" and "sordidness," that assault his sensitive consciousness after his "Ptolemaic" universe (which he diagrams on the fly-leaf of his geography book) has been utterly shattered during the catastrophic and traumatic Christmas dinner, is primarily or, at any rate, ontologically, a matter of random motion:

He sat near them [his numerous brothers and sisters] at the table and asked where his father and mother were. One answered:
—Goneboro toboro lookboro atboro aboro houseboro.
Still another removal! A boy named Fallon in Belvedere had often asked him with a silly laugh why they moved so often. . . .
He asked:
—Why are we on the move again, if it's a fair question?
The sister answered:
—Becauseboro theboro landboro lordboro willboro putboro usboro outboro. . . .
He waited for some moments, listening [to the children sing "Oft in the Stilly Night"], before he too took up the air with them. He was listening with pain of spirit to the overtones of weariness behind their frail fresh innocent voices. Even before they set out on life's journey they seemed weary already of the way.
. . . All seemed weary of life even before entering upon it. And he remembered that Newman had heard this note also in the broken line of Virgil *giving utterance, like the voice of Nature herself, to that pain and weariness yet hope of better things which has been the experience of her children in every time.*

(Walter Pater too had heard this sad Virgilian note and in quoting the passage in *Marius the Epicurean*, another novel having its setting in a disintegrating world, established the nostalgia for rest as the essential motive of the aesthetic movement in England.)

Seen in the light of his discovery that random motion is the radical category of modern urban life—that existence is prior to essence, which the postmodern writer will later present as the Un-Naming in the Garden-City—Stephen's well-known aesthetic or rather (to clarify what persistent critical reference to Stephen's "aesthetic" has obscured) his iconic poetics of stasis, both its volitional ground and its formal character, becomes clear. He wants, like T. E. Hulme, like Proust, like Virginia Woolf and like most other symbolists, a poetry the iconic—and autotelic—nature of which *arrests* the mind—neutralizes the anguish, the schism in the spirit—and *raises* it above desire and loathing, which is to say, the realm of radical motion, of contingency, of historicity, in the distancing moment when the whole is seen simultaneously.

The "epiphanic"—one is tempted to say "Oriental"—nature of this iconic poetic is further clarified in Stephen's amplification of the principle of *stasis* in terms of Saint Thomas's "*ad pulcritudinem tria requiruntur, integritas, consonantia, claritas*," especially the first and, above all, the most important third categories. *Integritas* or "wholeness," Stephen observes, is the apprehension of "a bounding line drawn about the object" no matter whether it is in space or in time: "temporal or spatial, the esthetic image is first luminously apprehended as selfbounded and selfcontained upon the immeasurable background of space or time which is not it. You apprehend it as *one* thing. You see it as one whole." *Consonantia* or "harmony" is the apprehension of the "rhythm of its structure"; the feeling that "it is a *thing*," "complex, multiple, divisible, separable, made up of parts, the result of its parts and their sum, harmonious." Finally, and most important for Stephen, *claritas* or "radiance" (the etymology of his translation—"radiance" is the light emitted in rays from a center or *logos*—and his analysis of the term clearly suggest its relation with revelation) is the apprehension of "that thing which it is and no other thing. The radiance of which [Saint Thomas] speaks is the scholastic *quidditas,* the *whatness* of a thing. This supreme quality is felt by the artist when the esthetic image is first conceived in his imagination. . . . The instant wherein that supreme quality of beauty, the clear radiance of the esthetic image, is apprehended *luminously by the mind which has been arrested by its wholeness* and fascinated by its harmony in the *luminous silent stasis of esthetic pleasure*" (my emphasis).

So also in "Sailing to Byzantium"—though the metaphysical context is more ontological than social in orientation—Yeats's speaker, like

Stephen, is articulating, both in the content and form of the poem, an iconic poetic that has its source in an impulse for epiphanic transcendence—what Wilhelm Worringer (the proponent of primitive and oriental, including Byzantine, artistic models who influenced T. E. Hulme) in *Abstraction and Empathy* calls the "urge to abstraction." As fully, if more implicitly, conscious of the paradoxical horror of the modern Western City as Stephen, the poet has come to the City of the iconic imagination—the City of Phase 15—to pray his mosaic models to teach him *an art of poetry* that will "consume my heart away"—a heart like Stephen's which, "sick with desire / And fastened to a dying animal / . . . knows not what it is." Such a heart is ignorant because, as Yeats says here and reiterates in innumerable ways throughout his early and middle poetry, its *immediate* relationship to history makes everything appear to be random motion, that is, absurd. Clearly, to continue with the phenomenological language of existentialism, this heart is a synecdoche for the dislodged and thus anguish-ridden man-in-the-world, the alienated man in the dreadful realm of *das Unheimliche*. And, as in Stephen's iconic poetic, Yeats's moment of consummation (the parallel with "radiance" should not be overlooked) which negates the human heart and neutralizes (arrests) desire—the Western, the empathetic urge "to possess, to go to something"—is the consummation of the creative act, the metamorphosis of kinesis into stasis, becoming into being, the uncertain temporal life into assured iconic artifact, "selfbounded and selfcontained upon the immeasurable background of space or time which is not it." (Similarly, the image of a Byzantine mosaic Panaghia or Saint is sharply articulated upon a depthless and vast gold space that suggests the absolute purity of eternity.) Like Stephen's "instant" of "luminous silent stasis," Yeats's moment of consummation is thus the distancing moment when all time can be seen simultaneously. Whereas the real birds of the first stanza—"those dying generations"—know not what they are because they are "caught" *in* time, the poet in this moment of consummation, having assumed the form "as Grecian goldsmiths make / Of hammered gold and gold enamelling," can sing in *full knowledge* from a perspective beyond or "out of nature" of the world below, which is to say, of history seen all at once, that is, spatially: "Of what is past, or passing, or to come." In the words that Yeats's myth or rather his "sacred book" insists on, this burning moment, like that of Joyce's "priest of the eternal imagination," and of so many other symbolist poets and novelists, is, in Ortega's term, the "dehumanizing" epiphanic moment of transcendence.

IV

Committed to an iconic poetic of transcendence, the literature of early modernism thus refused to engage itself in the history of modern man. Though it was able to reveal the squalor of the "Unreal City" of the West, where, as one of T. S. Eliot's Thames daughters puts it, "I can connect / Nothing with nothing," and even point with Dickens and Dostoevsky to the ontological invasion that had already begun, it did not challenge the positivistic structure of consciousness which organizes and sustains it. Despite, therefore, the terrible lessons of World War I and again World War II, especially of the genocidal holocaust perpetrated in the name of "the final solution," it is still the positivistic frame of reference that determines the questions-and-answers, that delineates the Western image of the universe and creates Western man's values. From the governing bodies and the scientific-industrial-military complex and even our educational and religious institutions to the so-called hard hat and blue collar workers, it is this well-made world, the world pointing toward a materialist utopia, toward a Crystal Palace end, that appears real. And as Sartre suggests in his assault on *les salauds* in *Nausea* and "The Childhood of a Leader," it is the certainty of the *rightness* of this fictional image of the macrocosm that continues to justify the coercion of the unique and disturbing deviant into its predetermined role—or its elimination ("liquidation" or "wasting")—when it does not fulfill the rigid and inexorable expectations established by a preconceived end. Indeed, this world-picture, as a book like Lewis Mumford's *The Pentagon of Power* suggests, becomes more rigid and inclusive, that is, totalitarian, in proportion to the irrationality it generates. The investigator and monstrous proliferation: these are the *presences* of contemporary life. And this is no accident.

As I have already suggested, my definition of the Western structure of consciousness as one which perceives the world as a well-made melodrama is not a *tour de force* of the critical imagination. It is discoverable everywhere in the language and the shape of action of men from all social levels of the Western City. All that is necessary to perceive it is attention. It is impossible in this limited space to support this claim in any detail. But perhaps a quotation from an editorial on the subject of literature that appeared some time ago in the *Daily News,* the New York tabloid with a circulation of over two million, may suggest how rooted and inclusive this perspective is:

Winner and Still Champ

For generations William Shakespeare has been recognized as the greatest English master of the drama, and quite possibly the greatest handler of the English language, that ever yet has trod this earthly ball. . . .

Shakespeare and Dickens had several things in common. They . . . composed stage or fictional pieces which had definite beginnings, unmistakable climaxes and positive endings.

Neither Dickens nor Shakespeare wrote so-what tripe that gets nowhere and is in some fashion nowadays. Nor did they glorify characters whom even the ablest of modern psychiatrists couldn't help.

End of today's discussion of matters literary.

This obsession for the "positive" and comforting *ending* in the face of Shakespeare's—and even Dickens's—disturbing ambiguities, to say nothing of the uncertainties of contingent existence, I submit, lies behind this newspaper's editorial support of all causes "grounded" in a storybook patriotism (such as United States involvement in Vietnam, President Nixon's invasion of Cambodia, Vice-President Agnew's political rhetoric) and vilification of all others "grounded" in storybook treachery (such as the peace movement, senatorial opposition to unilateral policy-making by the executive branch, and even Scandinavian anti-Americanism). More pernicious, because its implications are harder to perceive, this structure of consciousness also lies behind this newspaper's *presentation* of the news, whether a tenement murder, a campus uprising, or an international incident, as sensational melodrama whose problem-solution form not only neutralizes the reader's anxieties but even makes him a voyeur. To forestall the objection that this evidence is unreliably partisan, let me parenthetically refer to the parallel with, say, *Time* or *Newsweek,* where the narrative structure of every article is conceived as a well-made fiction, that is, written—manipulated—from the end.

Further, as even the most cursory examination of "The Pentagon

Papers" clearly suggests, this positivistic structure of consciousness also lies behind the actions that constitute the news. It has governed the United States' involvement in Vietnam from the overthrow of Diem, the Tonkin Bay incident, and the ensuing large scale "retaliatory" bombing of North Vietnam to the Vietnamization—which means the American-ization or rather the Westernization—of Vietnam. It is, then, no accident that *everywhere* in these secret documents the Southeast Asian situa-tion is seen by their American authors as a problem to be solved; that the planning to solve the problem—to achieve conclusive American ob-jectives—is referred to in the metaphor of plotting a scenario; that the execution—the acting out—of the *scenario* in this recalcitrant theater of operations is to be accomplished, first, by the CIA—the international detective agency whose job it is to coerce the reality under investiga-tion to conform to a preconceived order—and, then, by the military arm by way of a massive assault on the "criminal" enemy. In short, what emerges in these disturbing documents, if we pay critical attention to the language (especially to its trite metaphors), is an image of an action in which virtually everyone involved in this terrible human disaster—from the executive branch and its councils to the intelligence agencies and the military and the American press and its public—speaks and acts as if he is playing a role in a well-made fiction in the utterly dehuman-ized mode of a play by Eugène Scribe, a novel by Sir Arthur Conan Doyle, or closest of all, an episode of *Mission Impossible.*

I will refer specifically to only one concrete but representative action of the war in Vietnam: the large-scale interservice rescue operation staged against the Son Tay prisoner-of-war camp in North Vietnam in December 1970. Seen in the light of my discussion, this melodramatic action constitutes an illuminating paradigm not only of the war that America has been waging against Southeast Asia since 1954, but also—and more fundamentally, for it is not so much politics as ontology that concerns me here—of the war that the West has been waging against the world, indeed against Nature itself, ever since the seventeenth century. It reveals, that is, how embedded—how *located*—in the Western con-sciousness is the metaphor of the well-made universe and how intense the conditioned psychological need behind it. This elaborately plotted action, the "scenario" of which, according to the *New York Times* report, "was rehearsed for a month in a stage-set replica of the objective on the

Florida Gulf Coast," did not achieve its objective, that is, did not end, because, despite the split-second timing with which all the roles were acted out, there was no one there to rescue at the climactic moment. "It was like hollering in an empty room," one of the bewildered actors in this dreadful experience put it. "When we realized that there was no one in the compound," said another—his language should be marked well— "I had the most horrible feeling of my life." And *Time* summed up in language that unintentionally recalls Watt's agonized quest for or rather his futile effort to take hold of the elusive Knott in Beckett's novel: "All the courage, the long training, the perfectly executed mission, had come to naught."

Despite these revelatory glimpses into the horror, the secretary of defense was driven to declare reiteratively in the following days that the Son Tay affair was a successfully completed operation. It is this metamorphosis of the absurd into manageable object, into fulfilled objective, into an accomplishment, which is especially revealing. For the obvious incommensurability between the assertion of successful completion and the absurd and dreadful non-end constitutes a measure of the intensity of the need that the power complex and the people that depend on it feel for definite conclusions. Returning to the ontological level, it is a measure of modern Western man's need *to take hold of the Nothing* that despite, or perhaps because of, his technics is crowding in on him. To put it in the central metaphor of the existential imagination, it is the measure of his need to flee from the Furies of the not-at-home and its implications for freedom.

V

In the past decade or so there have emerged a variety of "postmodern" modes of writing and critical thought that, despite certain resemblances to aspects of the existential imagination, are ultimately extensions of early iconic modernism. I am referring, for example, to the structuralist criticism of Roland Barthes, the phenomenological criticism of consciousness of Georges Poulet and Jean-Pierre Richard, and the neo-imagism of Marshall McLuhan; the "field poetry" of Charles Olson and the concrete poetry of Pierre Garnier, Ferdinand Kriwet, and Franz Mon;

the *roman nouveau* of Robbe-Grillet and Michel Butor; the "Happenings" of Allan Kaprow and Claes Oldenburg; and the Pop Art literature advocated by critics such as Leslie Fiedler (who, it is worth observing, wants to reconcile the sensibilities of Henry Wadsworth Longfellow and Stephen Foster with those of the Beatles, Bob Dylan, Leonard Cohen, etc., all of whom have in common not only the clichés and the assertive end rhymes he admires for their expression of childlike innocence, but also, and in a way at the source of these characteristics, the desire to go home again: the nostalgia for the hearth). These modes of creativity and critical speculation attest to the variety of the postmodern scene, but this pluralism has also tended to hide the fact that, in tendency, they are all oriented beyond history or, rather, they all aspire to the spatialization of time. As a result the existential sources of the primary thrust of the postmodern literary imagination have been obscured, thus jeopardizing the encouraging post-World War II impulse to recover the temporality of the literary medium from the plastic arts, which is to say, to engage literature in an ontological dialogue with the world in behalf of the recovery of the authentic historicity of modern man.

Seen in this light, the "Pentagon Papers" not only emerge as a stark reminder that the totalizing structure of consciousness of the "straightforward" Gentlemen who built the modern City continues to coerce history with missionary certainty into well-made fictions. Because they resemble so closely the kind of fiction and drama associated with the rise of science, technology, and middle-class culture in the nineteenth century, they also emerge as a paradigm capable of teaching both the contemporary writer and critic a great deal about the Western mind and the popular arts and the media that nourish it. In so doing, finally, they suggest a way of discriminating between modernisms and of clarifying the direction that the main impulse of the postmodern sensibility has taken and, I think, should continue to take in the immediate future.

Ultimately, one would like a literature of generosity, a literature, like Chaucer's or Shakespeare's or Dickens's or George Eliot's or Tolstoy's, that acknowledges, indeed celebrates, the "messiness" of existence, as Iris Murdoch puts it, in the context of discovered form. But at the moment, Western man as a cultural community or rather public is simply incapable of responding to the generosity—the humane impulse, having its source in the humility of acknowledged uncertainty, to let Being be—

that, on occasion, infuses Shakespeare's stage and his world as stage. (As the editorial quoted above suggests, the ungenerous effort of the "Enlightenment" to rewrite the "endings" of Shakespeare's "inconclusive" plays continues down to the present, though it takes the form of accepting the rewritten version as myth while the plays themselves are locked up in university libraries.) For, to put the point in the familiar language of the historical critical debate, unlike the Western past, when Art (*The Odyssey*, for example) was justifiably a taxonomic model for ordering a brutal and terrifying Nature (existence) or a mode of psychological consolation in the face of its catastrophic power, the Western present, as the "Pentagon Papers" and the Son Tay "scenario" and the *Mission Impossible* series and the *Daily News* and *Time* suggest, is a time that bears witness to a Nature whose brutal and terrifying forces have been coerced—and domesticated—into a very well-made and therefore very dangerous work of Art.

The Western structure of consciousness is bent, however inadvertently, on unleashing chaos in the name of the order of a well-made world. If this is true, contemporary literature cannot afford the luxury of the symbolist, or, as I prefer to call it, the iconic literary aesthetic nor of its "postmodern" variants. For ours is no time for psychic flights, for Dedalean "seraphic embraces," however enticing they may be. Neither, for that matter, despite its more compelling claim as an authentic possibility, can it afford the luxury of the aesthetic implicit in the concept of the later Heidegger's *Gelassenheit* (that receptivity which might disclose the Being of Not-being and thus the sacramental at-homeness of the not-at-home), the aesthetic of "letting be" or, perhaps, of letting Being be, that Nathan Scott seems to be recommending in his important recent books, *Negative Capability* and *The Wild Prayer of Longing*. For, in the monolithic well-made world that the positivistic structure of consciousness perceives—and perceiving, creates—it is the Detective who has usurped the place not only of God but of Being too as the abiding presence and, therefore, has first to be confronted.

Our time calls for an existence-Art, one which, by refusing to resolve discords into the satisfying concordances of a *telos*, constitutes an assault against an *art*-ificialized Nature in behalf of the recovery of its primordial terrors. The most immediate task, therefore, in which the contemporary writer must engage himself—it is, to borrow a phrase ungratefully from Yeats, the most difficult task not impossible—is that of undermining the detective-like expectations of the positivistic mind, of unhoming Western man, by evoking rather than purging pity and terror—anxiety. It must, that is, continue the *iconoclastic* revolution begun in earnest after World War II to dislodge or, to be absolutely accurate, to *dis-occident,* the objectified modern Western man, the weighty, the solid citizen, to drive him out of the fictitious well-made world, not to be gathered into the "artifice of eternity," but to be exposed to the existential realm of history, where Nothing is certain. For only in the precincts of our last evasions, where "dread strikes us dumb," only in this silent realm of dreadful uncertainty, are we likely to discover the ontological and aesthetic possibilities of generosity.

In this image-breaking enterprise, therefore, the contemporary writer is likely to find his "tradition," not in the "anti-Aristotelian" line that goes back from the Concrete poets to Proust, Joyce, the imagists, Mallarmé, Gautier, and Pater, but in the "anti-Aristotelianism" that looks back from Beckett, Ionesco, and the Sartre of *Nausea* and *No Exit* through the Eliot of *Sweeney Agonistes,* some of the surrealists, Kafka, Pirandello, Dostoevsky and the "loose, and baggy monsters" of his countrymen, Dickens, Wycherley, and—with all due respect to the editor of the *Daily News*—the Shakespeare of *King Lear, Measure for Measure,* and the ironically entitled *All's Well that Ends Well,* in which one of the characters says:

They say miracles are past, and we have our philosophical persons to make modern and familiar things supernatural and causeless. Hence it is that we make trifles of terrors, ensconcing ourselves into seeming knowledge when we should submit ourselves to an unknown fear.

David Antin

Modernism and Postmodernism
Approaching the Present in American Poetry

A few years ago Roy Lichtenstein completed a group of works called the "Modern Art" series. The paintings—there were sculptures too, aptly labeled "Modern Sculpture"—were mainly representations of Art Deco settings, groups of recognizable abstract forms derived primarily from circles and triangles, situated in a shallow virtual space, derived from a late and academic cubism, and treated to Lichtenstein's typical, simulated benday dot manner in uninflected shades of blue, red, yellow, black and white, and sometimes green. The paintings were amusing. It was absurd to see the high art styles of the early twenties and the "advanced" decorative and architectural styles of the later twenties and early thirties through the screen of a comic strip. It was also appropriate, since these design elements found their way into the backgrounds of Buck Rogers and the lobby of the Radio City Music Hall. At the same time there was something pathetic and slightly unnerving in this treatment of the style features that had long appeared as the claims to "modernism" of Futurism, Purism, Constructivism, and the Bauhaus. What is particularly unnerving about the series is what is most relevant to the subject of modernism versus postmodernism.

Clearly the sense that such a thing as a "postmodern" sensibility exists and should be defined is wrapped up with the conviction that what we have called "modern" for so long is thoroughly over. If we are capable of imagining the "modern" as a closed set of stylistic features, "modern" can no longer mean present. For it is precisely the distinctive feature of the present that, in spite of any strong sense of its coherence, it is always open on its forward side. Once "modern" presents itself as closed, it becomes modern and takes its place alongside Victorian or baroque as a period style. Perhaps it was this sense that led furniture salesmen back in the fifties to offer us a distinction between modern and contemporary furniture, in which modern referred to a specific group of degraded Futurist and Bauhaus characteristics, signified by particular materials like glass and stainless steel or chromium, or by particular design features, such as the "laboratory look" or "streamlining," whereas contemporary signified merely the absence of any strongly defined period features. The pathos of modern art is particular to itself. There is after all nothing pathetic about baroque or Victorian art. But it was the specific claim of "modernism" to be finally and forever open. That was its "futurism," and now that its future has receded into the past it can be had as a sealed package whose contents have the exotic look of something released from a time capsule. This is true for Schoenberg and Varèse, Ruth St. Denis and Isadora or Martha Graham, for Picasso, Malevitch and Moholy Nagy, and for Eliot and Pound. There is nothing surprising about this. The impulses that provided the energy for modern art came from artists who had arrived at their maturity, as human beings if not as artists, by the beginning of the First World War. Since then the world has changed not once but twice. To read the letters or diaries of these artists is to realize that it would take almost as much effort to understand them as to understand the letters of Poussin. But while this is so evident to really contemporary artists as to be almost platitudinous, it is not so evident to anyone else, mainly because the truly contemporary artists of our time are known primarily to a community consisting of themselves. In a sense it is this capacity of the contemporary artist to recognize his contemporaries that is the essential feature of his contemporaneity. For two reasons, I would like to discuss the nature of this contemporaneity in particular for American poetry: because the course of American poetry from 1914 to 1972 is characteristic of the changes in our culture and attitudes, and because our poetry is in an extraordinarily healthy state at the moment and there is no need to consider what is being produced today as in any way inferior to the works of the supposed masters of modernism.

The most artificial and consequently the most convincing way to do this would be to compose a short continuous history of American poetry beginning at the turn of the century and showing how poetry and sensibility continued to change from salient moment to salient moment till we run out of salient moments. I will not do this because, whatever the ontological facts of change through time may be, it is a fact of our experience that it is the past not the present which changes. We go on for a long time taking the present for a constant, much as the self. At some point we raise our heads and are surprised at what lies behind us and how far away it is. The first questions I would like to raise then are when and to whom did the career of "modern" American poetry appear to be over and what did this mean? Taken precisely these questions are very difficult to answer because, among other things, they raise the preliminary question of what "modern" American poetry was, and fluctuations in the answer to this question will produce fluctuations in the answers to the other questions. But in a casual sort of way it is possible to ask these questions in terms of the average, college educated, literate American as of, say, 1960. (1960 is a turning point because it is the date of publication of Donald Allen's anthology *The New American Poetry*, which presented the same college student *moyen* with evidence for an alternate view of the history of American modernism.)

Allen Tate provides a standard list of "masters" in a 1955 essay that was reprinted as an introduction in his part of *An Anthology of British and American Poetry, 1900–1950*, which he compiled with David Cecil. It includes Frost, Pound, Eliot, Stevens, Marianne Moore, Ransom, Cummings, and Crane and is more or less typical for the period during which it was given and for the kind of critic making it. A few years later (1962) Randall Jarrell gives pretty much the same list in his essay "Fifty Years of American Poetry," but he includes William Carlos Williams and omits Crane and Cummings from the "masters" class. It is also worth noting that for this group of critics the period of "modernism," in Tate's words, has "Frost and Stevens at the beginning, Hart Crane in the middle, and Robert Lowell at the end," which situates the period of "modernism" roughly between 1910 and 1950, with Frost at the end of one period and Lowell at the end of the newer one. The fact that it is now 1972 and that the list seems open to reconsideration, to say the least, should not obscure the degree of agreement in established academic circles at that time on this history of the "modern American tradition." From Pound and Eliot to Robert Lowell. This was the view held by the *Kenyon Review, Partisan Review, Sewanee Review, Hudson Review, Poetry Maga-*

zine and perhaps even the *Saturday Review of Literature.* If these authorities were concerned with modern poetry in English, they would generally include Yeats and Auden and Dylan Thomas, though the precise relations of the English to the Americans in the "modern" tradition were not worked out in great detail, except that it was clear that Yeats was among the beginners (after Pound), Auden in the middle (after Eliot), and Thomas toward the end (much like Lowell).

Almost all of the critics who wrote in these magazines held important university positions and taught this view of the tradition as an uncontroversial body of facts. The conviction that in 1950 we were at the conclusion of this period was as much a matter of agreement as everything else, though the feeling surrounding this conviction was somewhat equivocal. In a 1958 lecture on "The Present State of Poetry" Delmore Schwartz offered this summary of the situation:

the poetic revolution, the revolution in poetic taste which was inspired by the criticism of T.S. Eliot . . . , has established itself in power so completely that it is taken for granted not only in poetry and the criticism of poetry, but in the teaching of literature.

Once a literary and poetic revolution has established itself, it is no longer revolutionary, but something very different from what it was when it had to struggle for recognition and assert itself against the opposition of established literary authority. Thus the most striking trait of the poetry of the rising generation of poets is the assumption as self-evident and incontestable of that conception of the nature of poetry which was, at its inception and for years after, a radical and much disputed transformation of poetic taste and sensibility. What was once a battlefield has become a peaceful public park on a pleasant Sunday afternoon, so that if the majority of new poets write in a style and idiom which takes as its starting point the poetic idiom and literary taste of the generation of Pound and Eliot, the motives and attitudes at the heart of the writing possess an assurance which sometimes makes their work seem tame and sedate.

Or to quote Auden, "Our intellectual marines have captured all the little magazines." Whatever one thinks of Schwartz's equivocal characterization of the poets he is describing as the somewhat "sedate" heirs of Eliot and Pound, it is now baffling to hear him refer to new poets writing in a "style which takes as its starting point the poetic idiom and literary taste of the generation of Pound and Eliot" and find him quoting as a specimen of this style:

The green catalpa tree has turned
All white; the cherry blooms once more.
In one whole year I haven't learned
A blessed thing they pay you for.

The comparison between this updated version of *A Shropshire Lad*, whatever virtues one attributes to it, and the poetry of *The Cantos* or *The Waste Land* seems so aberrant as to verge on the pathological. At first sight it is nearly impossible to conceive what Schwartz could possibly have imagined the "poetic idiom" of Pound and Eliot to be, if it could have bred such children as Snodgrass. But the problem is not that Schwartz did not understand what Pound or Eliot sounded like or how their poems operated. His essays demonstrate his grasp of the individual characteristics of both these poets. The etiology lies deeper than that. It lies in his genealogical view of what implications are to be drawn from the work of these "masters," and how these implications validate a succession of poetic practices which inevitably move further and further from the originating styles to the point at which the initiating impulses have lost all their energy. In Schwartz's view Snodgrass and the rest of the poets of the Pack, Hall and Simpson anthology are merely "the end of the line." The important question then becomes: how did the line arrive at this place? The easiest way to answer this question is not to explore the various aspects of the nearly stillborn descendants, but to find the next to the last place—the last "living" generation within the tradition. This group would include Robert Lowell, Randall Jarrell, Theodore Roethke, Karl Shapiro, and Delmore Schwartz himself. If we can understand the curve of connection that joins these poets to Eliot and Pound, we can understand what this tradition of "modernism" was thought to be.

Though he is neither the weakest nor the strongest of these poets, Schwartz is in some ways the most characteristic of this "generation." Schwartz's first book of poetry, *In Dreams Begin Responsibilities*, was published in 1939. It was greeted with enormous enthusiasm. Allen Tate described Schwartz's style as "the only genuine innovation since Pound and Eliot came upon the scene twenty-five years ago." The description is strange, especially in view of Schwartz's own more modest description of the poems as "poems of Experiment and Imitation." The imitations were obvious. "In the Naked Bed in Plato's Cave" is an exercise in what formalist critics like to call Eliot's "late Tudor blank verse."

Hearing the milkman's chop,
His striving up the stair, the bottle's chink,
I rose from bed, lit a cigarette,
And walked to the window. The stony street
Displayed the stillness in which buildings stand,
The street-lamp's vigil and the horse's patience.

But somehow the poem, like most of Schwartz's poems, manages to jog along in the sound of Auden from whom he had acquired the gift of versified platitude, which is so well exemplified in

Tiger Christ unsheathed his sword,
Threw it down, became a lamb.
Swift spat upon the species, but
took two women to his heart.

which concludes in true cautionary style:

"—What do all examples show?
What can any actor know?
The contradiction in every act,
The infinite task of the human heart."

Not only does the sound belong to Auden, but the wisdom, often complete with capitalized nouns:

May memory restore again and again
The smallest color of the smallest day:
Time is the school in which we learn,
Time is the fire in which we burn.

Since the title of Schwartz's first book is derived from the epigraph to Yeats's 1914 volume *Responsibilities* one might have expected some Yeats, and it's there:

All clowns are masked and all *personae*
Flow from choices; . . .

Gifts and choices! All men are masked,
And we are clowns who think to choose our faces
And we are taught in time of circumstances
And we have colds, blond hair and mathematics,
For we have gifts which interrupt our choices.

It is a selection from the imagery of Yeats screened through Auden's bouncing sound. In fact, both the Eliot and Yeats in Schwartz's early work are strained through a screen of Auden. Since Schwartz was twenty-five when the first book came out, the only surprising thing about this is Tate's enthusiasm. For if, as Tate had argued, poetry is "a form of human knowledge," Schwartz's first book neither adds anything to it nor even takes anything away. As for Schwartz, the early work is smooth and trivial but the later work cannot even be said to attain this level. If Auden stood between Schwartz and the "modernist" masters, this fact was not peculiar to Schwartz for the blight of Auden lay heavy on the land. Shapiro's "Elegy for a Dead Soldier" begins matter of factly enough in spite of the rhymes:

> A white sheet on the tail-gate of a truck
> Becomes an altar; two small candlesticks
> Sputter at each side of the crucifix. . . .

but soon swings into Auden's lush rhetorical style:

> No history deceived him, for he knew
> Little of times and armies not his own;
> He never felt that peace was but a loan,
> Had never questioned the idea of gain.
> Beyond the headlines once or twice he saw
> The gathering of power by the few
> But could not tell their names; he cast his vote,
> Distrusting all the elected but not the law.
> He laughed at socialism; *on mourrait*
> *Pour les industriels?* He shed his coat
> And not for brotherhood, but for his pay.
> To him the red flag marked a sewer main.

Even Randall Jarrell, who in 1942 was struggling with a swarm of other voices, had contracted the Auden disease.

> But love comes with its wet caress
> To its own nightmare of delight,
> And love and nothingness possess
> The speechless cities of the night.

At the same time that these younger poets were inundated by Auden they were very busy attempting to exorcise him from their minds. Schwartz sets the style for this procedure by dividing Auden into "The Two Audens." One is "the clever guy, the Noel Coward of literary Marxism," one who speaks in the voice of the "popular entertainer, propagandist, and satirist." This is the Auden "of the Ego," an unauthentic Auden. The other is the "voice of the Id," who is "a kind of sibyl who utters the telltale symbols in a psychoanalytic trance," that is, an authentic Auden. The first Auden writes lines like "You were a great Cunarder, I / Was only a fishing smack"; the second writes passages like:

> Certain it became while we were still incomplete
> There were certain prizes for which we would never compete;
> A choice was killed by every childish illness,
> The boiling tears among the hothouse plants,
> The rigid promise fractured in the garden,
>   And the long aunts.

If the distinction appears oversubtle to us now it did not appear so to Randall Jarrell, who two years later in a somewhat schoolboyish essay tried to work out the precise stylistic differences that encoded the distinction between the more and less authentic Audens. For Jarrell this comes down to the distinction between an early Auden and a late Auden. Early Auden (the authentic one) employs a peculiar *language*; late Auden employs a peculiar *rhetoric*. Though Jarrell seemed at the time fairly satisfied with this tautology, he was apparently unable to provide any reasonable distinction between a "language" and a "rhetoric," because he characterized both of them with the same sort of lists of stylistic literary devices, some of which he merely seems to like better than others. Four years later he returned to the Auden problem, this time approaching it from the point of view of changes in "Auden's Ideology." He finds not two but three Audens—Revolutionary Auden, Liberal Auden, and Fatalist-Christian Auden. It is hard to understand why versified Kierkegaard should appear fundamentally different from versified Marx. No matter what Auden says, it's still chatter. The difference between the Auden of 1930 and 1940 is merely that people are saying a few different things at the same cocktail party. The only "position" one can attribute to Auden is a mild contraposto, one hand in his pocket, the other holding the martini. Which is what is modern about his work. It is modern because he has a modern role to play. The scene is always some kind of party, "Auden" is the main character, and the name of the play is "The Ridiculous Man." Original Sin, the Oedipus Complex, the Decline of the West, the Class Struggle, the Origin of the Species are the lyrics of a musical. There are no changes of opinion, because there are no opinions, just lyrics; there are no changes in style—even at a cocktail party a man may place one finger in the air as he moves to a high point. The Icelandic meters, Piers Plowman, the Border Ballads, syllabics are all made to jog along with a very modish sound. If there is something lethal in this outcome, it is not a viewpoint. Auden has occupied this position with his life.

But Schwartz and Jarrell did not regard Auden as a "modernist" master merely because he was a splendid example of a modern predicament. There are two verbal habits or strategies which Auden has always employed and which these poets regard as fundamental categories of the "modern" mind, appeals to "history" and to "psychoanalysis." Talking about Eliot in a 1955 essay Schwartz refers to a "sense of existence which no human being, and certainly no poet, can escape, at this moment in history, or at any moment in the future which is likely soon to succeed the present." According to Schwartz two aspects of this "view of existence which is natural to a modern human being" are "the development of the historical sense and the awareness of experience which originate in psychoanalysis." Though the "awareness of experience" originating in psychoanalysis may seem somewhat fin-de-siècle or Wagnerian to us now, what Schwartz means by this is fairly clear. What he means by the "historical sense" is not so clear. One would normally suppose a "historical sense" to consist of some view of the relations between sequentially related epochs. Marxism supplies a kind of eschatological view of history and Auden frequently refers to this, along with several other views which are by no means consistent with it. Still, if you look for it, you can find several antihistorical senses, in Auden's poetry. But a "historical sense" is the one thing you cannot find in poems like *The Waste Land* or *The Cantos*, which we may assume Schwartz would have considered the principal "modern" works. *The Waste Land* and *The Cantos* are based on the principle of collage, the dramatic juxtaposition of disparate materials without commitment to explicit syntactical relations between elements. A "historical sense" and "psychoanalysis" are structurally equivalent to the degree that they are in direct conflict with the collage principle. They are both strategies for combating the apparently chaotic collage landscapes of human experience and turning them into linear narratives with a clearly articulated plot. It is not easy to see what advantage such systems offer a poet unless he was convinced of their truth, which would, I suppose, mean either that it would be relevant to some purpose to use these systems as conceptual armatures upon which to mount the diverse and colorful individual facts of sociopolitical and personal human experience, or else that these systems conformed more perfectly than any other with a vaster system of representations to which the poet was committed for some valued reasons. If this was what Schwartz intended we would be confronted with a truly "classical" poetry which would devote itself to the particularization of general truths. While we might imagine such a poetry, we have never really been confronted with it. The poets of Schwartz's generation never presented anything like the kind of detailed particularity of human or political experience in their poems that would have been a necessary condition for such a poetry of metonymy. Even if the poems had fulfilled this necessary condition, such a poetry would require either a commonly accepted theory of history or psychoanalysis or at least a precise knowledge of the details of such a theory and the additional knowledge that such a theory was being referred to, as well as a set of rules for referring the concrete particulars of experience to particular aspects of the theory. Such a situation only obtains for a few people in narrowly circumscribed areas of what we generally call science; that is to say, it obtains only for those who share what Thomas Kuhn in his book *The Structure of Scientific Revolutions* calls a paradigm. Even in a rather trivially reduced form of this situation such as *The Waste Land*, where Eliot has himself advised us that the poem is built on the plan of a particular mythical narrative, there is no agreement on the way the particular parts of the poem relate to the myth. There is so little agreement on this that most critics who are involved with such concerns cannot decide whether the poem does or doesn't include the regeneration which is intrinsic to the myth.

For better or worse "modern" poetry in English has been committed to a principle of collage from the outset, and when "history" or "psychoanalysis" are invoked they are merely well-labeled boxes from which a poet may select ready-made contrasts. For relatively timid poets this strategy may have the advantage of offering recognizability of genre as an alibi for the presentation of what he regards as radically disparate materials, somewhat in the manner in which a sculptor like Stankiewicz used to throw together a boiler casing, several pistons and a few odd gears, and then arrange them in the shape of a rather whimsical anthropomorphic figure. In the main, poets have not resorted to "a sense of history" or to "psychoanalysis" because of the success of these viewpoints in reducing human experience to a logical order, but because the domains upon which they are normally exercised are filled with arbitrary and colorful bits of human experience, which are nevertheless sufficiently "framed" to yield a relatively tame sort of disorder.

If there is any doubt that it is the "sense of collage" that is the basic characteristic of "modernist" poetry, it is mainly because of the reduced form in which the principle of collage had been understood by the Nashville critics and the poets who followed them. Poets of this group, like Jarrell or Robert Lowell, tend to produce this attenuated collage with the use of a great variety of framing devices. In a poem only sixteen lines long Jarrell ticks off the names of Idomeneo, Stendhal, the Empress Eugenie, Maxwell's demon, John Stuart Mill, Jeremy Bentham, William Wordsworth, Charles Dodgson, and Darwin's son, a fair-sized list of figures from the arbitrary procession of history, but the poem is carefully rationalized (framed) by its title, "Charles Dodgson's Song." The author of Alice in Wonderland ought to be able to sing history in any order, and the poem is presented as a supposed "inversion" of a supposed "logical" view of history. But there is no "logical" target of the poem, which is not a parody at all. It is merely a pleasant historical collage with a title that takes the edge off. To poets like Jarrell, Europe after the end of the Second World War offered an unparalleled opportunity. It presented them with a ready-made rubble heap (a collage) that could be rationalized by reference to a well-known set of historical circumstances, and it is no accident that nearly half of his book *The Seven League Crutches* (published in 1951) is devoted to a section called "Europe." The strongest of the poems in this section, "A Game at Salzburg," is also typical:

A little ragged girl, our ball-boy;
A partner—ex-Africa Korps—
In khaki shorts, P.W. illegible.
(He said: "To have been a prisoner of war
In Colorado iss a privilege.")
The evergreens, concessions, carrousels,
And D.P. camp of Franz Joseph Park;
A gray-green river, evergreen-dark hills.
Last, a long way off in the sky,
Snow-mountains.

Over this clouds come, a darkness falls.
Rain falls.
         On the veranda Romana,
A girl of three,
Sits licking sherbet from a wooden spoon;
I am already through.
She says to me, softly: *Hier bin i'*.
I answer: *Da bist du*.

This is a kind of covert collage, the girl ball-boy, the ex-enemy tennis partner, the P.W. camp in Colorado, the evergreens, concessions, carrousels, the girl on the veranda eating sherbet, the dialogue "Here I am," "There you are." And while it masquerades in the guise of a realist narrative, there is no "narrative"—or to be even more precise, what it shares with "short stories" of this type is the characteristic of a covert collage masquerading behind the thin disguise of pseudo-narrative. The poem would have been a lot more effective had it ended here, but Jarrell, who is obsessed with the necessity for framing at the same time that he is always tempted by his vision of the arbitrary, goes on for two more stanzas past some more local color—Marie Theresa's sleigh and some ruined cornice nymphs—to the obligatory pseudo-epiphany in which such pseudo-narratives normally culminate:

But the sun comes out, and the sky
Is for an instant the first rain-washed blue
Of becoming . . . .

In anguish, in expectant acceptance
The world whispers: *Hier bin i'*.

Jarrell may have a strong sense of the arbitrariness of experience, but the experience is not so arbitrary that it cannot be labeled in terms of "local color" as well as the "revelational experience." Still, "A Game at Salzburg" is the strongest poem in the book and is a marked improvement over *Little Friend, Little Friend*, in which the only poem that isn't smothered in framing devices is the epigraph to the volume:

Then I hear the bomber call me in: "Little Friend
Little Friend, I got two engines on fire. Can you see
me, Little Friend?"
         I said, "I'm crossing right over you. Let's go home."

The only reason that Jarrell didn't frame this piece was that he didn't think of it as a poem.

The use of covert collage was very widespread among the poets of the forties and early fifties. Robert Lowell's *Lord Weary's Castle* abounds in it and employs a great variety of framing devices: collage as biography ("Mary Winslow," "In Memory of Arthur Winslow"), as elegy ("The Quaker Graveyard in Nantucket"), as psychological fiction ("Between the Porch and the Altar"), as history ("Concord," "Napoleon Crosses the Berezina"); and there is a considerable overlap of genres in single poems. A sonnet like "Concord" is a fairly good example of this type of history collage:

Ten thousand Fords are idle here in search
Of a tradition. Over these dry sticks—
The Minute Man, the Irish Catholics,
The ruined bridge and Walden's fished-out perch—
The belfry of the Unitarian Church
Rings out the hanging Jesus. Crucifix,
How can your whited spindling arms transfix
Mammon's unbridled industry, the lurch
For forms to harness Heraclitus' stream!
This Church is Concord—Concord where Thoreau
Named all the birds without a gun to probe
Through darkness to the painted man and bow:
The death-dance of King Philip and his scream
Whose echo girdled this imperfect globe.

If it is obvious that Lowell has attitudes toward American history, it is even more obvious that they do not represent an "historical sense." The poem is a collage made up of remnants of the past thrust into the present in the form of worn-out monuments. Thoreau, the Minute Man, the Unitarian Church share a salient characteristic for Lowell's imagined tourists in their Fords; they are all out of the elementary school history text. King Philip would also share this characteristic, but he doesn't make it into most grade school histories. Lowell throws him into the list of contrasting figures on the battlefield of history to add the one that inhabits his mind along with the rest of them. The poem is filled with sets of clear and not so clear dramatic oppositions. Thoreau, the peaceful resister, against the Minute Man, the warlike resister; King Philip, the Indian rebel, who shares a feature with Thoreau (perhaps) in resisting the inevitable advance of technology (if we discount Thoreau's pencil factory), and shares warlikeness with the Minute Man; the Irish Catholics who inherit the energy of Christianity (we all know about Irishmen), which contrasts with the pallid lack of energy of the "higher class" Unitarians. The Irish probably drive the Fords; the Unitarians were there forever, at least since King Philip's War was settled. The figures in the poem carry a barrage of coupled features—High Energy/High Value; High Energy/Low Value; Low Energy/Low Value; Low Energy/High Value—though in a number of cases the feature assignments are not by any means clear from the poem, only from a general likelihood, considering the places from which Lowell acquired the material. Thus, Melville's "Metaphysics of Indian Hating" lies somewhere behind the poem, as does Hawthorne; but it is not clear how far behind the poem they lie. That is to say, it is clear from the poem that the arbitrary selection of figures who appear in it, including Christ, have strong evaluative interpretations attached to them, but it is not at all clear what they are or how securely they are attached. So that the attitudes toward history in the poem merely guarantee various charges of intensity. The poem, however, is securely situated in a genre that is more appropriately called "The New England Myth." This is not so much history as a communal fiction carried out by Hawthorne, Melville, Henry James, a host of minor writers, and, at the very beginning of his career, by T. S. Eliot, where we might have expected it to end for sheer lack of relevance to any contemporary reality. But it is from this reservoir of attitudes that Lowell persists in pulling his pieces.

"Concord" is not a major effort for Lowell and whatever strength it has it draws from its position among the other pieces in *Lord Weary's Castle,* but it is characteristic of Lowell's manipulation of history, which turns out to be neither history nor Lowell's manipulation of it. It is the "New England Myth" reduced still further to the cryptic commonplaces of the sort of *Partisan Review* essay that used to draw upon the well-known ironic collisions of Hawthorne, Melville, and James with grade school textbooks and Fourth of July speeches. It is cocktail-party intellectual history. It requires no theory and very few facts and is a natural collage. In defense of Lowell, the poet, one may say that it has the singular advantage of appealing to a coherent group that is not interested in history or fact or poetry, but in its own conversation—the literary community of the *New York Review of Books.* So it is not surprising to find Lowell still exploiting the same strategy at the end of the 1950s in

"For the Union Dead." This poem is on a larger scale, and because it is somewhat expanded it superimposes a screen of pseudo-narrative over its pseudo-history. Or more correctly the "history" is partially dissolved in a standing liquid of pseudo-narrative. Where "Concord" begins with the anecdotal realism of the Fords stalled on the highway, "For the Union Dead" begins with a walk through South Boston:

> The old South Boston Aquarium stands
> in a Sahara of snow now. Its broken windows are boarded.
> The bronze weathervane has lost half its scales.
> The airy tanks are dry.

This triggers the memory of watching the fish as a child, and emergence from this memory leads to the memory of a different walk across Boston Common. Here the Heraclitian flux of "Concord" is expanded to:

> One morning last March,
> I pressed against the new barbed and galvanized
>
> fence on the Boston Common. Behind their cage,
> yellow dinosaur steamshovels were grunting
> as they cropped up tons of mush and grass
> to gouge their underworld garage.
>
> Parking spaces luxuriate like civic
> sandpiles in the heart of Boston.
> A girdle of orange, Puritan-pumpkin colored girders
> braces the tingling Statehouse,
> shaking over the excavations, as it faces Colonel Shaw
> and his bell-cheeked Negro infantry
> on St. Gaudens' shaking Civil War relief,
> propped by a plank splint against the garage's earthquake.

There are several worn-out monuments of New England virtue (mythical virtue) here also: Colonel Shaw, who

> has an angry wrenlike vigilance,
> a greyhound's gentle tautness;
> he seems to wince at pleasure,
> and suffocate for privacy.
>
> . . . he rejoices in man's lovely,
> peculiar power to choose life and die—
> when he leads his black soldiers to death,
> he cannot bend his back

—and the usual "old white churches" which "hold their air / of sparse, sincere rebellion," to which pair is added William James, who "could almost hear the bronze Negroes breathe." Lowell, who always manages to get as much grade school history into a poem as he can, manages to turn the protective red lead paint on the brand new girders into "Puritan-pumpkin colored girders." Only Squanto and the turkeys are missing, but this is probably for the very good reason that they do not immediately lend themselves to the "dark view" of New England history appropriated from Hawthorne et al. by the Southerners of the *Partisan Review*. If the churches are "sincere," they are also "sparse"—that is, Puritanical, rigid, probably even antisexual. The bronze statue of Colonel Shaw "cannot bend his back," which looks at the least like some sort of "abstract" arrogance. ("The stone statues of the abstract Union Soldier / grow slimmer and younger each year—.") For the inhabitants of Boston "Their monument sticks like a fishbone / in the city's throat." William James, whose wholesome virtue seems to have blinded him to St. Gaudens' aesthetic limitations, apparently did not anticipate this. Although the poem at times seems so, it is not a form of cryptic Southern propaganda. The ironies are merely obligatory parts of the poem's machinery; grammar school history is only a target for parlor conversation. William James knew about Northern negro lynchings and the famous draft riots, and it is doubtful that Lowell would deny this. The "William James" of the poem is not William James, it is a "Great Optimist" speaking, also an invention of literary gossip. The real concern of this poem is what its "urban collage"—"la forme d'une ville / Change plus vite, hélas! que le coeur d'un mortel."

"For the Union Dead" is so much like Baudelaire's "Le Cygne" that it is instructive to examine the similarities and differences between these two poems separated by a hundred years time. The Baudelaire poem is also triggered by a walk past something that is no longer there: "as I was crossing the new Carrousel." The Place du Carrousel, or that part of it situated between the Arc de Triomphe du Carrousel and the Louvre, had been occupied until about 1840 by a snarl of narrow streets that Louis Philippe started to clear in a vast demolition program that was completed by Napoleon III. The renovations were not completed much before the composition of the poem. So that for Baudelaire the area, for most of the length of his experience of Paris, had been the site of temporary structures and things rising and falling, a situation not unlike the post-Second World War renovation of the older Eastern American cities like New York or Boston. It is hardly necessary to point out that the area around the Tuileries and the Boston Common have certain similarities for their respective cities. Baudelaire does not begin directly with a description of the city but with an apostrophe to Andromache, an image of loss which, it turns out, takes its point of departure from the presence of the Seine on the poet's right as he faces the Louvre; but with the second stanza he moves directly into the "city collage":

> That little river
> . . . .
> Fecundated my fertile memory,
> As I was crossing
> The old Paris is no more (the form of a city
> Changes faster, alas, than the human heart);
>
> Only in my mind can I see that camp of shacks,
> Those piles of roughed-out capitals and columns,
> The weeds, the great blocks grown green from the water
>   in the puddles
> And the confused pile of rubble gleaming among the tiles.

Where Lowell has an Aquarium, Baudelaire has a menagerie that is no longer there. For Lowell:

> Once my nose crawled like a snail on the glass;
> my hand tingled
> to burst the bubbles
> drifting from the noses of the cowed, compliant fish.
> My hand draws back. I often sigh still
> for the dark downward and vegetating kingdom
> of the fish and reptile . . . .

And for Baudelaire:

> There, one morning, I saw . . .
>
> A swan that had escaped its cage
> And with its webbed feet scraping on the dry pavement
> Dragged its white plumage on the rough earth
> Along a dried up gutter . . .
>
> In whose dust it nervously bathed its wings.

These are both poems of intense nostalgia, where the city becomes the site of arbitrary historical change. The city as collage is a sort of model of the menace of history viewed as deterioration from some "non-fragmented" anterior state. The similarities in the poems are more surprising than the differences, which are to a great extent differences in presentational strategy. Baudelaire has no reason to suppose that he should not explicitly comment on the "meaning" of the presented material:

> Paris changes! But in my melancholy nothing
> Budges! New palaces, scaffoldings, blocks of stone,
> Old quarters, the whole thing becomes an allegory for me
> And my fond memories are heavier than the stones.

The result of this is that he winds up as a figure inside the poem. Lowell plays it cooler. Though it is the poet who crouches at his television set, it is Colonel Shaw who "is riding on his bubble" waiting "for the blessed break." Which may seem like a thin distinction, but it corresponds rather closely to Allen Tate's distinction between a romantic and a modern poet.

the Romantic movement taught the reader to look for inherently poetical objects, and to respond to them "emotionally" in certain prescribed ways, these ways being indicated by the "truths" interjected at intervals among the poetical objects. Certain modern poets offer no inherently poetical objects, and they fail to instruct the reader in the ways he must feel about the objects. All experience, then, becomes potentially the material of poetry—not merely the pretty and the agreeable—and the modern poet makes it possible for us to "respond" to this material in all the ways in which men everywhere may feel and think . . . for to him [the modern poet] poetry is not a special package tied up in pink ribbon: it is one of the ways that we have of knowing the world.

With careful qualifications Tate is here defining his idea of the "modern" poet. His argument rests on two ideas: that all experience is a legitimate arena for poetry and that the interjection of the poet's opinions into a poem is an act of coercion that narrows the possibilities of response in the reader by constraining him to take up certain attitudes in regard to the objects presented. If you follow this line of reasoning, Baudelaire shares the "modernist" appetite for dealing with "all experience . . . not merely the pretty and the agreeable," but he is not a "modern" poet insofar as he instructs the readers not once but several times in the ways they must respond to the objects he has presented. By this formula, subtract from Baudelaire his remaining "romanticism" and we get Lowell's "modernism." Since Tate was arguing for a poetry of pure presentation, in which the reader's response to the "objects" in the poem is based entirely upon a kind of object semantics, he would seem to be for a poetry of pure collage. Given this attitude toward "modernism," it is surprising that critics like Tate did not respond with great enthusiasm when a poet like Charles Olson appeared on the scene shortly after the end of the Second World War.

> I thought of the E on the stone and of what Mao said
> la lumiere"
> > but the kingfisher
> de l'aurore"
> > but the kingfisher flew west
> est devant nous!
> > he got the color of his breast
> > from the heat of the setting sun!
>
> The features are, the feebleness of the feet
> > (syndactylism of the 3rd and 4th digit)
> the bill, serrated, sometimes a pronounced beak, the wings
> where the color is, short and round, the tail
> inconspicuous.

This should have fit Tate's theory perfectly. The objects are there in all their autonomy—the enigmatic mark on the stone, Mao's injunction to action, the kingfisher as bird of the imagination, the kingfisher out of the natural history book. "The Kingfishers" is filled with many interjections, but none of them advises the reader how to react to the other "objects" in the poem. The interjected "truths" have an objectlike status which they share with Mao's words, the natural history text, the mythical material, the fragment of a contemporary party, bits of communication theory, the inventory of plundered Indian treasure, the elliptical anecdote of human slaughter. But if it fits Tate's theory, Tate was apparently unaware of it; one may search Tate's *Essays of Four Decades*, published as late as 1968, and not find a single mention of one of the most powerful poets and certainly the most graceful poet of the fifties.

But Tate was not alone in ignoring Olson, and there is no obligation on the part of a poet-critic to try to take a reasonable view of the contemporary poetic situation. Certainly both John Crowe Ransom and Delmore Schwartz, who had more reason to consider a force as powerful as Olson when they were reviewing at the Library of Congress the state of American Poetry at mid-century, managed not to notice him and to conclude, since they were apparently unaware of every significant younger poet in the country, that the "newest poets appear much more often than not to be picking up again the meters, which many poets in the century had thought that they must dispense with." As a statement of fact this was a complete misrepresentation of what was going on in American poetry in 1958. An alphabetical list of poets besides Olson who had already published at least one book and who were not "picking up again the meters" includes John Ashbery, Paul Blackburn, Gregory Corso, Robert Creeley, Robert Duncan, Larry Eigner, Lawrence Ferlinghetti, Allen Ginsberg, David Ignatow, Kenneth Koch, Denise Levertov, Michael McClure, Frank O'Hara, Joel Oppenheimer, and Jack Spicer, to name only the ones that come to mind most easily. These poets were very different from each other, then as now; and some of them, perhaps as many as half, may have seemed to represent a neoromantic sensibility, which the Southern formalists had opposed to a "modern" sensibility. Specifically a poet like Ginsberg might seem to have ushered in a return to Blake or Shelley (romantic = unmodern), and while this particular opinion is worth discussing, that's not what happened. As usual Tate is typical. In a 1968 essay he suggests that "much of the so-called poetry of the past twenty or more years [is merely] anti-poetry, a parasite on the body of positive poetry, without significance except that it reminds us that poetry can be written." What is shocking about this suggestion is that it is based on what seems like a nearly trivial characteristic of this great body of diverse poetry: its disregard for metrical organization. In the paragraph I have quoted Tate explains that "formal versification is the primary structure of poetic order, the assurance to the reader and to the poet himself that the poet is in control of the disorder both outside him and within his own mind." This bizarre statement seems very far from the immense human dignity of Tate's definition of the "Modern Poet": "Certain modern poets offer no inherently poetical objects, and they fail to instruct the reader in the ways he must feel about the objects. All experience, then, becomes potentially the material of poetry." Certainly the "assurance to the reader that the poet is in control" instructs the reader quite precisely in the ways he must feel about the objects. He must feel poetical about them, that is, he must experience no equivocal impulses that are likely to threaten the poetical frame that wraps these objects like a "pink ribbon." It is the pathetic hope of a virgin for an experienced lover whose competence (detachment) is sufficient to lead her to an orgasm, and all to be achieved by mere maintenance of a regular rhythm.

The great importance attributed to something so trivial as regularization of syllable accent by such relatively intelligent people as Tate, Ransom, and Eliot is so remarkable that it deserves an essay of itself. But it is probably sufficient for our purposes here to point out that the value attributed to this phonological idiosyncrasy is symbolic. So that when Eliot insists on the value of the ghost of a meter lurking "behind the arras," it is because the image of meter is for him an image of some moral order (a tradition). It is this aspect of Eliot that is not "modern" but provincial. This becomes clearer in Ransom, who is very precise about the symbolic nature of meter.

I think meters confer upon the delivery of poetry the sense of a ritualistic occasion. When a ritual develops it consists in the enactment, or the recital over and over again, of some experience which is obsessive for us, yet intangible and hard to express. The nearest analogue to the reading of poetry according to the meters, as I think, is the reading of an ecclesiastical service by the congregation. Both the genius of poetry and the genius of the religious establishment work against the same difficulty, which is the registration of what is inexpressible, or metaphysical. The religious occasion is a very formal one, with its appointed place in the visible temple, and the community of worshippers congregated visibly.

You don't have to be especially committed to ritual or religion to observe that this is a kind of poetical Episcopalianism. The Sermon on the Mount was also a religious occasion; it didn't take place in a "visible temple" and wasn't delivered in meter. But if the meaning of meter for Ransom is amiable and nostalgic, that is a triumph of personality. For Eliot and for Tate, as for their last disciple, Lowell, the loss of meter is equivalent to the loss of a whole moral order. It is a "domino theory" of culture—first meter, then Latin composition, then In'ja. This persistent tendency to project any feature from any plane of human experience onto a single moral axis is an underlying characteristic of the particular brand of "modernism" developed by Eliot, Tate, and Brooks. It is not a characteristic of Pound or Williams, and it is why Eliot and Tate will lead to Lowell and even Snodgrass, while Pound and Williams will lead to Rexroth, Zukofsky, Olson, Duncan, Creeley and so on.

The mentality behind this "moral" escalation is clumsy and pretentious. It has its roots in Eliot's criticism, in which it is so totally pervasive that a single instance should be sufficient to recall the entire tonality. In his essay on Baudelaire Eliot offers to gloss Baudelaire's aphorism: la volupté unique et suprême de l'amour gît dans la certitude de faire le mal. According to Eliot, "Baudelaire has perceived that what distinguishes the relations of man and woman from the copulation of beasts is the knowledge of Good and Evil (of *moral* Good and Evil which are not natural Good and Bad or puritan Right and Wrong). Having an imperfect, vague, romantic conception of Good, he was able to understand that the sexual act as evil is more dignified, less boring, than as the natural 'life-giving,' cheery automatism of the modern world. . . . So far as we are human, what we do must be evil or good." Which suggests that Baudelaire is, like Eliot, a moral social climber, energizing his sexual activity by reducing the whole complex domain of its human relations to a single moral axis with two signs: Good and Evil. The most amusing thing about Eliot's reading is that Baudelaire in no way suggests that "the sexual act" is Evil; what he says is that "the unique and supreme voluptuousness of love lies in the certainty of [its leading to] doing evil"—presumably because of the complex set of nonidentical desires, expectations, and frustrations and their consequences in so close a terrain. The "voluptuousness" is like that of stock car driving, which will certainly lead to injury, though one does not seek it. Baudelaire was not from St. Louis.

This tendency to reduce all variation to clashes of opposites is part of what critics like Cleanth Brooks and I. A. Richards imagine to be characteristic of metaphysical poetry. Richards provides a theoretical analysis of two types of poetry which becomes the basis of Brooks's theory of the distinction between modern and romantic poetry. Richards distinguishes between a poetry of "inclusion" (for Brooks, modern and metaphysical) and the poetry of "exclusion" (for Brooks, romantic and unmodern). The poetry of exclusion "leaves out the opposite and discordant qualities of an experience, excluding them from the poem," the poetry of inclusion is a "poetry in which the imagination includes them, resolving the apparent discords, and thus gaining a larger unity." From this definition it follows that these two types of poetry are structurally different: "the difference is not one of subject but of the relations *inter se* of the several impulses active in the experience. A poem of the first group [exclusion] is built out of sets of impulses *which run parallel, which have the same direction.* In a poem of the second group the most obvious feature is the *extraordinary heterogeneity* of the distinguishable impulses. But they are *more than heterogeneous, they are opposed* [my emphasis]." This remarkable idea is based on a metaphorical vector analysis, in which it is absolutely necessary to imagine a poem as consisting of "impulses" seen as directed movements in a single plane for which a fixed set of coordinates has been chosen. It is only when we make all these assumptions that we fully understand Richards's idea of "opposed" impulses. They are magnitudes of opposite signs considered with respect to their projections on a single axis (toward or away from a zero point). It is because Richards has this precise analysis in mind that he substitutes the idea of "opposition" for the idea of "heterogeneity." Heterogeneity does not immediately simplify into a contrast along a single axis. To support this simplified vector analysis further, Richards redefines "irony" as a single dimensional reversal. "Irony in this sense consists in the bringing in of the opposite, the complementary impulses." This predictably leads to the tautologous observation that the poetry of exclusion is vulnerable to irony while the poetry of inclusion is not (because it includes it—which is like saying that Czechoslovakia was not vulnerable to the Russian Army because it included it). Brooks seizes upon this analysis and identifies both the nervous and elusive, quibbling style of Donne and his version of "modernist" tradition with this trivial idea of monodimensional contrast. That the idea is trivial will become clear if we consider the situation of semantic contrast. For any two words in a language it may be possible to find a common semantic axis along which they may be ranked. For example: two adjectives "colloquial" and "thrifty" may be regarded as antonymic (possessing opposed signs) along the axis running from "Closed" to "Open," with "colloquial" moving toward "Open" and "thrifty" moving toward "Closed," though the extent to which either word is intersected by that semantic axis may not be equivalent or specifiable. Even "colloquial" and "blue" may have a semantic axis in common, for example, Abstract—Concrete (which might be exploited by a poet like Auden in a hypothetical line such as "They lived in houses / that were colloquial and blue"); and while it's obvious that from most viewpoints "colloquial" will run toward Abstract and "blue" toward Concrete, it should be equally obvious that the number of possible axes would consist of all the innumerable antonymic pairs of the language and the most commonplace utterances would have to be mapped in terms of "hyperspaces" that defy the imagination. But no one has attempted such mapping except Osgood, and he has not been concerned with relating his Semantic Differential to poetry. The effect of this imaginary vector analysis was largely to reduce the idea of complex poems to an idea of ironic poems, which is to reduce the complex "hyperspace" of modernist collage (Pound, Williams, Olson, Zukofsky) to the nearly trivial, single-dimensional ironic and moral space of Eliot, Tate, Lowell, and so on. This is the reason for not recognizing Olson. It was the same reason for not recognizing Zukofsky. They do not occupy a trivial moral space. The taste for the ironic, moral poem is a taste for a kind of pornography which offers neither intellectual nor emotional experience but a fantasy of controlled intensity, and like all pornography it is thoroughly mechanical. But machinery is quite imperfectly adapted to the human body and nervous system, which operates on different principles. As a result poetry such as Lowell's seems terribly clumsy as it continually seeks to reach some contrived peak of feeling while moving in the machine-cut groove of his verse. So lines like "I could hear / the top floor typist's thunder" or "I sit at a gold table with my girl / whose eyelids burn with brandy" come to be judged by Lowell himself in other lines like "My heart you race and stagger and demand / More blood-gangs for your nigger-brass percussions," but they are misjudged. Lowell attempts to energize a poem at every possible point and the result is often pathetic or vulgar; Baby Dodds didn't push and was never vulgar. But it is the decadence of the metrical-moral tradition that is at fault more than the individual poet. The idea of a metrics as a "moral" or "ideal" traditional order against which the "emotional" human impulses of a poet continually struggle in the form of his real speech is a transparently trivial paradigm worthy of a play by Racine and always yields the same small set of cheap musical thrills.

The appearance of Olson and the Black Mountain poets was the beginning of the end for the Metaphysical Modernist tradition, which was by no means a "modernist" tradition but an anomaly peculiar to American and English poetry. It was the result of a collision of strongly antimodernist and provincial sensibilities with the hybrid modernism of Pound and the purer modernism of Gertrude Stein and William Carlos Williams. Because of the intense hostility to "modernism" of Eliot, Ransom, and Tate, it was not possible for them to come into anything but superficial contact with it except as mediated through Ezra Pound, whom Eliot at least was able to misread as a fellow provincial, chiefly because of Pound's "Great Books" mentality. This was a mistake, for regardless of the material that he was manipulating, Pound as a poet was an inherent modernist committed to the philosophical bases of collage organization, both as a principle of discovery and as a strategy of presentation. But it was a fortunate mistake for Eliot, because whatever is interesting about *The Waste Land* is only visible and audible as a result of Pound's savage collage cuts. Whatever is interesting and not vulgar—because it is the speed of the collage-cut narration that rushes you over the heavy-handed parodies and the underlying sensibility, which is the snobbery of a butler. The return of collage modernism in the fifties had both semantic and musical implications. If it meant a return to the semantic complexities of normal human discourse in the full "hyperspace" of real language, it also meant an end to the ideal of "hurdy gurdy" music, finishing off once and for all the "dime store" eloquence of Yeats and the "general store" eloquence of Frost, along with the mechanical organ of Dylan Thomas, as anything more than shabby operatic genres that might be referred to out of nostalgia or an equivocal taste for falseness and corrupted styles. The appearance of Olson in *Origin* and in the *Black Mountain Review* signified the reappraisal of Pound and Williams, the return of Rexroth, Zukofsky, and the later return of Oppen, Rakosi, Reznikoff, and Bunting; and it was quite appropriate for Williams to reprint Olson's essay on "Projective Verse" in his own autobiography, because it was the first extended discussion of the organizational principles of this wing of modernist poetry.

Starting as he does from Pound it is inevitable that Olson should see these organizational principles in "musical" terms. But Olson reads Pound very profoundly and locates the "music" of poetry in the origins of human utterance, the breath:

If I hammer, if I recall in, and keep calling in, the breath, the breathing as distinguished from the hearing, it is for cause, it is to insist upon a part that breath plays in verse which has not . . . been sufficiently observed or practiced, but which has to be if verse is to advance to its proper force and place in the day, now, and ahead. I take it that PROJECTIVE VERSE teaches, is, this lesson, that the verse will only do in which a poet manages to register both the acquisitions of his ear *and* the pressures of his breath.

It follows from the brief mythical description Pound gave to it in 1913:

You begin with the yeowl and the bark, and you develop into the dance and into music, and into music with words, and finally into words with music, and finally into words with a vague adumbration of music, words suggestive of music, words measured, or words measured in a rhythm that preserves some accurate trait of the emotive impression, or of the sheer character of the fostering or parental emotion.

Pound's is the expressivist theory suggested by Vico and the eighteenth-century music theorists and lurking for a long time in the European imagination. Olson places this idea, or that part of it he is interested in, on the plane of a kind of psycholinguistics: the pressure to utterance is supported by a surge of breath, which is alternately partially checked and released by what presents itself as a phonological entity—the syllable—until the breath charge is exhausted at the line ending. So Olson's Projective Verse is a theory of poetry as well-formed utterance, where "well-formed" means that it provides an adequate traversal of the poet's various energy states. This is full-fledged romantic theory, and whatever weaknesses it has, it offers the poet a broad array of new phonological entities to discriminate and play with, and it places its reliance on the well-formedness of the language itself. So Olson will seek to articulate vowel music, to play upon patterned contrasts between tense and lax vowels, or compact and diffuse vowels, or vowels with higher and/or lower pitched prominent formants, to dispose of these under varying conditions of tenseness or laxness, or brevity or length in the environment of differentially closed, or closed versus open, syllables, under varying accentual conditions resulting from different position in words, in word groups, in sentences and whole segments of discourse. To this Olson adds a final discrimination in the notation of pausal juncture and of shifts of attention and general speaking tempo and pulse. This vast repertory of possibilities inherent in the language was partially exploited by Pound and Williams, though Pound's overattachment to crude extralinguistic song and dance rhythms superimposed on the language tends to obliterate his linguistic refinement. It is possible that the weak point of this whole group of poets—Pound, Williams, Zukofsky, Bunting, Olson, Duncan, Creeley, etc.—is the metaphor of music itself, for the "music" they have in mind is based on a relatively conventional organization of pitches and accents. But because they are not dealing with "music" but language, and because there is a very imprecise analogy between language and music (as for example in the case of so-called "vowel pitch," where it is notorious that vowels do not have "pitches" but, all other things being equal, consist of variously amplified frequency bands impressed upon a fundamental carrier tone), they are not so seriously affected by the inadequacy of their theory of music (or dance), which still represents an enormous advance over the absurdly trivial repertory of possibilities offered by meter.

It is this vastly enlarged repertory of possibilities that makes it possible for these poets to sustain with unerring, abundant, and casual subtleties poems hundreds of lines long. Poems like "As the Dead Prey Upon Us" or "To Gerhardt, There Among Europe's Things . . ." are each cantilenas of nearly 200 lines. They are difficult to give any reasonable impression of through quotes because the large curve of the music subsumes without blurring many sequences of intricately various detail whose sequential relations form a large part of Olson's poetics. To indicate how original this unforced sound was, one is compelled to quote mere fragments:

I pushed my car, it had been sitting so long unused.
I thought the tires looked as though they only needed air.
But suddenly the huge underbody was above me, and
        the rear tires
were masses of rubber and thread variously clinging together

as were the dead souls in the living room, gathered
about my mother, some of them taking care to pass
beneath the beam of the movie projector, some record
playing on the victrola, and all of them
desperate with the tawdriness of their life in hell

I turned to the young man on my right and asked, "How is it,
there?" And he begged me protestingly don't ask, we are poor
poor. And the whole room was suddenly posters and
        presentations
of brake linings and other automotive accessories,
        cardboard

displays, the dead roaming from one to another
as bored back in life as they are in hell, poor and doomed
to mere equipments

Then this moves quickly back to his mother in the "rocker / under the lamp" ("she returns to the house once a week") and, picking up on the bit of Indian song "we are poor poor," swings into

O the dead!
        and the Indian woman and I
        enabled the blue deer
        to walk
        and the blue deer talked,
        in the next room,
        a Negro talk

        it was like walking a jackass,
        and its talk
        was the pressing gabber of gammers
        of old women

        and we helped walk it around the room
        because it was seeking socks
        or shoes for its hooves
        now that it was acquiring

        human possibilities

In the five hindrances men and angels
stay caught in the net, in the immense nets
which spread out across each plane of being, the multiple nets
which hamper at each step of the ladders as the angels
and the demons
and men
go up and down

        Walk the jackass
        Hear the victrola
        Let the automobile
        be tucked into a corner of the white fence
        when it is a white chair. Purity

is only an instant of being, the trammels

recur

In the five hindrances, perfection
is hidden

        I shall get
        to the place
        10 minutes late.

        It will be 20 minutes
        of 9. And I don't know,
        without the car,

        how I shall get there

Which raises the difficult if somewhat academic question of whether
this is a return to "modernism." In principle it is built on Pound, and
some details, taken out of context, sound like Williams ("I shall get / to
the place / 10 minutes late"); but other details sound of surrealism, translations of American Indian poetry, and so on. In the end this powerful
and light way of moving is Olson's own. But even assuming that Olson
and the other Black Mountain poets are thoroughly individual, which
they are, it is still possible to see them as renovating and deepening the
"modernist" tradition of Pound and Williams. There is certainly a transformation of Pound's idea of culture. Where Pound set out on a course to
recover the cultural heritage of poetry, what he had in mind seemed at
times to mean a collection of "touchstones." He was a collector of literary specimens. (But there was also the Frobenius, and Confucius and the
Founding Fathers, and so on). Olson shifts the whole emphasis into an
attempt to recover the cultural heritage of *humanity*, "The Human Universe." Similarly Robert Duncan, the other main theorist of the group,
sets out to recover his version of the human universe and starts out to
look for it in the exiled, abandoned and discarded knowledges, hopes and
fears, magic, alchemy, the Gnosis, Spiritualism, etc. It is a deepening and
widening of Pound's cultural career, though to the extent that Pound was
involved in a cultural career he was not any more of a "modernist" than
Matthew Arnold. Unlike the Frenchmen who were his contemporaries
Pound had the advantages and disadvantages of provincialism. In 1914
Pound was still translating Latin epigrams, worrying about Bertran de
Born, and advising his songs how to behave, while Blaise Cendrars had
already completed "The Transsiberian Prose and Little Jeanne of France"
and "Panama or the Adventures of my Seven Uncles." There was nothing
that Pound had written that could compare to the "modernism" of:

Those were the days of my adolescence
I was just sixteen and I could no longer remember my childhood

I was sixteen thousand leagues from the place of my birth
I was in Moscow in the city of one thousand and three bells
        and seven railroad stations
And I wasn't satisfied with the seven railroad stations and the
        thousand and three towers
Because my adolescence was so hot and crazy
That my heart burned in its turn like the temple at Ephesus
        or the Red Square in Moscow
When the sun sets
And my eyes were lighting up old roads
And I was already such a lousy poet
That I could never go all the way to the end

The Kremlin was like an immense Tartar cake
Encrusted with gold
With the giant almonds of the cathedrals all white
And the honeyed gold of the bells . . .
An old monk was reading the lay of Novgorod
I was thirsty
And I was deciphering cuneiform characters
When the pigeons of the Holy Ghost suddenly flew up from
        the square
And my hands flew up too with the rustling of an albatross
And those were my last memories of my last day
Of my very last voyage
And of the sea

And I was a very lousy poet
And I could never go all the way
And I was hungry
And all the days and all the women in the cafes and all
        the glasses
I would have liked to drink them and break them
And all the shopwindows and all the streets
And all the cabwheels whirling over the rotten pavement
I would have liked to plunge them into a furnace of swords
And grind up their bones
And pull out their tongues
And liquify all those huge bodies strange and naked under the
        clothes that drive me crazy
I sensed the coming of the great red Christ of the Russian
        Revolution
And the sky was a nasty wound
That opened up like a brasier . . . .

Those were the days of my adolescence
And I could no longer remember my birth.

It drives on for more than four hundred lines of campy power, without
a thought of the *Odyssey* or the decline of French letters, just the poet
and a little French girl in the sleeping compartment of a train moving
through Siberia past the dead and the wounded of the Russo-Japanese
war. This is what we have come to know as the voice of the international
"modern" style—Cendrars and Apollinaire in France, Marinetti in Italy,
Mayakovski, Khlebnikov and Yessenin in Russia, Attila Joseph in Hun-
gary, and in the Spanish speaking countries Huidobro, Vallejo, Neruda,
and Lorca. But in 1917 and 1918 Pound was writing for *Poetry* magazine
on the work of Gautier, Laforgue, Corbière, Heredia, Samain, Tailhade,
De Régnier and so on. Pound was twenty-five years behind European
time, which does not mean that he was in 1890 Paris either. Pound never
occupied Europe, present or past. He was living in American time, and in
a truly provincial fashion he was trying to construct a literary methodology, a "language," that Americans could use out of a nearly random
array of foreign excellences. In the case of French poetry the excellences
of Gautier and Jammes, say, are in direct conflict with each other and
cannot be combined. Pound, who was both intelligent and sensitive, was
well aware of this, but apparently unaware of the fundamental direction
of French (or European) poetry, a growing hostility to and finally hatred
of literature. And how could he have realized that, since the one thing he
loved was literature? This was also naturally American and provincial.
America had so little real literature that it must have seemed obvious
to almost all Americans of Pound's generation and cultivation that what
was required was a general reform of literary sensibility. The idea was
that the genteel and trivial would fall by the wayside, and that a tough
literary critical stance would result in literary masterpieces comparable
to the *Odyssey* or the *Canterbury Tales*. The idea that these were not
"literary" masterpieces and were not recoverable or even intelligible to
"literary" men was not yet possible in America. But for the French it was
another thing. Even in a sweet literary lyricist like Verlaine, the message
of French poetry was clear: what is alive is poetry; "the rest is literature." So Pound and Eliot, both quite fluent at French, cannot even read
Laforgue, not the Laforgue of *Hiver* or *Dimanches*, the casual tossed-off
lines, lightweight and ridiculous. Everyone says that Eliot got his early

style from Laforgue. Maybe. If you can imagine a provincial Laforgue amalgamated with Gautier's hard line and Tudor poetry as soon as it comes over into English. In French Eliot is different, as is Pound, but there it's possible to follow the actual sound of a French poet. Both Eliot and Pound carve at English, and when Pound doesn't carve it's all fin-de-siècle, like Swinburne. It is important to remember that the Americans were trying to get into literature and the French were trying to get out. And it is ironic that those of the French who didn't follow Rimbaud or Lautréamont into their version of the antiliterary looked to Whitman to lead them out, while the Americans of the Pound-Eliot variety were embarrassed by the great predecessor because of his overt romanticism and because of the antiliterary impulses embodied in the great catalogs and the homemade tradition of free verse. As Pound says in the poem to Whitman in *Lustra*,

> I have detested you long enough.
> I come to you as a grown child
> Who has had a pig-headed father;
> I am old enough now to make friends.
> It was you that broke the new wood,
> Now it is time for carving.

From the French point of view "breaking the new wood" is poetry, "carving" is literature. American poetry had not had this kind of modernism since Whitman, and the Pound-Eliot tradition does not contain it.

While Olson's representation of the Pound-Eliot-Tate tradition as the Pound-Williams-Zukovsky tradition went more or less unnoticed by anyone not directly involved with this recreation of American modernism, Ginsberg's amalgamation of Whitman, Williams, Lawrence, Blake, and the Englished versions of the French, German, and Spanish modern styles out of the chewed-up pages of old copies of *Transition, View, Tiger's Eye,* and *VVV* produced instant panic and revulsion. This is probably the poetry that Tate was referring to as "anti-poetry" in 1968. This was the only poetry that Delmore Schwartz knew the existence of back in 1958, outside the suburban lawns of the poetry by those he designated as "the new poets":

Before saying something more detailed about the character of the majority of new poets, some attention must be given to the *only recent new movement and countertendency* [my emphasis] that of the San Francisco circle of poets, who, under the leadership of Kenneth Rexroth, have recently proclaimed themselves super-Bohemians and leaders of a new poetic revolution. . . . Since these poets recite their poems in bars and with jazz accompanists, and since one poet aptly calls his book of poems "Howl," it is appropriate to refer to them as the Howlers of San Francisco.

The wonderful thing about Schwartz's response to this poetry is that it is couched entirely in political terms and takes the form of a defense of America presumably against

> America I've given you all and now I'm nothing
> America two dollars and twenty-seven cents January 17, 1956
> I can't stand my own mind.
> America when will we end the human war?

on the grounds that "since the Second World War and the beginning of the atomic age, the consciousness of the creative writer . . . has been confronted with the spectre of the totalitarian state, the growing poverty and helplessness of Western Europe, and the threat of an inconceivably destructive war which may annihilate civilization and mankind itself. Clearly when the future of civilization is no longer assured, a criticism of American life in terms of a contrast between avowed ideals and present actuality cannot be a primary occupation and source of inspiration. . . . Civilization's very existence depends upon America, upon the actuality of American life, and not the ideals of the American Dream. To criticize the actuality upon which all hope depends thus becomes a criticism of hope itself." All this artillery marshaled against a poem that goes on:

> America stop pushing I know what I'm doing
> America the plum blossoms are falling
> I haven't read the newspapers for months, everyday some-
>   body goes on trial for murder.
> America I feel sentimental about the Wobblies
> America I used to be a communist when I was a kid I'm
>   not sorry
> I smoke marijuana every chance I get.
> I sit in my house for days on end and stare at roses in
>   the closet
> When I go to Chinatown I get drunk and never get laid

The success of the style can be measured by the degree to which the "establishment" critics responded to this poetry as antipoetry, antilit-erature, and as sociopolitical tract. While there may have been contributory factors in the political climate of the cold war and Schwartz's own mania, it is still hard to believe that this alternately prophetic, rhapsodic, comic, and nostalgic style could appear unliterary. But it did appear unliterary, primarily because the appropriate devices for framing "modern" poetry and literature in general were nowhere in sight. Instead of "irony," it had broad parody and sarcasm; instead of implying, the poem ranted and bawled and laughed; learned as it was in the strategies of European poetry, it was seen as the poetry of the gutter. Which demonstrates that a major factor that separated the Beat Poets from the Academic Poets was education, which the Beat Poets had and the Academic Poets did not have. They had been to school not only with Williams and Pound, but also with Rexroth, who managed to blend the Williams-Pound modernism with the European romantic modernist style. So that it was natural for an alliance of sorts to form between the Beat Poets and the Black Mountain Poets. At about the same time a slightly more dandyish version of the European style appeared in New York. It was also "antiliterary" but advanced against literature the strategy of a gay and unpredictable silliness:

Be not obedient of the excellent, do not prize the silly with an exceptionally pushy person or orphan. The ancient world knew these things and I am unable to convey as well as those poets the simplicity of things, the bland and amused stare of garages and banks, the hysterical bark of a dying dog which is not unconcerned with human affairs but dwells in the cave of the essential passivity of his kind. Kine? their warm sweet breaths exist nowhere but in classical metre, bellowing and puling throughout the ages of our cognizance like roses in romances. We do not know anymore the exquisite manliness of all brutal acts because we are sissies and if we're not sissies we're unhappy and too busy.

It is a collage of poetic echoes, which gradually slides into a more straightforward assault:

I don't want any of you to be really unhappy, just camp it up and whine, whineola, baby. I'm talking to you over there, isn't this damn thing working? . . . It's not that I want you to be so knowing as all that, but I don't want some responsibility to be shown in the modern world's modernity, your face and mine dashing across the steppes of a country which is only partially occupied and acceptable, and is very windy and grassy and rugged. I speak of New Jersey of course.

In Frank O'Hara's hands it is a poem like a ridiculous telephone conversation, moving between a preposterous high style ("oh plankton /

mes poèmes lyriques, à partir de 1897, peuvent se lire comme un journal in-time"), bits of gossip and pseudogossip ("John, for instance thinks
I am the child of my own old age; Jimmy is cagy with snide remarks
while he washes dishes and I pose in the bathroom"), bits of pop song
and Silver Screen nostalgia, and sometimes a very precise "run" on real
(unpromoted) and false (promoted) feeling:

> why do you say you're a bottle and you feed me
> the sky is more blue and it is getting cold
> last night I saw Garfinkel's Surgical Supply truck
> and knew I was near home though dazed and thoughtful
>> what did you do to make me think
>> after we led the bum to the hospital
>> and you got into the cab
>> I was feeling lost myself

There were sufficient reasons for these different groups—Black Mountain, the Beats, and the New York school—to quarrel among themselves,
and there were such quarrels. In one issue of *Yugen* Gregory Corso,
representing the rhapsodic tendencies of the Beats, took a swipe at what
he considered the pedantic musical concerns of Olson and was promptly
stepped on by Gilbert Sorrentino, who dismissed him as a presumptuous
idiot. But quarrels like this were minor and trivial in duration. These
poets all read together and published together in magazines like *Yugen*,
which formed a common ground for the New York and San Francisco
scene and for publications of translations of various European modernist poets. The bonds that held these poets together were more profound
than any differences: a nearly complete contempt for the trivial poetry
of the last phase of the "closed verse" tradition and more significantly
the underlying conviction that poetry was made by a man up on his feet,
talking. At bottom all their images of "writing a poem" are a way of
being moved and moving, a way of walking, running, dancing, driving.

> The dance
>> (held up for me by
> an older man. He told me how. Showed
> me. Not steps, but the fix
> of muscle: to move
> —

> I do not seek a synthesis, I seek a melee.
> —

It's like going into a spin in a car—you use all
the technical information you have about how to get
the car back on the road, but you're not thinking
"I must bring the car back on the road" or else you're
off the cliff.

—

If someone's chasing you down the street with a knife
you just run, you don't turn around and shout, "Give
it up! I was a track star for Mineola Prep."

It was not quite an idea of an "oral" poetry, not yet. Outside of Parry
and Lord's work on the South Slavic guslar poets and some well-reasoned
speculations about Homer and *Beowulf*, nobody knew much about that.
But a change was coming over the idea of "writing" poetry, perhaps re-
inforced by the proliferation of readings. Although these poets did not
identify the "performance" of a poem with the poem itself, they also
did not identify the text of a poem with the poem itself. Olson calls
it a "notation," and the idea of the text of a poem as a "notation" or
"score" occupies a middle ground between an idea of oral poem and an
idea of literature. It is easiest to see this in music, where it is abundantly
clear that eighteenth- and nineteenth-century scores are insufficient to
yield a skilled performer enough information to play the music reason-
ably. An adequate performance of Bach or Mozart or Beethoven requires
a familiarity with the conventional context that directs the performer
how to read (interpret) a score. Obviously the figured bass tradition relied more on the musical civilization of the performer than did the later
nineteenth century. And there was a lesson to be learned from this too.
Who can play the Hammerklavier at the instructed tempo? And how
much *brio* is *con brio*? This shifting view of the relation between text
and poem, which was not something these poets were thoroughly aware
of, led to two totally different conclusions in the poetry of the sixties:
Concrete Poetry, which assumes sometimes with marvelous perversity
that the text is the poem, and direct composition on tape recorder. But
for America both of these possibilities were played out in the sixties
by many other poets. In fact it was the sixties that saw the great explosion of American poetry. If there were perhaps twenty or thirty strong
poets among the Black Mountain, Beat poets and the first generation of
the New York school, it is probable that the number of impressive poets
to appear in the sixties is more than double that. For those of us who

came into the arena of poetry at the end of the fifties and the beginning of the sixties, the Beats, the Black Mountain poets, the New York poets represented an "opening of the field." They had swept away the deadwood, the main obstacle to the career of poetry; and they offered a great claim for the meaning of poetry: that phenomenological reality is "discovered" and "constructed" by poets. Speaking for myself I thought then and still think that the claim, when its implications are clearly articulated, is quite reasonable. It is part of a great romantic metaphysic and epistemology that has sustained European poetry since Ossian and Blake and Wordsworth and is still sustaining it now. If the particular representations of reality offered by these poets of the fifties seemed less useful or adequate, this seemed less important and partially inherent in the romantic metaphysic itself, according to which reality is inexhaustible or, more particularly, cannot be exhausted by its representations because its representations modify its nature. The poets of the sixties simply went about the business of reexamining the whole of the modernist tradition. By now we have had to add to the fundamental figures Gertrude Stein and John Cage, both of whom seem much more significant poets and minds than either Pound or Williams. This itself is the merest of indications. All of European dada and surrealism were reconsidered in the sixties; poets like Breton, Tzara, Arp and Schwitters, Huidobro, and Peret were reclaimed along with many others. But beyond this there was the recognition that the essential aspiration of romantic poetry was to a poetry broad enough and deep enough to embody the universal human condition. We are better equipped now linguistically and poetically and perhaps shrewder about what is at stake in this type of project. At present there is now going on a total revolution in the consideration of the poetry of nonliterate and partially literate cultures; and this reevaluation is not a mere collecting of texts but a reevaluation of the genres, with enormous implications for the work of present poets. This surge of activity is already transforming the poetry of the sixties, which is itself far too rich to treat in this essay.

Ihab Hassan

The New Gnosticism

Speculations on an Aspect of the Postmodern Mind

Thine own consciousness, shining, void, and inseparable from the Great Body of
Radiance, hath no birth, nor death, and is the Immutable Light.
The Tibetan Book of the Dead

The Gospel of Truth is joy for those who have received the *grace* of *knowing*
from the Father of Truth. . . . He who knows is a being from above. If he is called,
he hears, he replies, he turns to him who calls him, in order to come back to
him. . . . He who thus possesses *gnosis* knows whence he has come and whither
he goes. *The Gospel of Truth*

The Circumference is Within, Without is formed the Selfish Center, / And the
Circumference still expands going forward to Eternity. . . .
William Blake, *Jerusalem*

The origins of the process of mechanization are more mystical than we imagine.
Henri Bergson, *The Two Sources of Morality and Religion*

Spiritualized Energy is the flower of Cosmic Energy. To dominate and canalize
the powers of the air and the sea is all very well. But what is this triumph,
compared with the world-wide mastery of human thought and love?
Teilhard de Chardin, *Building the Earth*

Today computers hold out the promise of a means of instant translation of any
code or language into any other code or language. The computer, in short, promises by technology a Pentecostal condition of universal understanding and unity.
The next logical step would seem to be, not to translate, but to by-pass languages
in favor of a general cosmic consciousness.
Marshall McLuhan, *Understanding Media*

All scientific generalizations
Are pure metaphysics

All metaphysics are weightless
And physically unlimited.
R. Buckminster Fuller, *Intuition*

Because of the millennial nature of the goal of extending consciousness, we can
expect that, if we adopt it, it will exert a small but persistent influence on human
activities over a very long period of time.
Gerald Feinberg, *The Prometheus Project*

We are actually born out of light, you might say. I believe light is the maker of
all material. Material is spent light.
Louis Kahn, *Time*, January 15, 1973

But what do epigraphs prove?

Surely they do not answer an appeal to authority since few of
us now accept the same authorities.

Do they evoke a mood, declare a theme, insinuate a conclusion? Possibly. Yet, coming at the start, they do nothing that the text itself will
not confirm or deny. Thus epigraphs become a kind of preparation for
failure.

Or is the function of epigraphs to release metaphors and ideas from
the bounds of a single time, place, and mind? Can quotation marks hold
back a thought from seeking a larger identity in Thought? And what are
the walls within Language made of?

These are questions that the im-mediate mind sometimes asks.

The Convergence of Consciousness

The theme of this
paracritical essay
is   the growing
insistence of Mind
to apprehend reality im-mediately;
to gather more and more mind
in itself:
thus to become
its own
reality.
Consciousness becomes all.
And as in a gnostic

                    dream,
                        matter dissolves
                                    before the
            Light.

Certainly, Consciousness has become one of our key terms, replacing Honor, Faith, Reason, or Sensibility as the token of intellectual passion, the instrument of our cultural will. Cold-eyed behaviorists may eschew the term; yet its nimbus still hangs over our rhetoric as we discourse of politics and pornography, language and literature, morality and metaphysics. Thus we "raise," "expand," "alter," "criticize," and "bracket," consciousness, among so many other things we do to it nowadays.

This cultural chatter may not be wholly idle. A certain dematerialization of our world is taking place, from the "ephemeralization" of substance (Buckminster Fuller) to the "de-definition" of art (Harold Rosenberg). How many forms, disciplines, institutions, have we seen dissolve, in the last few decades, into amorphous new shapes? How many objects, solidly mattered, have we seen dissolve into a process, an image, a mental frame?

The New York Times, *October 22, 1972:*

The impact of the computer is felt in virtually every corner of American life, from the ghetto to the moon. And data-processing is the world's fastest growing major business; sometimes during the next decade, it is expected to become the world's largest industry.

From hardware to software, from software to pure mind?

This process may be one of convergence far more than of dissolution. The "syntropic" force of consciousness is remaking our world in every way. As Teilhard de Chardin put it: "Everything that rises must converge." That is a hypothesis that we need, at least, to entertain.

Teilhard's famous phrase, however, provides Flannery O'Connor with an ironic title to a collection of stories. Why ironic? Because the stories reveal isolation, terror, and waste, reveal life without Grace. Here is another hypothesis of the human condition that we cannot entirely repudiate. The radical insufficiency of that condition—I do not wish to say: of man—still offers intractable resistance to the old gnostic dream. Whether we call it Evil, Ananke, or (mawkishly) The System, this resistance must be acknowledged. *Without assent.*

Beyond Arcadians and Technophiles

The New Gnosticism is the result of various synergies. Myth and Technology, for instance, now easily blend in the mind. A great part of our culture, however, still abets opposition, division. Consider, for instance, the current distinction between Arcadians and Technophiles:

The Arcadians look for the unspoiled life in nature. They tend to be mythically minded and edenic. Hostile to technology, they like communes, ecology, health foods, folk music, occult and visionary literature. They are children of the Earth, mother-oriented, ruled by the great archetypes. See Charles Reich's *The Greening of America*, Theodore Roszak's *Where the Wasteland Ends*, or George B. Leonard's *The Transformation*.

The Technophiles favor the active life of cities. They tend to be technically minded and utopian. They like gadgets, science fiction, electronic music, space programs, futuristic designs of their environment. They are children of the Sky, father-oriented, struggling to create neotypes. See Zbigniew Brzezinsky's *Between Two Ages: America's Role in the Technetronic Era*, F. M. Esfandiary's *Optimism One: The Emerging Radicalism*, or Victor Ferkiss's *Technological Man*.

These, to be sure, are stereotypes. Yet their tensions inform such serious works as Leo Marx's *The Machine in the Garden*, Arthur Koestler's *The Ghost in the Machine*, and Lewis Mumford's *The Myth of the Machine*—note the titles—works that prefigure some of our postmodern perplexities.

Though the antipathy between Arcadians and Technophiles may derive from an ancient wound in the human psyche, there is nothing ineluctable about it. Earth and Sky, Myth and Technology have joined before and their gap is narrowing. Eden and Utopia, the first and last perfection, are homologous imaginative constructs, mirror images of the same primal desire. Furthermore, the laws of myth and of science have this in common: both are partial codifications of reality, ways in which the mind imitates itself. Their structures, their functions, their predictive logic may not be identical; yet neither myth nor science escapes the influence of the imagination. Thus Einstein notes in *Ideas and Opinions:* "The axiomatic basis of theoretical physics cannot be extracted from experience, but must be freely invented." And again J. Bronowski: "The step by which a new axiom is added cannot itself be mechanized. It is a free play of the mind, an invention outside the logical processes.

This is the central act of imagination in science and it is in all respects like any similar act in literature" (*The American Scholar* [Spring 1966]). Why, then, should we wonder that Isaac Newton labored secretly in alchemical pursuits, seeking the universal signature of life in all matter? And who knows what hieratic converse Newton carried with Paracelsus across the centuries? The origins of mechanization are indeed more mystical than we suppose.

That is a crucial intuition Arcadians tend to ignore even as they belabor Technophiles for their "Single vision and Newton's sleep." Roszak's *Where the Wasteland Ends*, for instance, a work that engages some of my deepest sympathies, resolutely denies the potential of spiritual transformation contained in modern science. In so doing, it banishes imagination from a large area of consciousness and evades the metaphysical meaning of change, innovation, and human evolution. I think it more likely that "mystics" and "mechanists," as William Irwin Thompson calls them, will move toward a new issue:

Western civilization is drawing to a close in an age of apocalyptic turmoil in which the old species, collectivizing mankind with machines, and the new species, unifying it in consciousness, are in collusion with one another to end what we know as human nature. (*At the Edge of History*)

But the convergence of which I speak manifests itself not only in broad cultural contexts; it finds a voice in private lives when least we expect it. Here is the late Jimi Hendrix:

It's music. . . . It's electric-icity . . . that will take us all to that spiritual high I call the electric church. . . .

Mind expansion . . . I expanded mine the first time I turned on and plugged into an electric amplifier . . . someday it's going to carry me all the way there, too: pure mind. (Bibliographic reference lost)

The mythological bard becomes a technological mystic. Consider now a high-flier of a different kind, not a freaked-out black musician but a shy exemplar of WASP rectitude. Here is Charles Lindbergh:

Gradually, I diverted hours from aviation into biological research. How mechanical, how mystical was man? Could longevity be extended? . . .

Decades spent in contact with science and its vehicles have directed my mind and senses to areas beyond their reach. I now see scientific accomplishment as a path, not an end; a path leading to and disappearing in mystery. (*Life*, July 4, 1969)

Lindbergh, the romantic adventurer, evolves into a technocrat, and the technocrat soon becomes a nature mystic. Does his vision blend into that of Jimi Hendrix?

Admittedly, two instances do not prove a trend. Yet the instances are scattered throughout our lives, as if each of us were compelled to discover his own Beulah, his own "place where Contrarieties are equally True." We have seen computer art aspire to Pythagorean mysteries. And even the dark avatars have disengaged themselves from our dreams to become, as in "2001: A Space Odyssey," technological prophecies.

The New Gnosticism eludes distinctions of the old mind, seeking yet unknown synergies.

Entropies:
> Does the mind also create unknown entropies?
> Ivan Karamozov: "It's not that I don't accept God, you must understand, it's the world created by him that I don't accept."
>> And still it seems the same:
>> Death
>>> Dearth
>>>> Deceit.
>> Everywhere the fullness of decay.

A Digression on Prometheus

Myth, Technology, and Literature meet in the various figures and fables of Prometheus.

As a Titan, Prometheus reverts to the chthonic forces of the Earth, of nature and instinct. Yet this Titan is clever; he allies himself with the new Parnassian order of Zeus. He reaches for the sky, and his name means foresight.

This Titan may be too clever. A natural trickster, he represents the creative principle of intelligence, creative yet essentially flawed because it is ignorant of its limit, its purpose. Prometheus begins lacking in wisdom.

Gaston Bachlard, The Psychoanalysis of Fire:

This, then, is the true basis for the respect shown to flame: if the child brings his hand close to the fire his father raps him over the knuckles with a ruler. Fire, then, can strike without having to burn. Whether this fire be flame or heat, lamp or stove, the parents' vigilance is the same. Thus fire is initially the object of a general prohibition; *hence this conclusion: the social interdiction is our first general knowledge of fire.* . . . *Consequently, since the prohibitions are primarily social interdictions, the problem of obtaining a personal knowledge of fire is the problem of* clever disobedience. *The child wishes to do what his father does, but far away from his father's presence, and so like a little Prometheus he steals some matches.*

At Mecone, where gods and men come to settle their dispute, Prometheus tricks the gods of their share of the feast's meat. Henceforth, gods and men will stand ever apart. Prometheus defies Zeus again by bestowing fire on man, and bestowing mind (alphabet, number, all the practical and occult arts).

Prometheus: Titan of nature, creative Trickster, master of Technics. His sufferings begin. Perhaps he acquires dignity only on the terrible rock, spiked, chained, liver torn. Some say his torment is redemptive (Aeschylus), some say it proves only the absurdity of gods (Goethe). It is certain only that Prometheus suffers on Tartarus and that his suffering creates an ambiguous prophecy. Or is it simply another trick?

> The prophecy promises—if you can penetrate it—deliverance:
> deliverance of Prometheus,
> deliverance really of man.
>> Does it also promise the abolition of the gods?
>> The matter is not yet clear.

> Consider the Promethean fable in these texts:
> A. Hesiod's *Theogony, Works and Days*
> B. Aeschylus's *Prometheus Bound*
> C. Goethe's *Prometheus: A Dramatic Fragment*
> D. Percy Bysshe Shelley's *Prometheus Unbound*
> E. Mary Shelley's *Frankenstein: or, the Modern Prometheus*
> F. Gerald Feinberg's *The Prometheus Project*

At the origin, there is an action: trickery, defiance, creation, hope, an alliance with man that defines the human condition in terms of limits and transgressions, lapses and transcendences. Fire is stolen, yes, and with it consciousness is wrested from its divine place. But like fire, consciousness is dialectic; it seeks its solid opposite; and it devours its own pain. Released in the world, consciousness questions all, questions matter and every matter, vexing itself to the last. What, then, is the Promethean answer?

A. Hesiod largely reports the myth. Here and there he speaks with some didactic relish; but the redemption of Prometheus scarcely troubles his mind.

B. Aeschylus adheres to prophecy and patience. Let us wait for the advent of heroes (Herakles) who can mediate between men and gods, between death and eternity. But who are "heroes?" For us they are past; for Prometheus they are future. Or does Prometheus know some other secret about the end of Zeus?

C. Goethe explores revolt. As C. K. Kerényi puts it: "Goethe's Prometheus is no God, no Titan, no man, but the immortal prototype of man as the original rebel and affirmer of his fate: the original inhabitant of the earth, seen as an antigod, as Lord of the Earth. In this connection he seems more Gnostic than Greek" (*Prometheus: Archetypal Image of Human Existence*). Above all, he seems romantic and therefore nearly modern.

D. Percy Shelley will not fully explain his Prometheus, a creature both of will and vision. Shelley sees him as kin to Milton's Satan, yet exempt from the "pernicious casuistry" of the rebel archangel. Bound by his own hate, by his own divided faculties, Prometheus strives to liberate himself from himself. To become whole again, he must find renewal in the Imagination. This Imagination is also teleological. At the end, Demogorgon assures Prometheus: "to hope till Hope creates/From its own wreck the thing it contemplates/ . . . This is alone Life, Joy, Empire, and Victory."

E. Mary Shelley divines the point at which scientism and idealism, reason and revelation, meet. It is a point shrouded in terror. Frankenstein, the modern Prometheus, surrenders to Albertus Magnus and Paracelsus before he masters the exact sciences. "I was required," he says, "to exchange chimeras of boundless grandeur for realities of little worth." But his great error lies elsewhere. Self-absorbed and self-obsessed, he blights the powers of sympathy in himself. His solitary "fiend" returns to haunt him and haunt us, a ghastly embodiment of Prometheanism without responsibility or love. "Hateful day when I received life!" the fiend cries. Is that the curse of life born of pure mind? Frankenstein and his fiend are neither twain nor really one; but in this they are compact: both together adumbrate the perils of consciousness in its (heroic-demonic) labors of self-creation. This Promethean adventure ends in a world not of fire but of ice.

F. Feinberg has fewer qualms about Prometheanism, about the increase of self-consciousness without bound. That increase is his project, and his Prometheus is ourselves. His premise is this: "My own feeling is that the despair of the conscious mind at the recognition of its own finitude is such that man cannot achieve an abiding contentment in his present form or anything like it. Therefore, I believe that a transformation of man into something very different from what he is now is called for." Calmly, lucidly, simplistically, Feinberg argues that mankind needs to set long-range ends for itself and to devise corresponding means. The goal he proposes as the most likely human destiny is Promethean indeed: man will become a total consciousness. "Because of the inner logic of the conflict between the unity of one consciousness and the diversity of phenomena in the external world, there is probably no level of consciousness in which the conscious being will rest content until the sway of consciousness is extended indefinitely." We do not require the theology of Teilhard de Chardin to achieve this extension nor the science fiction of Olaf Stapledon. "I firmly believe," Feinberg notes, "that in trying to predict the future of technology, reality is likely to outstrip one's most extreme vision." The postmodern Prometheus reaches for the fire in distant stars.

The Promethean archetype is a focus on convergences that reappear in our midst. The archetype contains a gnostic dream or project:

the creation and continual recreation
of human consciousness
until consciousness redeems itself in complete knowledge.

This project implies will: Prometheus wills, and even wills to be wrong.

It implies also prophecy: Prometheus, that far-seer, falls forward into the fullness of time.

Above all
it implies imagination: Prometheus attempts a radical reconstitution of the given world, the fixed order of things.

Hence Prometheanism remains the arch human endeavor for that "visionary company" of poets about whom Harold Bloom has so vividly written. Yes, there are acute dangers: solipsism, willfulness, self-corruption. Yet only in a spirit of extreme piety can we conclude, as William F. Lynch does in *Christ and Prometheus*, that "Prometheanism is the project of a will separated from the imagination and from reality, separated, therefore, from most of the human." Prometheanism, I think, veers toward the demonic when it denies the female principle of creation. Therefore, Aeschylus includes in his fable both Themis and Io, and Percy Shelley includes Asia. (Significantly, Mary Shelley's Frankenstein never consummates his relation to Elizabeth, nor is his relation to any man or woman but perfunctory.) There is a dark, moon-like side to

Promethean nature, Kerényi insists, a side shaped by maternal forces. That side Prometheus can never afford to ignore.

No more than the Sky can ignore the Earth, or Technology, Mythology.

Myth

I do not for a moment suggest that the New Gnosticism reverts directly to those ancient or medieval cults expounded, say, in Hans Jonas's excellent work, *The Gnostic Religion*. Still, new and old forms of gnosis may find a common source in certain myths, in certain persistencies of human dreams.

As in the beginning, so in the end; as above, so below. Such are the principles of mythical thought. Yet myth appears mainly retrograde, its focus on some event in the immemorial past, *in illo tempore* (Eliade). Into that far, dim, and sacred time, a privileged state of existence is usually projected. Is that state one of universal consciousness?

We know the story of the Garden of Eden. There is also that other strange story in the *Book of Genesis:*

> And the whole earth was of one language and of one
>   speech . . .
> And they said, Go to, let us build us a city and a tower
>   whose top may reach unto heaven . . .
> And the Lord said, Behold, *the people is one, and they
>   have all one language;* and this they begin to do:
>   and now nothing will be restrained from them,
>   which they have *imagined* to do.
> Go to, let us go down, and there confound their
>   language, that they may not understand one
>   another's speech. (all italics mine)

Just what was that unitary language of mankind before God struck it into a babel of tongues? Music? Mathematics? Telepathy? Chomsky's deep structures of the mind or linguistic universals ringing each to each? Or was it the same language Orpheus spoke in distant Thrace, singing Orpheus, he who became himself bird and tree and rock and wolf and cloud? Was it a poetry of silence? The silence of mind and nature when they perfectly meet? The silence that Norman O. Brown calls "the mother tongue?"

According to Erich Neumann, the ancient pleromatic or uroboric condition of existence is less conscious than unconscious, a state ruled by the Great Mother, a state, therefore, of *participation mystique*. Gnosticism, however, insists on spiritualizing this condition. "Consequently, in Gnosticism," Neumann says, "the way of salvation lies in heightening consciousness and returning to the transcendent spirit, with loss of the unconscious side; whereas uroboric salvation through the Great Mother demands the abandonment of the conscious principle and a homecoming to the unconscious" (*The Origins and History of Consciousness*).

The shift, then, seems to be from unconsciousness to consciousness. Teilhard agrees: "Mythology and folklore . . . are, in fact, filled with symbols and fables expressing the deeply rooted resolve of Earth to find its way to Heaven" (*The Future of Man*). Yet if Beginnings and Ends are cognate, they must express, on some concealed level at least, a point of contact, perhaps even of identity. In the Jewish *Midrash*, for instance, the unborn babe in its womb carries a prophetic light around its head in which it sees the end of the world. (Recall, again, the eschatological image of the luminous intergalactic foetus at the end of "2001.") Furthermore, the mystic trance and shamanistic journey are both ways of recovering the First and Last moment into the present.

Can it be, then, that the shift from unconsciousness to consciousness is true only in a partial perspective of reality? Can it be that conscious and unconscious are both implicit in the larger state of mind that myth projects far back into the sacred past and far forward into the sacred future? The state of mind that dream, vision, and trance recover in the im-mediate present?

Mircea Eliade, Myths, Dreams, and Mysteries:

In India a whole literature has been devoted to explanations of this paradoxical relationship between what is pre-eminently unconscious—Matter—and pure "consciousness," the Spirit, which by its own mode of being is atemporal, free, uninvolved in the becoming. And one of the most unexpected results of this philosophic labor has been its conclusion that the Unconscious (i.e., pakriti), moving by a kind of 'teleological instinct,' imitates the behaviour of the Spirit; that the Unconscious behaves in such a way that its activity seems to prefigure the mode of being of the Spirit.

I doubt that such questions can be answered at this time in any terms that would satisfy those who insist on an answer; yet they are the very questions that myth raises repeatedly before the skeptical mind. Behind these questions lurks a desire, an intuition, perhaps even a gnosis of a universal consciousness that transcends time, and transcends the organization of our most complex language.

Technology

We all acknowledge that science and its extension in technology are the major agents of transformation in our world. Sometimes we acknowledge it fearfully, and like Jacques Ellul in *The Technological Society*, we see only dark portents of our future. "Enclosed within his artificial creation," Ellul writes, "man finds that there is 'no exit'; that he cannot pierce the shell of technology to find again the ancient milieu to which he was adapted for hundreds of thousands of years." Certainly, anyone over thirty will remember that the earth was a cleaner place in the past, more surprising, and more sensuously various. Science and technology, however, also operate in other dimensions, silently, invisibly, making always a little more life available to us.

Consider that familiar rubric, "the communication explosion." Quite precisely, a layer of sentience or awareness now envelops the earth, much like Teilhard's "noosphere," moving ever outwards.

Query

The communication explosion is a product not only of technology but also of the population explosion. There are, literally, more brains on earth, working all at the same time. How does this fact affect the degree of sentience on earth?

End of Query

Furthermore, communication itself is becoming increasingly immediate, requiring less and less mediation. It is a far cry from a stone hieroglyph weighing five tons, to a wireless set weighing less than a pound. Even now we casually use "slow motion telepathy," as Barry Schwartz puts it, devices that require only microseconds to elapse between coded communication, decoded message, and feedback (*Arts in Society* [Summer–Fall 1972]). The process can be extended by radio or laser far into the universe. There are also other means.

The New York Times, *February 27, 1972:*

Tonight, if all goes well, the United States will launch the longest space mission in history. . . . It is the first official effort of mankind to draw attention to itself. As the vehicle, Pioneer 10, passes Jupiter, the gravity of that planet will seize it and hurl it out of the solar system. It will sail indefinitely through the vast reaches of the Milky Way Galaxy, carrying a message.

The message is not composed of quotations from Shakespeare. It includes visual representations of the male and female figures, and mathematical symbols referring to the structure of the hydrogen molecule and the frequency of pulsars. Can the basic rhythms of the universe provide a kind of alphabet of a universal intelligence?

The process is itself part of what Buckminster Fuller calls "ephemeralization:" doing constantly more with constantly less. As a result, matter intervenes less and less in the transactions of mankind. And the mind is free to pursue its destiny: to become the antientropic, or syntropic, force in the universe, gathering knowledge, expanding consciousness, regenerating *metaphysically* a *physically* decaying universe. "Einstein's mind discovered and generalized the comprehensive law of physical energy universe as $E = mc^2$ and the process of metaphysical mastery of the physical is irreversible," Fuller says in *Utopia or Oblivion;* to which he adds his great, optimistic principle: "Energy cannot decrease. Knowhow can only increase." In this ambience of sentience, telepathy becomes a new possibility. Thus Fuller again: "I think that possibly within ten years we'll discover scientifically that what has been telepathy and has been thought of as very mysterious is, in fact, ultra, ultra, high frequency electromagnetic wave propagation" (*House and Garden*, May 1972).

Telepathy, the gnostic language, in technology?

A. In 1954, Norbert Wiener, father of Cybernetics, said in his book, *The Human Use of Human Beings:*

Let us admit that the idea that one might conceivably travel by telegraph, in addition to traveling by train or airplane, is not intrinsically absurd, far as it may be from realization.

Within two decades, we hear that Japanese researchers are trying to develop "Intersex" or "Cybersex:" long-distance sex between consenting partners. The idea is to record as fully as possible—oh, much more than Masters and Johnson ever dreamed—all sexual stimuli, visual, tactile, auditory, olfactory, and even kinetic, and to transmit these stimuli, through electronic devices and computers, to sexual partners. Furthermore: "By the end of the century, Hikari expects to see commercial Cybersex tapes, recorded by prominent male and female celebrities, generally available, much as one buys a phonograph recording today" (*Architectural Design*, September 1969).

B. In 1964, Marshall McLuhan stated in his book, *Understanding Media:*

Electric technology does not need words any more than the digital computer needs numbers. Electricity points the way to an extension of the process of consciousness itself, on a world scale, and without any verbalization whatever.

Within less than a decade, we hear that Dr. José Delgado at Yale has implanted electrodes in special brain areas of a fighting bull. By pushing a button, he was able to stop the bull in the middle of the fiercest charge. There is nothing to prevent Dr. Delgado from "wiring" his bull to a computer and programming its existence. There is no theoretical difficulty to prevent us from doing the same thing with human beings, as the television program "Search" weekly suggests to oblivious audiences. "Soon," Dr. Delgado says, "with the aid of the computer, we may have direct contact between two different brains—without the participation of the senses" (*New York Times Magazine*, November 15, 1970). Soon, too, with the aid of "Dream Machines" acting directly on the brain, we may simulate, we may *possess*, any sensuous experience while sitting at home: a three-star meal at Lasserre in Paris or free-fall from a plane over the Andes.

We can imagine the utopian and dystopian possibilities of these and other developments; indeed, many of them have been imagined already in science fiction. Yet a hysterical rejection of science and its applications will not do; for there is no way for us to repress what we already know, what we already are and can be, without grave consequences to our psychic health. We cannot wish away what we have already done; we can only do otherwise, on pain of extinction as a race. We must find a way to restore the deep rhythms of life within us without foregoing the dream that may be leaving its imprint—a biological code?—on our evolution.

Already, our senses are becoming coextensive with the cosmos: we can "touch" things on the moon and "hear" quasars at the edge of the universe. Slowly, we are all entering a multidimensional, non-Euclidean, and still sensuous—for sense and mind are one—realm of existence. We can begin to "speak" to one another, and to the animals at hand, as well as to invite, as we have done, voices farther out in space to speak to us.

John C. Lilly, Man and Dolphin:

Within the next decade or two the human species will establish communication with another species: nonhuman, alien, possibly extraterrestrial, more probably marine; but definitely highly intelligent, perhaps even intellectual. . . . Our own spot in the universe, our own view of ourselves, will be tremendously modified if such a communication is established. Any other species that could talk with us on our own level will give us a perspective of which we can only be dimly aware at the present time. Our own communication among ourselves will be enhanced and improved by such contact. Our own views of one another will change radically under the influence of interspecies communication. The very fact that we try to communicate with them is an important indication of our own stage of evolutionary maturity.

We can further insist that technology become not only pollution-free but also invisible. There are those who believe—are they gnostics?—that technology can imitate the inherent order of things. Here, for instance, is John Cage:

Just as Fuller domes (dome within dome, translucent, plants between) will give impression of living in no home at all (outdoors), so all technology must move toward the way things were before man began changing them: identification with nature in her manner of operation, complete mystery. (*A Year From Monday*)

In short, like Myth, Technology suggests that man is creating a universal consciousness which renders mediated action and speech gradually obsolete. A measure of radical American Innocence is required to hold this view. Cage has it. So has Charles Lindbergh who may be even a greater technological gnostic: Will we discover that only *without* spaceships can we reach the galaxies; that only *without* cyclotrons can we know the interior of atoms? (*Life*)

Literature

Men of letters tend to believe that the word gives the mind its flesh; and critics are even more stringent than the authors they criticize in defense of that view. Literature is the keystone of the humanities; it stands, like Man, between Earth and Sky, severed from neither. We expect it, therefore, to show a certain recalcitrance toward the im-mediate mind.

Yet there are signal exceptions. William Blake, for instance: "Mental Things are alone Real; what is called Corporeal, Nobody knows of its Dwelling Place: it is in Fallacy, & its Existence an Imposture" ("A Vision of the Last Judgment"). Curiously enough, Blake's contemporary, Donatien-Alphonse-François de Sade, would have agreed entirely for reasons demoniac of his own. One is tempted to argue—as I have in *The Dismemberment of Orpheus*—that Blake and Sade stand at the threshold of the modern experience, exemplars of two kinds of gnosticism. But there are, of course, other kinds; the gnostic impulse, restricted as it may be in literature, touches visionary, antinomian, or romantic writers of every age.

The unmediated will, however, asserts itself as a cultural phenomenon in the late eighteenth century. The artist begins his journey to the interior, there to end by discovering the languages of silence. Hegel provides romanticism with a point of philosophical reference, and also of reaction.

Erich Heller, The Artist's Journey into the Interior:

> In both the early Romantics and Hegel, the human mind puts forward a total claim for itself, a claim in which revolution and eschatology are uneasily mingled. The world must become imagination and poetry, say the Romantics; and Hegel says, the world must become rational consciousness. But the poetry meant by the Romantics, and the rational consciousness meant by Hegel, have much in common: above all the ambition of the human mind to dominate the real world to the point of usurping its place.

The world becomes poetry even as the final unfolding of the World-Spirit makes all poetry redundant, all art obsolete. That is the paradoxical prophecy of the romantic "soul."

The journey into the interior is a journey toward consciousness, toward mind claiming more and more for itself in terms less and less conditional. It is a gnostic journey only in the very broadest sense, and its shadowy paths may be discerned in various human endeavors. Philosophy, for instance, moving from Hegel to Husserl, Heidegger, Sartre, and Wittgenstein, finds itself in an immense new field of subjectivity which it hopelessly sets out to survey. Literary criticism follows a similar path in the different works of Poulet, Blanchot, Barthes, Foucault,

Derrida, a path that leaves "texts" behind, wanders brilliantly through language, and vanishes finally into consciousness.

As for literature itself, we have heard its story told many times, going as far back as Erich Kahler does in *The Inward Turn of Narrative*, or as far forward as Sharon Spencer in *Space, Time and Structure in the Modern Novel*. From the great modernists—Valéry, Proust, Rilke, Kafka, Joyce, Yeats, Pound, Eliot, Stevens, etc.—to the enigmatic postmodernists—Beckett, Borges, Genet, Butor, Cortazar, Barth, etc.—the tendency of literature has been to escape itself, to subvert or transcend its forms, to re-imagine imagination; and, as it were, to create a state of unmediated literary awareness. Yet a generalization of this kind cries for qualifications that I can scarcely begin to make here. We need a narrower focus: not gnostic tendencies in their shadowy outlines but the New Gnosticism in American literature particularly. This will bring us eventually to science fiction.

An Aside: Burroughs and Others

Ever since *Naked Lunch*, William Burroughs has declared himself, in words certainly, the enemy of language: "To speak is to lie;" "Rub out the Word Forever." Or in *The Ticket That Exploded:* "The word is now a virus. . . . The word may once have been a healthy neural cell. It is now a parasitic organism that invades and damages the central nervous system. Modern man has lost the option of silence."

Burroughs's icy rage against language is partly self-parodic. But it is also directed against the Old Consciousness, all its deceptions, inhibitions, and controls, which he identifies with the Word. Above all, his rage sustains a failed dream of pure consciousness. "Words—at least the way we use them—can stand in the way of what I call non-body experience," he says. "It's time we thought about leaving the body behind" (*Writers at Work: The Paris Review Interviews, Third Series*). And leaving also the earth behind, Burroughs insists; for in doing so, we gain a new perspective on our conditioned existence, on the meaning of gravity. Burroughs, then, is a technological gnostic; quite explicitly, he hopes that science will help to remake man. Autonomic processes, hallucinogenic drugs, electric stimulation of the brain, telepathy and telekinesis—all these interest him because they exercise the powers of the mind to transform itself, to act directly upon itself without tiresome interventions of body or matter ("Interview," *Penthouse,* March, 1972).

But is the case of Burroughs relevant to our general cultural condition or is it simply a terminal case of literature? The answer, I suspect, depends on how we value other writers, mentalists all of different kinds. Consider the playful ultimacy of John Barth's *Chimera;* the entropic indeterminacy of Thomas Pynchon's *The Crying of Lot 49;* the pop or "dreck" surrealism of Donald Barthelme's *City Life;* the oneiric death-denying abandon of Robert Coover's *The Universal Baseball Association;* the epistemological introversion of Rudolph Wurlitzer's *Flats;* and the regenerative narrative blanks of Ronald Sukenick's *Out.* Admittedly, these fictions are distinct, and their postmodern authors even more so. But do not these authors share with Burroughs a complex desire to dissolve the world—or at least to recognize its dissolution—and to remake it as an absurd or decaying or parodic or private—and still imaginative—construct? Geomancers more than mystics, they still abolish the terror, dreariness, and hazards of given things by FANTASY. Is this FANTASY, then, a novel type of secular gnosis? Perhaps we need a still narrower focus.

Ronald Sukenick, The Death of the Novel and Other Stories:

The contemporary writer—the writer who is acutely in touch with the life of which he is part—is forced to start from scratch: Reality doesn't exist, time doesn't exist, personality doesn't exist. God was the omniscient author, but he died; now no one knows the plot, and since our reality lacks the sanction of a creator, there's no guarantee as to the authenticity of the received version.

Also quoted in Jerome Klinkowitz & John Somer, eds., Innovative Fiction: Stories for the Seventies.

Science Fiction

A sharper view of the New Gnosticism in American literature would focus on science fiction. This may appear the easy way out of certain cultural and aesthetic complexities. Yet it is right for us to be curious about science fiction at this time. It is the imaginative form that creates new myths of our machines, new models of our social existence, new images of our destiny in the universe. As fable, as satire, as prophecy, then, the best science fiction deserves a quality of critical attention that we have tended to deny it. This attention may be forthcoming, particularly since so many "serious" novelists—as different from one another as Burgess, Burroughs, and Vonnegut—are finding the genre congenial.

And here is the point: some of the finest science fiction concerns itself, like its two parents, Myth and Technology, with the question of a universal consciousness. Sometimes the assumption appears to be that wherever life obtains in heightened forms, intelligence also functions in im-mediate ways. At other times, the assumption is simply that human minds are good enough to imagine better minds with, but good for little more.

British science fiction has richly rendered its own versions of this theme (see Fred Hoyle's *The Black Cloud* or Olaf Stapledon's *Last and First Men*). My examples, however, will refer to three works that are part of the American scene. The first is widely popular; the other two have literary distinction:

A. Robert Heinlein's *Stranger in a Strange Land*
B. Alfred Bester's *The Demolished Man*
C. Theodore Sturgeon's *More Than Human*

A. There are rumors that Heinlein's famous work, full of dull and jolly claptrap, has influenced the commune of Charles Manson. But the erotic and religious cults that fill the novel are less crucial than the "grokking" powers of its presumably Martian hero. These cults confess that Earthlings are still corporeal, that their imperfect grokking faculties must be mediated mystically through the flesh. Grokking itself means complete identification, total understanding, a momentary fusion of two beings into a larger awareness. The concept carries the mythic feeling of *participation mystique* and the technological idea of telepathy to their point of contact.

B. Bester's novel shows that in some distant future the fate of the human race depends on a nearly incorruptible society of mind readers, called "Espers" or, colloquially, "peepers." Third-class peepers can penetrate the conscious mind of "normals;" second-class, the preconscious mind; and first-class, the deep subconscious. But the whole society of mind readers constitutes a link with the future development of man, his evolution toward a larger consciousness. When a powerful, egotistic, and homicidal tycoon threatens this evolution, his "normal" brain is flooded with the collective psychic energy of all the peepers. Thus he receives illumination, perceives the mystery of his own identity and of cosmic love. He is "demolished" only as a willful and isolate self, caged in its obsolete needs.

C. But the most subtle of the three science fictions may be Sturgeon's. The time is the present; somewhere in the woods of America, a community accidentally takes shape. This community is composed of a grown telepathic idiot; twin little black girls who are teleports; a slightly older white telekineticist; and her charge, a mongoloid infant with the mind of a computer and extraterrestrial connections. Solitary and freakish apart, together they form a preternatural organism, a new kind of intelligent life, called *homo gestalt*, that also possesses the means to conquer gravity. "Gravitics," it seems, would add Psyche to the Unified Field that already includes Matter, Energy, Space, and Time. But as it turns out, *homo gestalt* must learn from *homo sapiens* something about a moral ethos before making its quantum spiritual jump. That, in hasty outline, is the story of *More than Human*.

These three science fictions are by no means unique in presaging the transformation of man into a vast noetic reality, a universal consciousness capable of im-mediate exchanges of knowledge. Can such anticipatory myths become slow, self-fulfilling prophecies? Or is the future simply our most widely shared, treasured, and revised fantasy?

Coda

Once again, I should stress that we are not concerned here with the old Gnostic religions, their theories of creation and apocalypse, their dualisms and demiurges, their Elohims, Sophias, and Helens. We are concerned, however, with a new sense of the im-mediacy of Mind, of complete gnosis or knowledge. This sense implies a vast, new role of Consciousness in the universe. Curiously or uncuriously, this role was vaguely prefigured by the ancient Gnostics, authors of a passionate subjectivity.

But the New Gnosticism does not rest only on mystical experiences or mythical archetypes; it insinuates itself into postmodern literature; and it appears as a condition of our science, of our technology. The New Gnosticism, in fact, presupposes convergences that are silently altering the definitions of culture. Will they not end by changing the definitions of man?

I have spoken in a speculative voice. I have assumed, as some others have, that we are witnessing a transformation of man more radical than anything Copernicus, Darwin, Marx, or Freud ever envisaged. But there are alternatives to this assumption. We may, for instance, obliterate ourselves as a race. Or we may develop apace, doing more or less what we do now, without any radical change in our destiny. Or again, we may indeed change radically in a way that entails no universal consciousness. Everything that rises must converge? Perhaps it is only everything that falls.

I have spoken in a speculative voice to raise questions, not to foreclose them; but speculations may also clear the way for theory, judgment, or belief. No doubt, every reader will have his responses. The questions that remain concern us, more specifically, as readers and writers of literature. How shall we respond to these new realities? Should we sever ourselves from the sources of imagination and change in our time? Can we enter the gnostic dream to give it a larger and richer shape? Or will we continue to sustain ourselves on our own traditions, with piety, skepticism, and complex hope?

An Exemplum: Norman Mailer

He has become exemplary and, many also say, the foremost author in America. His home, we know, is the domain of the Self: power, instinct, vision. Closer to the old magic than to the new, he has been a deep and ambiguous critic of technology. Yet here, perhaps, is a failure: he conceals from himself what I think he senses, that magic and technology meet at a vital point of human evolution. Mailer, at any rate, sees that shamans and computers enjoy their intercourse in the surreal world of today and tomorrow:

Yet even this model of the future was too simple. For the society of the rational and the world of the irrational would be without boundaries. Computersville had no cure for skin disease but filth in the wound, and the guru had no remedy for insomnia but a trip to the moon, so people would be forever migrating between the societies. Sex would be a new form of currency in both worlds—on that you could count. (*Of a Fire on the Moon*)

Sex—and also its primordial equivalents, Gravity and Light? Who knows what the sexual consciousness—body seeking body, energy freed from itself—might become?

The example Mailer sets before the community of letters is that of its own endeavor, that of the literary act itself, in our time. His vaulting ambition, imagination, irony attempt to comprehend some final facts and fancies of the age. But the recalcitrance of our palpable life, the persistence of our prejudice and pain, contrast so sharply with the invisible possibilities of the human race that even the most extreme vision must hedge itself. In our quotidian existence, hunger and anger still rule the day far more than the imagination. This is to say that our Promethean crisis is at heart still RELIGIOUS. (*End of Exemplum*)

The New Gnosticism assumes that the more consciousness increases, the more Fact and Fancy will converge, the more Is and Can, Sensation and Thought, become one. The Literary Imagination can only hold the New Gnosticism in suspicion; the latter doubts that Imagination will still find its primary fullfilment in Literature.

Quite probably, the great chain of being, extending from hell to heaven, running through all the intermediate forms of creation, is broken. Or more precisely: the great chain of being is reconstituting itself in one great link or loop of consciousness, not linear but multiform. Man no longer stands between Earth and Sky; he is becoming both and either.

Yet how many
        within or without
        academies of mind
                of every kind
can truly perceive
        Where this metaphor
        of our friend   (Blake)
          ends?
            (Not I).

   . . . each grain of Sand,
   Every stone on the land,

Each rock & each hill,
Each fountain & rill,
Each herb & each tree,
Mountain, hill, earth, & sea,
Cloud, Meteor, & Star,
Are Men Seen Afar.

Charles Altieri

From Symbolist Thought to Immanence
The Ground of Postmodern American Poetics

I

Recent criticism has shown a remarkable measure of agreement on the following generalizations about contemporary poetry: (1) three overlapping modes of contemporary poetry can be distinguished—confessional and less extreme forms of highly personal poetry, poetry based on Olson's Projectivist aesthetic which ranges from objectivist poems to the fantasies of the New York Poets, and poetry of the deep-image self-consciously utilizing in a controlled fashion a surrealist poetic; (2) contemporary poets prefer the direct, the personal, the local, the anti-formal, and the topical to the traditional modernist emphases on impersonality (i.e., formalism, overtly mythical themes and constructs, the use of persona, and a stress on complex and paradoxical statements), literary tradition, historicism and universal statement; (3) contemporary aesthetic calls for participation far more than for interpretation; (4) the custom of poetry readings has become very influential and has led away from complex meditative poetry to a more oral, communal style; and (5) the contemporaries are often directly religious or "sacramental" in their poetry, while at the same time rejecting traditional Western religious codes and seeking their religious meaning in some kind of "natural supernaturalism."[1]

Precisely because these generalizations are well-founded, the field of critical inquiry is enlarged rather than closed off. What, we are tempted to ask, lies behind these traits; what common ground of philosophical or mythical assumptions informs the sensibilities nurturing the poems?

The pursuit of such a question requires a cavalier willingness to generalize and to take certain poets as representative, but the rewards seem worth the risks. Since we have by now a pretty good idea of the philosophical and aesthetic assumptions behind high or traditional modernism and the poetry and poetics it spawned from about 1935 to the early sixties, we can perhaps best discover the ground of a postmodern poetics through its contrasts with that tradition. Once we have discovered the underlying philosophical framework, it becomes possible to map a kind of logical geography which explains the relationship between recurrent contemporary themes.

What unity we find in postmodern poetry derives from a common approach to two philosophical crises which have seriously affected poetics—the first stemming from the tensions which led the romantics to redefine poetry as a unique way of knowing the world and discovering or creating significance within it, and the second, a sense of the inadequacy of the answers to those romantic problems posed by the earlier generations of modern poets. We can formulate these basic problems in many ways: it is possible to speak, for example, of the need to reconcile a series of dichotomies—substance with quality, body with mind, feeling with thought, passive with active man, and the pressure of reality with the liberating power of imagination. All these, however, seem to me versions of the one central dichotomy between fact and value. In other words, the romantics were essentially responding to the tensions man experiences between definitions of his relationship to the world which do and do not affirm as "real" those projections of human subjectivity we find most pronounced in mythic thinking. The distinction is ultimately between a dead world and a live world, a world that can be satisfactorily explained without analogues from man's experience of his own being in the world and one where he imagines the world beyond his self to complement and extend the experience he has of his own body and immediate surroundings.[2] The problem of finding a place for value in a world of fact existed, of course, long before the romantics, but in the period immediately preceding theirs, it came more and more to permeate the general intellectual culture. One need only reflect on the turmoil caused by Hume and the French materialists. And even Hume's opponents are faced with similar tensions—in Burke's sense of the need for myth or in Johnson's Rasselas, who is always on the verge of learning that it is his own quest and not its objects which creates the values he wants to find. When we turn to the romantics themselves, we need only think of Whitehead's description of Wordsworth and Shelley in his *Science and the Modern World,* or of anti-Lockean thought, convinced that associationism left no place for the value-creating faculty which alone could satisfy inherited expectations about human dignity.

To mediate fact and value, the romantics explored two modes of thought, often interrelated but worth distinguishing if we are to see how both modern and postmodern poetry derive from romanticism and differ from each other. We can, for example, differentiate between Wordsworth (particularly in his early years as a poet) and Coleridge in their approach to associationism and hence to the way one can bring together subject and object, fact and the interrelations of fact which in part constitute the experience of value. Where Coleridge tries to refute Lockean associationism through the Kantian epistemological revolution and its focus on creative imagination, the Wordsworth of the "Preface to the *Lyrical Ballads*" counters it by pointing to the presence of laws in nature and to the way the movements of the mind are linked to those laws: "Reflecting upon the magnitude of the general evil, I should be oppressed with no dishonorable melancholy, had I not a deep impression of certain inherent and indestructible qualities of the human mind, and likewise of certain powers in the great and permanent objects that act upon it which are equally inherent and indestructible?"[3] In the contrast between the two men we have the essential terms and inner logic which informs the modernist poles of symbolism and imagism and their postmodern transformations. Wordsworth's essay for the most part stresses the power of nature to create and sustain value (its corollary to contemporaries like Charles Olson is a heavy stress on Keats's letter on negative capability) and offers the following theses which recur in later poetics calling for a similar "immanentist" position on value: the stress on natural law and its harmonic relation with the mind (245, 249–50), the priority of subject matter or content to form (249–50), the call for simplicity of style and a language theory insisting that the world need not be distorted by the words which express it, the precept of looking steadily at one's subject, and finally the opposition between various convention-bound ways of viewing the world and fresh ones which allow its value to manifest itself. In Coleridge, on the other hand, we find a model in English for symbolist theories of value (in the sense of the term exemplified by thinkers like Ernst Cassirer who stress the creative faculties by which the collective mind imposes its forms on reality and responds to its own creations). For him the creative imagination is the principle of form responsible for generating the value of the particulars in a poem; complexity and fusion are his primary aesthetic values; organic unity is a creation of the poet and (at least in the poem) not a fact of prior experience; and poetry is in no way imitative, rather it is "secondary creation" (Kant's term) and thus takes its purposiveness from an act of mind and appeals primarily to the meditative faculties of the audience. The argument can be summarized by distinguishing between Coleridge's recreation of the object through the subject and early Wordsworth's sense that the subject is created by means of its participation in the object.

We cannot overlook here, in our zest for distinction, the basic fact that almost all major romantic and postromantic poets have shared the ideal of creating through the imagination a world in which nature and mind are correlative and extend one another. Nonetheless, it remains possible to identify the central position informing their quest as rooted in one of the two traditions. Furthermore, acceptance of the two poles enables us to see the kind of problems and tensions which beset a poet who takes his initial ground at either one. For example, when Wordsworth tells us that his associations "must have been sometimes particular instead of general" (268), and thus without life for the reader, he is warning us that a poetry of immanence constantly flirts with the danger of appearing as a dead collection of facts. (One thinks of criticisms of Gary Snyder or of Pound's need to develop imagism into vorticism.) And Coleridge's criticism of his "Preface" reminds us that poetry of immanence tends toward a reverence for simplicity and sheer presence and thus continually flirts with primitivism and with an inability to measure properly man's creative powers in the world. For symbolist thinking, the dangers are two kinds of dualism—the linguistic Platonism of Mallarmé and the skeptical view that all created orders are sheer fiction and man is perpetually alienated from any experience of truth in the world. The tensions in Wordsworth and Coleridge grow far more problematic when men can no longer accept the God who assured Wordsworth that human and natural orders are in fact harmoniously blended in the laws of association and who grounded for Coleridge the integrative role played in the objective world by the synthesizing imagination. Perhaps a final and almost absurd manifestation of the dangerous extremes at each pole can be found in contemporary American fiction with one exemplified by reporter novelists and the other by elaborate explorations of the theme of fiction and of the fantasies of the fictive mind.

Modernist poetry and poetics are informed almost entirely by the symbolist tradition. Even imagism, the modernist poetic closest to Wordsworth, places a heavy stress on artifice and on the creative, transcendent word. More important is the fact that most imagist and objectivist poets have become more important to the contemporaries than they were to their most influential peers. It is no accident that modernist poetry produced the symbolist-oriented New Criticism and no popularly accepted objectivist aesthetic. The change then to the postmoderns and their revival of Pound and Williams is a crucial one. Dating perhaps from Roethke's "The loneliest thing i know/is my own mind at play," postmodern poets have been seeking to uncover the ways man and nature are unified, so that value can be seen as the result of immanent processes in which man is as much object as he is agent of creativity.

We can draw the distinction sharply between these orientations by examining their perspectives on two topics—the place of nature in man's value schemes, and the relation between concrete and universal. As J. Hillis Miller has made clear, the symbolist tradition is essentially dualist, and one can readily illustrate this dualism by pointing out the modernist tendency to view experiences as data incomplete until complemented by some creative activity of mind. The world without man is always lacking something, or in Randall Jarrell's phrase, "when art goes what remains is life." Yeats and Stevens, with their explorations of the dialectic between objective and imaginative poles of meaning most obviously illustrate the modernist sense of the ways values come to exist. And a similar perspective is evidenced in Eliot's need for tradition and later for Incarnation, a metaphor which both in poetry and in the poetics of the New Criticism expressed the miraculous fusion felt to be necessary if men were to unite the contradictory pulls of objective fact and the orders created by the value-giving imagination. Allen Tate's lifelong struggle with the dangers of narcissism provides a good example of a man aware of the ultimate logic of his dualist position yet trying to modify it into some acceptable compromise. The more distant the God grows who helped Tate reach his compromises, the more evident becomes the menace of narcissism in this symbolist tradition, and radical anti-humanist thought becomes the necessary antidote.

The metaphor of incarnation has specifically poetic implications as well as axiological ones. Incarnation interpreted by Christian writers as diverse as Dante and Augustine is a historical concrete event which mediates and guarantees the transformation of fact into allegory. Now while the New Critics were opposed to allegory, they did devote a lot of energy to explaining ways in which logical structure and local texture, the realm of discourse and the realm of particular experience are miraculously joined in the poem as concrete universal. Their stress on the poem as artifact was essentially a way of keeping in mind the two facets of all acts of making—the object to work on and principles the maker refers to in his activities. Because these principles or forms exist essentially in the realm of discourse, poetry is communication at least as much as it is experience. So poetic theorists stress both participatory and communicative aspects of the poem, and critics come more and more to treat the poem less as phenomenon than as key to enter the order of relationships to be found behind and beyond the particulars. Form becomes "informing" particulars with some interpretative frame, while form for a postmodern like Robert Duncan, manifests itself as "information," as an immediate relationship with particulars in process.

Louis Simpson suggests that while particular poetic styles manifest a complex multiplicity, the common ground underlying that multiplicity can become apparent when we look at what the poets refuse to do. The value of this suggestion becomes evident as soon as we turn to postmodern thought on the topics we've been discussing. Charles Olson and those he influenced have rejected modernist assumptions most fully, but I hope to show that their sentiments are for the most part indicative of the less explicit assumptions shared by a good majority of those poets arriving at mature styles in the 1960s. Their primary concern is a rejection and reformulation of the humanist framework which they see underlying modern poetics. Here, for example, are two reactions by Robert Duncan and by Olson against the idea that value and order depend on man's creative imagination:

Central to and defining the poetics I am trying to suggest here is the conviction that the order man may contrive or impose upon the things about him or upon his own language is trivial beside the divine order or natural order he may discover in them.

(PP, 139)[4]

Hanging over into the present from the old cosmology are three drags, each of them the offsets of the principal desire of man for Kosmos during the two millenia and a half preceding us. And the three hang about people's necks like dead birds. They are Void, Chaos, and the trope Man. Or, to put them down in the order of their occurrence, Chaos, Man, Void; that is, Chaos was the imagined unformed on which the order Kosmos set form. Man was the later child of the same act—a teleology of form as progressive was the hidden assumption of the old cosmology, and Void is what's left when the Kosmos breaks down as the interesting evidence of order, Man falls when that purpose falls, and so Void is the only assumption left; that is, Kosmos infers Chaos as precedent to itself and Man as succeeding, and when it goes as a controlling factor, only Void becomes a premise of measure. Man is simply filling an empty space. Which turns quickly by collapse into man is skin and flesh surrounding a void as well. Void in, void out. It is the counsel of despair.

(SVH, 47–48)

While incarnation for the moderns exemplified the union of form and significant value on an otherwise empty and chaotic natural world, God for the contemporaries manifests himself as energy, as the intense expression of immanent power. Thus they refer frequently to D. H. Lawrence's gods, who do not descend from heaven but emerge from the soil. Consequently, sacramentalism takes on radically different implications. Compare Allen Tate's view of sacramentalism as the miraculous union of concrete and universal, intension and extension, with Nathan Scott's Heideggerean definition of the same process in contemporary poetry: "Certain objects or actions or words or places belonging to the ordinary spheres of life may convey to us a unique illumination of the whole mystery of our existence, because in these actions and realities . . . something numinous is resident, something holy and gracious."[5] To Scott and the contemporary poets sacrament equals radical presence while the more traditional humanist interpretation views it as essentially symbolic, structuring as well as intensifying experience.

Symbolism, however, is always distrusted in Protestant cults of presence, and postmodern poetics are radically Protestant.[6] It is only logical then that there should be a redefinition of the symbolist interpretation of the concrete universal. Thus we find Robert Duncan calling for:

---

a poetics not of paradigms and models but of individual variations and survivals, of the mutual affinities of organic beings and the evolution of living forms. . . . The old poetic intuition remained true, that God created Man in His own Image; but now to be read true, it must be read in the light of our science, of a new acknowledgement. The Image of God is primordially present; it is in our own time, in our immediacy—'our' here referring to the immediate locus of consciousness each of us is *alone*.

(*NG*, ii)

The key words here are "primordially present"; a poem is significant not because it leads us out to meaning or embodies significant themes or dramatizes human problems but because it captures in its own processes the basic forces or presences which give human existence its meaning. Concrete universal gives way to an exploration of the many ways the universal—be it "being" or energy or the collective unconscious—manifests itself in the concrete moment. Instead of raising particulars to the level of universals whereby they come to provide models for experience (Croce on *Don Quixote* is the classic text), the postmoderns seek to have the universal concretized, to see the particular as numinous, not as representative.

The difference, of course, remains essentially one of emphasis. In one way Duncan's statement, "It is not that poetry imitates, but enacts in its order the order of first things" (*PP*, 138) can be seen as merely an extension of New Critical arguments for the poem as dramatic event not statement. But when we ask what is being enacted, we see there remains a strong philosophy of representation and consequently of interpretation in New Criticism radically different from Duncan's ontological concern for the presence of an ordering force analogous to (or the same as) the ordering force in nature. Interpretation of experience gives way to the ideal of invoking numinous power in such diverse poetic enterprises as those of James Dickey, with his attempts to merge animal and human consciousness, and Charles Olson, with his attack on "energy referred to" as opposed to "energy made present":

What Socrates did was to isolate the value and thus raise and isolate the man-time from space-time. What he performed, however, was a removal from the particular, which, as Whitehead, in calling any occasion the actual, is the absolute, because it is in fact the way the absolute energy asserts itself.

(*SVH*, 27)

Even Robert Bly, so often an adamant critic of Olson, comes to sound exactly like him on the idea that poetry is a way man uncovers "secrets objects share" (SW, 25): "The poem is an extension of the substance of the man, no different from his skin or his hands. The substance of the man who wrote the poem reaches far out into the darkness and the poem is his whole body, seeing with his ears and his fingers and his hair" (WT, 38).

The postmodern insistence that value is not mediated but stems from a direct engagement with the universal forces of being manifest in the particular has important implications which transcend poetics. We have seen how the idea of concrete universal complements the modernist insistence that value is a human creation in the universe. Before the particular can be significant, it must fit some larger human interpretive framework. The doctrine of concrete universal arose as a nineteenth-century means (especially in Hegel) for preserving the sense of a universe responsive to human forms even when the God had died who guaranteed that man does indeed possess the potential to measure the universe. This idea then goes hand in hand with Matthew Arnold's attempt to preserve the ethical power of "the best that is known and thought," even as he denied the theological base for so much of what he needed to continue believing. The creative imagination as form-giver and as creator of ethical principles became a way for modernism to retain and restate a humanism it could no longer defend philosophically. This tenuous humanism becomes the first object of attack when poets no longer accept the primacy of human creativity. If the subject is created by the object at least as much as it creates the object, value need not depend on human choice or on the universals men refer to in making their choices. Value instead emerges from the ways man participates in the world beyond himself, and thus value can be conceived in biological and psychological terms. Value is a way of being informed, not of informing. Primary in the reaction against humanism is the model of ecological thinking. It is not enough for man to assume he can determine the measure of things; rather he must try to discover how he himself is an object given his "orders" by the general schemes of creative nature in which he is only another participant. "Decreation" then is a basic process for the postmodern arts: human forms must first be destroyed, if we are to be open to the true sources of value manifest in the natural processes which create forms. Though many of my references later in the paper will be relevant, it is sufficient here to recall radical movements in the other arts like John Cage's negation of musical structure as a means for focusing attention on natural events or Alain Robbe-Grillet's manifesto for a new novel devoted to objects seen in themselves and not through humanized interpretation. In poetry, the distrust of humanly imposed form manifests itself in Olson's attack on what he calls "the suck of the symbol" or in Kenneth Koch's cry for "Fresh Air" as a relief from the poetic scene where,

> I am afraid you have never smiled at the hibernation
> Of bear cubs except that you saw in it some deep
>   relation
> to human suffering and wishes. . . .
>   The white and pink roses are slightly agitated
>   by the struggle,
> But afterwards beside the dead "poet" they cuddle up
>   comfortingly against their vase.
> They are safer now, no one will compare them to the
>   sea.

In ethical thought, anti-humanism has two basic themes. There is first of all a renewed attention to the biological and the domestic, the necessary as opposed to the creative. Here are sections of Anthony Hecht's poem "The Dover Bitch: A Criticism of Life":

> Well now, I knew this girl. It's true she had read
> Sophocles in a fairly good translation
> And caught that bitter allusion to the sea,
> But all the time he was talking she had in mind
> The notion of what his whiskers would feel like
> On the back of her neck. . . .
>   To have been brought
> All the way down from London, and then be addressed
> As a sort of mournful cosmic last resort
> Is really tough on a girl, and she was pretty.

Second is a kind of anarchic individualism. When the presence of the universal becomes more important than its structure, value comes to reside more in intensity than in the meaning of actions, more in the fact of participation with the forces of process than in the results achieved by action and the community's approval of them. Infinite modes of authenticity become possible when communal measures of the results accomplished no longer matter. The secular thinking of the postmoderns is amazingly close to Protestant doctrines of the relationship between man and the absolute, and as a result, contemporary poets replace humanist thinking with metaphors like the "Ground" and the "Way"—the "ground" expressing the need for a foundation in radically non-human sources of value and the "way" calling up the structured, yet immediate and nonreflective processes in which these values become actualized.

II

I have up to now been overemphasizing the mentalist aspects of the great modernists, who Monroe Spears is the latest to remind us were essentially in quest of a rich balance between Dionysiac energy and Apollonian form. The bent of my argument, however, does call attention to those aspects of modernism which were most influential on the generation of poets preceding the contemporaries. Josephine Miles offers the following generalizations of the poetry of the 1940s (which apply equally well to the fifties):

> The poetry is therefore of pattern. It is devoted to the linear, tonal, and qualitative arrangement of things according to a perspective in a state of mind. Its truth and beauty are in arrangements. . . .
> The poetry of the decade is, in its whole make-up, opposed to direct apprehension or intuition through substance. It is made out of abstract consideration. . . .
> The varying styles, while they shade from brief immediacy to ironic analysis and to splendid encompassment, persist always in their emphasis on the pattern of things, made and natural, in the presence of mind.[7]

We can then trace a logical (and in part chronological) movement from the poetry of the forties to the contemporaries in three stages—poetry inspired by New Critical ideals, confessional poetry, and a poetry of numinous presence. Richard Wilbur's "A World Without Objects is a Sensible Emptiness" exemplifies the first stage and makes a useful contrast with Robert Lowell's *Life Studies:*

> The tall camels of the spirit
>   Steer for their deserts, passing the last groves loud
> With the sawmill shrill of the locust, to the whole honey of the arid
>   Sun. They are slow, proud,
>
>   And move with a stilted stride
> To the land of sheer horizon, hunting Traherne's

Sensible emptiness, there where the brain's lantern-slide
   Revels in vast returns.
. . . .
               . . . Turn, O turn
From the fine sleights of the sand, from the long empty oven
   Where flames in flamings burn

      Back to the trees arrayed
   In bursts of glare, to the halo-dialing run
Of the country creeks, and the hills' bracken tiaras made
   Gold in the sunken sun,

      Wisely watch for the sight
   Of the supernova burgeoning over the barn,
Lampshine blurred in the steam of beasts, the spirit's right
   Oasis, light incarnate.[8]

Wilbur's poem is a hymn to the sensible world as source of value and true home of spirit. However the style conflicts sharply with the theme (deliberately, I suspect), depending as it does on Wilbur's confidence in the mind's elegant play with artifice and metaphor as it orients us to a different source of value. Lowell's *Life Studies* as a coherent volume also elaborates the tension between fictive order and animal faith. Now, though, the stakes have been raised: crossing the Alps and descending to earth necessitates a radical reorientation in one's sense of the sources of value. Not only does Lowell in this volume reject the typological and formal style of his earlier verse, he also rejects the mental landscape of Wilbur's imaginings for the concrete and prosaic world of fact and local detail, the bedrock zero where experiences of value can replace interpretations of it. And some experience of value is necessary, because after the rejection of Catholicism Lowell in effect surveys his life for some valid ground on which to affirm his own value and value outside of himself and finds only the emptiness of a decaying American and artistic tradition and of his family which embodied them. All this is recapitulated in the dark night of the soul or "everlasting nay" sections of "Skunk Hour," but Lowell then finds at least a provisional basis for value in the skunk's instinctive care for its own existence and sense of responsibility for its children. The skunk's rooting in the garbage takes on overtones of a sacramental meal, and the blending of religious overtones with radically de-sacralized phenomena creates an emblem which frequently recurs in contemporary poetry.[9]

Even if his change of perspectives is not total and the skunk comes to embody for Lowell many of the humanist values whose grounds he no longer shares, that shift is a representative one. John Logan, W. S. Merwin, James Wright, and even in part, Mr. Wilbur himself, move away from formal, intellectualized styles to more experience-oriented poetry. In Lowell's own case, *Life Studies* initiated the habit of conceiving human problems along the metaphorical lines of biological process, a tendency which has grown more and more pronounced in his subsequent poetry. Along with the emergence of the biological metaphor goes an increasing passivity, a surrender of a faith in man's creative processes in favor of at least the appearance of becoming merely a vehicle for experience.[10] And the political corollary of this passivity is, in *Notebooks*, an increasing note of self-pity and of pity for a culture whose death seems inevitable. This passivity, I should like to argue, is also a logical necessity of the bases of Confessional poetry. Confessional poetry is an attempt to solve value problems—both within the poem and for the individual—without reference to philosophical, cultural, or mythic universals. Poetically Confessional poetry generates the syntax of charged relationships primarily through the tortured presence of the individual speaker. His condition, rather than his frame of reference, creates whatever intensity the poem possesses beyond that established by its strictly aesthetic patterning. And on the ethical level (where *Notebooks* makes apparent what had been implicit in *Life Studies*) all the poet can affirm is what immediately touches on his subjective existence. Confessional poetry is the epic of what Hannah Arendt calls the economical man whose value frame extends only to the field of his domestic existence. And if Lowell is its Dante, its Aquinas is the existential Sartre, whose despair is never far in the background.

The final step in the logic leading to the positions of the postmodern poets is precisely this evaluation of Confessional poetry and the mythos of individualism justifying it. Robert Bly, for example, points out that Lowell's kind of poetry fails because the merely human cannot really generate value: "Only a person with really sluggish blood could put up with the average interior state of a human being without yawning, and to make art out of it is impossible" (*DW*, 5). Lyric poetry, by the very nakedness it gives its content (especially when mental play is eschewed), is a heightened test of the value possibilities of that content, and the confessional poet, with the sensitivity to realize his quotidian experience will not stand up (though *Notebooks* is a noble failure attempting to achieve this) is driven to present progressively more extreme situations. As Bly puts it:

> For the confessional poet anything less than an abortion or a cancer operation really doesn't justify the machinery. A poem becomes a tank that can't maneuver on soft ground without destroying it.

(DW, 6)

Bly's comments echo Kierkegaard's analysis of the despair of being oneself, for him the ultimate form of despair. Kierkegaard is an especially apt analogue here because his subjectivist theology works itself out in opposition to Hegelian and Catholic doctrines of the primacy of the universal concepts in which the individual can find his meaning. In his existential condition, Kierkegaard's self-conscious individual finds himself alone and forced to make his own particular definition of values, but without a ground, without a context complementing and supporting the individual's choice, he can ultimately choose only his own despairing isolation:

> Revolting against the whole of existence, it thinks it has hold of a proof against it, against its goodness. This proof the despairer thinks he himself is, and that is what he wills to be, therefore he wills to be himself, himself with his torment, in order with this torment to protest against the whole of existence.[11]

To transcend this state of despair, Kierkegaard needs to resurrect the Hegelian formulation of the problem of the self, though he continues to reject the Hegelian universal as its solution. Instead he defines the self's necessary ground as a presence, not a concept, and goes on to explain how this living ground can be discovered in faith: "despair is completely eradicated" when the self recognizes that it exists only in relationship and the relationship achieves equilibrium "only by relating itself to that power which constituted the whole relation" (146–47). The most complete relational term, that which constitutes and thus "measures" the whole relationship into which the self can enter is God (210). Kierkegaard speaks here for all those poets like Bly who will develop the metaphors of "measure" or (Kierkegaard's other term) "ground" as their antidotes to the "despair of being oneself." In fact, if we take into account the fact that the postmoderns will redefine Kierkegaard's "measure" in terms more amenable to their secular and naturalistic interests, we can see this quest for a viable "ground" within process to save the self from solipsistic despair as the central movement in contemporary poetic thought.

As Bly so nicely proposes, the "ground" of postmodern poetry tends to be an evanescent one, to be found as the horizon of experiences rather than as their conceptual background. Thinkers like Olson often cite a Heraclitean fragment which summarizes the kind of measure the poets are after, "Man is estranged from that with which he is most familiar." In addition to its implicit criticism of extremism or of elaborate conceptual or mythical systems, the fragment calls our attention to the possibility of whole value frames rooted in man's normal nonreflective experience of the world. Value must be rediscovered not recreated, and this is the challenge accepted by postmodern poetry. What is needed then are new ways of seeing and conceptualizing the familiar, and I shall suggest four interconnected conceptual frames through which the familiar can become "measure" for man's actions and locus of value. All four can be seen as ways of interpreting Charles Olson's influential definition of meaning, "That which exists through itself is what is called meaning" (CM, 2), or as some of my students put it, "a thing means what it does." Each of the four takes a different tack on exactly what activity is necessary for the thing to exist through itself, and the result is a kind of continuum running from visions of the inherent activity in objects, through interpretations of the way mind enters into and joins in the process of emergence, to views calling attention to the creative power of mind, not as creator of symbolic or fictive constructs but as the ultimate force enlivening the objects it encounters. We might define the first two frames as versions of objectivism—the first concerned primarily with the quality of objects in the world and the second calling attention to the ontological properties of those objects, the Being they share with man. The philosopher closest to the first is Husserl, to the second Heidegger. The second set of frames moves progressively inward from the qualities of things to the psychic meaning of things and finally to the processes by which a consciousness creates the world it inhabits. Whitehead's philosophy helps describe the third, Nietzsche's the fourth.

The first frame develops two basic aspects of the imagist, objectivist heritage—the sense of value in the sharp definition of particulars and the subsequent attention to the vital processes manifest when the particulars are treated as themselves active agents participating in the energies of the world. We find, for example, George Oppen asserting, "I do believe that consciousness exists and that it is consciousness of something, and that is a very complete but not very detailed theology." Seeing becomes for him the essential mode of implementing this theology and several contemporaries share his echo of Pound on the symbol and Williams on "no ideas but in things." Theodore Roethke, for example, made the influential assertion, "Intensely seen, image becomes symbol" and Robert Duncan bases his whole essay on Dante on the theme "an idea is a thing seen." But sight for postmodernism is usually more than a way of perceiving objects; it becomes a way of entering the duration of objects beyond the self and thus a way of participating in their becoming. It is possible, as Robert Kelly shows us, to formulate a poetics of the image based on this distinction between fact and process: the difference, he tells us, between imagism and the deep image is the difference between the world seen as fact and the world seen so that "the image is not a thing. It is process and discovered identity. It discovers its being in its function." Tate's meditation on tension, intension, and extension is replaced by the central concept of *attention* before the mysteries of process. A. R. Ammons provides a good example of the contemporary perspective:

> manifold events of sand
> change the dune's shape that will not be the same shape
> tomorrow,
> so I am willing to go along, to accept
> the becoming
> thought, to stake off no beginnings or ends, establish
>   no walls:
>
>   the news to my left over the dunes and
> reeds and bayberry clumps was
>   fall: thousands of tree swallows
>   gathering for flight:
>   an order held
>   in constant change: a congregation
> rich with entropy: nevertheless, separable, noticeable
>   as one event,
>
>   the possibility of rule as the sum of rulelessness:
> the "field" of action
> with moving, incalculable center:[12]

The eye will never force "a humbling of reality to precept"; Olson reminds us that unlike conceptual judging activity the eye allows free play to all that stands before one and can open man to the mysteries of being:

> We are in the presence of the only truth which the real can have, its own undisclosed because not apparent character. Get that out with no exterior means or materials, no mechanics except those hidden in the thing itself, and we are in the hands of the mystery.
>
> (*SW*, 45)

There is an interesting fragment of Heraclitus, (quoted in a different version by W. S. Merwin as an epigraph to *The Lice*) which illustrates how we move from the concern for delineating particulars to the second more metaphysical frame which interrogates the implications of that "mystery" embodied in the processes the particulars share:

> Men are deceived in their knowledge of things that are manifest—even as Homer was, although he was the wisest of all Greeks. For he was even deceived by boys killing lice when they said to him: 'What we have seen and grasped, these we leave behind; whereas what we have not seen and grasped, these we carry away.'

Kenneth Rexroth's restatement of the same theme, "We are in Being as fish in water, who do not know water exists," makes clear the possibility of reorienting our vision away from things becoming to the contemplation of what it is these becomings share. Perceptual aesthetics here become self-consciously ontological and the relevant philosopher is Heidegger with his central question, "on what ground? from what source does the essent derive?" [13] Heidegger's questionings actually help clarify two aspects of the postmodern scene—they illustrate what it is poets hope to find as source of value through their involvement in process and they show one philosophical way of explaining the union of thinking and being, of human activity and natural process, sought by poets like Gary Snyder and Robert Bly. The relevance of this philosophy becomes apparent if we notice the similarity between Denise Levertov's quotation from Heidegger's "Hölderlin and the Essence of Poetry" and a statement by Robert Bly opposing to "humanist poetry" the poetic sense of the universe in which "a person is not seen as an 'I' but as part of something else." First the quotation and then Bly:

> Poetry looks like a game and is not. A game does indeed bring men together, but in such a way that each forgets himself in the process. In poetry, on the other

hand, man is reunited on the foundation of his existence. There he comes to rest; not indeed to the seeming rest of inactivity and emptiness of thought, but to that infinite state of rest in which all powers and relations are active.

(OP, 236)

The human poets study the three classical faculties: feeling, will, and intellect. The poets of the universe accept these faculties, and are aware of an additional energy inside themselves. Groddeck calls this energy the 'Gott-natur' (the holy nature). The Gott-natur senses the interdependence of all things alive, and longs to bring them all inside a work of art. The work of these poets is an elaborate expression of the Gott-natur. What results is a calmness.

(DW, 3)

Heidegger's thinking nicely recapitulates the logical progression from an object-oriented value base to one grounded on some shared immanent process. One of the primary themes in his *Kant and the Problem of Metaphysics* is the finitude of human being, which the analysis of man's encounters with the world at once demonstrates and explains. Human knowledge is finite because it requires for its completion "essents" (*Seindes*) which it itself is not and which it has not created. This essent functions as object (significantly *Gegenstand*) because it throws itself forward in its self-contained completeness and thus negates the infinite freedom of consciousness. Kant, we remember, defined the real object as that which cannot be wished away; but that definition to Heidegger betrays a mentalist, humanist bias in which mind is the active power and nature sheer materiality. Heidegger instead develops the sense of Kant's definition in a more monistic way by claiming that what makes the object a negation of consciousness is its own activity, its own function of throwing itself "forward to be met" (*KPM*, 74–76).

In his *Introduction to Metaphysics* and his later work, Heidegger's interest in the object expands into an interest in the ground of the object, in whatever underlies the power of various objects to come forward. His basic question becomes, "How does it stand with being?" or in the terms I am using, "how does the universal manifest itself in the concrete?" To separate the ground from its object for the reflective consciousness, Heidegger distinguishes two aspects under which the "essent" can appear—one in which the vital force of its being is manifest and one in which it merely exists as material entity, "that which is at any time." He sounds here very much like T. E. Hulme with his Bergsonian distinctions between things seen merely to be manipulated and "intensive manifolds" whereby things retain their essential mystery, their participation in *durée*, but Hulme, like the imagists, is atomistic. Each intensive manifold can be expressed in its completeness and no universal manifests itself, so Hulme can continue to stress the artificial aspects of the art work. Because Heidegger's distinction is ontological, between object ready to hand as mere existence and being which runs through all objects and makes them stand—makes them enter consciousnes not as things but as the self-enclosing process of a thing encountering its limit (*IM*, pp. 23, 25–27, 49–50), his thinking leads in more religious directions. "Meta," he tells us, denotes going "beyond something to see its conditions," and *phusis* for the Greeks meant "self-blossoming emergence . . . opening up, unfolding" (*IM*, 11–14).

For one who recognizes the condition of "self-blossoming," strong ethical implications follow. First for Heidegger is the anti-humanist insistence on "letting-be," on substituting attention to the world for the creative desire to adapt the world to human purposes.[14] The corollary of this precept is an important one because it nicely expresses the ethical implications of attention and the fears contemporaries have of the fictive imagination:

> The essent is no longer asserted (i.e. preserved as such). Now it is merely found ready made, it is datum. The end result is no longer that which is impressed into limits (i.e. placed in its form); it is merely finished and as such available to everyone, already there, no longer embodying any world—now man does as he pleases with what is available. The essent becomes an object, either to be beheld (view, image) or to be acted upon (product and calculation). The original world-making power, *physics*, degenerates into a prototype to be copied and imitated.
>
> (*IM*, 52)

In other words as one loses his feel for the pressure of being, of nature as its own *telos*, he comes to feel free to make up fictions about it and to impose his own purposes on it until he can only find a world made by man.

Heidegger's two contrasted perspectives on being express the recurrent opposition in the poets between dead and live worlds, and his discussion of the two ways man can know the world as being likewise echo poetic meditations on how the world can be kept vital. First of all, to understand essents as more than sheer materiality, to comprehend how being functions as the ground of essents, one must, as only poetry and philosophy can, be able to speak about nothing. Since being is never exhausted in the essent seen as mere mass, the thinker must be able to negate the overwhelming facticity of mass, must grasp what is not obviously there and exhausted by objects:

What in all these things we have just mentioned is the being of the essent? We run (or stand) around in the world with our silly subtleties and conceit. But where in all this is being?

All the things we named *are* and yet—when we wish to apprehend being, it is always as though we were reaching into the void. The being after which we inquire is almost like nothing, and yet we have always rejected the contention that the essent in its entirety is not [that is its entirety or ultimate reality is not an absent Platonic ideal].

(IM, 29)

Yet nothingness is also the basic threat to being; and here we can grasp the importance of the second way man can apprehend being—in the creative power of human speech—"If he is to take over being-there [*da-Sein*] in the radiance of being, he must bring being to stand, he must endure it in appearance and against appearance, and he must wrest both appearance and being from the abyss of nonbeing" (93). Heidegger distinguishes a speech concerned with appearance (what in *Being and Time* he calls "idle talk," pp. 195–214) and an authentic poetic speech he explains in terms of the etymology of *Logos*. *Legein* means "to collect, to gather together," and authentic speech is a means for bringing appearances into relationship and opposition and thus for sharpening the myriad modes of emergence in the world. Human *logos* is defined as "apprehension," the power which completes being because, as "receptive questioning," it gathers into the unity of tension particular aspects of being and, by the tensions it creates, it allows the limits or forms of the essents to manifest their vitality. Art, intense authentic speech, "is disclosure of the being of the essent;" beauty is not pleasure but the manifest presence of being since "presence was pure radiance" (*IM*, 111).

Heidegger's meditation on speech has already involved us in a third frame for considering "a thing is what it does," this time on an epistemological rather than an ontological level. Heidegger's metaphor of "unfolding" entails the agent of the knower as well as the action Being, but we can more completely elaborate the epistemology behind postmodern poetics from the work of Alfred North Whitehead, the one philosopher frequently cited by the poets.[15] Whitehead emphasizes the idea that one cannot consider the action of a percept apart from the action of the perceiver; what a thing does is inseparable from what man does to it and in that interaction the subject-object problem of classical philosophy is considered to be resolved. Human knowledge is a way of uniting with the world, of creating meaning and of being created by what one perceives. This desire for a union of creative subject and creative object is everywhere in postmodern poetry: we can look for example, at Bly's definitions of the image as the moment where man and world blend or at James Dickey exploring what he calls "the union of inner and outer states" (BB, 285) or at the general interest in primitive poetry where the poets feel they can find a permanent union of affective consciousness and dynamic world. On a more contemporary secular level, Robert Creeley finds in the idea of "place" (for which he sometimes uses Whitehead's word "occasion") the same experience of union with his perceptual field Bly finds in the image of others in the primitive. "Place" he suggests is where "I love and am loved," where "poetry not only creates" the experience but "issues from it" (QG, 63). Creeley rejects what he calls the old poetics of description and reflective arrangement because it denies the immediacy of the poem as event, as itself the issue of authentic being, or more properly "doing," in the world: "It is, then, to 'return' not to oneself as some egocentric center, but to experience oneself as *in* the world, thus, through this agency or fact we call, variously, 'poetry' " (QG, 64). Poetry is the emergence of place into the energy of language.

Whitehead's philosophy allows more thorough explanation of what the poets are driving at. Like Heidegger, Whitehead begins with the recognition that traditional mind-oriented ways of thinking are encountering a state of crisis. Given the dichotomy between substance, or matter in location, and qualities created by the subjective perceiving mind, reflective men can only vacillate between the poles of nausea and narcissism:

Thus the bodies are perceived as with qualities which in reality do not belong to them, qualities which in fact are purely the offspring of the mind. Thus nature gets credit which should in truth be reserved for ourselves: the rose for its scent. . . . The poets are entirely mistaken. They should address their lyrics to themselves, and should turn them into odes of self-congratulation on the excellency of the human mind. Nature is a dull affair, soundless, scentless, colourless; merely the hurrying of material, endlessly, meaninglessly.

(SMW, 154)

To this "fallacy of misplaced concreteness" or philosophy of referential instances (to relate Whitehead to Gilbert Ryle), he opposes his own philosophy of event as the primordial concrete reality: "What the theory does is to edge cognitive mentality away from being the necessary substratum of the unity of experience. That unity is now placed in the unity of an event" (*SMW*, 92). Knowledge to Whitehead is the indestructible unity of the action of a prehending agent and a set of data. Knowing is prehensive unification, "the passing from the objectivity of the data" to the subjective "feelings of the prehending agent as it completes its intentional project" (*PR*, 54).

Meaning, then, in Whitehead is always a process of emergence, a union of energy of mind and the energy of the world in subjective realizations (or "satisfactions") of the world's potential for meaning. Through this definition of meaning we are given philosophical analogues for numerous topics in contemporary poetics. To appreciate the importance of the local and the theme of place, for example, we need only turn to the two basic steps in his definition of meaning. Meaning as becoming is also meaning locked into a specific place, "The real essence indicates where the entity is" (*PR*, 75). And from this ground situation, meaning reaches out to incorporate a field of interlocked energies: "An extensive continuum is a complex of entities united by the various allied relationships of whole to part, and of overlapping so as to possess common parts, and of contact, and of other relationships derived from these primary relationships" (*PR*, 82). The same line of reasoning makes possible a solution at once to the problems of subject and object and of the one and the many. Subject and object complement each other in bringing to satisfaction the potential inherent in the context of prehension, yet the individual prehending entity is itself a part of the world and potentially data for the prehending action of others or even of further stages in the life process of the prehending individual: "The organic philosophy interprets experience as meaning the 'self-enjoyment' of being one among many, and of being one arising out of the composition of many" (*PR*, 168–69). Finally, as we might expect in an age where meaning is problematic, Whitehead echoes Heidegger on value as realization, especially as realization of vital relationships between opposites:

Remembering the poetic rendering of our concrete experience, we see at once that the element of value, of being valuable, of having value, of being an end in itself, of being something which is for its own sake, must not be omitted in any account of an event as the most concrete actual something. 'Value' is the word I use for the intrinsic reality of an event. Value is an element which permeates through and through the poetic view of nature. . . . Realisation therefore is in itself the attainment of value. But there is no such thing as mere value. Value is the outcome of limitation. The definite finite entity is the selected mode which is the shaping of attainment; apart from such shaping into individual matter of fact there is no attainment. The mere fusion of all that there is would be the non-entity of indefiniteness.

(SMW, 93–94)

My fourth frame for comprehending the way postmodernism renders immanent values comes into play when the emergent manifests itself almost entirely in the human term of the prehension. Value here resides in the creative activity of the artist—not in the forms he creates but in the manifestation of creative energy itself. The postmodern artist differs from the modern on this topic as Nietzsche's theme of action as play differs from Hegel's teleological perspective on creative action: the first is an end in itself and the second is part of a human process of embodying a universal logic.[16] At its most simpleminded the postmodern formulation of the theme of creative energy generates dicta like Gregory Corso's claims that the poet is really the true poem and his life is the value-source for his words (PP, 172, 176, 181). But at its most complex, it leads to fascinating poetic speculations, like those of Robert Duncan and W. S. Merwin, on the sources of creativity and the nature of the creative Word which informs the spoken word.

Charles Olson's much maligned "Projective Verse" is the most obvious and influential treatment of the energizing power of the poet in the poem. Olson's metaphysics of the breath is dubious, but accompanying it are some sharp observations on the possibilities for poetry in an anti-symbolist age. Olson wants the poem to be a "high energy discharge," but he distrusts formal arrangement as a means for generating this second syntax and at the same time fears that sheer objectivism might fall flat. His last recourse is the energizing presence of the poet, not as psychological being involved in self-expression but as a nexus of energy prehending the energies outside him. Breath is a suggestive concept here because it is at once physical, a concrete aspect of one's involvement in an objective world, and spiritual, both in the etymological sense of "spirit" and "soul" and as principle of measure. Breath is in the natural order, a form of rhythm—in no way abstract or a priori creative of the shape of experience—but expressing the patterns of force in the engaged energies of the responder. Composition for Olson, then, is the embodied process of the energies of recognition.

Olson's theories might not have been so influential if poets like Creeley or Frank O'Hara could not have so easily linked them with Action-Painting as a dramatic analogue for their new view of the creative process (see *SW*, 7). The artist need no longer be conceived as creative mind outside of what he makes; the art object literally becomes a place (or in Whitehead's terms an "event") where artist and world meet and where the old aesthetics of the harmony and unity of the art work can now be related to the artist's existential relation with and literally *in* his work. Furthermore, the harmony is less a construct than it is a "condition" of process, and it is intensely personal without being self-expressive (which implies another absent referent). Finally, the analogue allows a way to conceive art as structured without positing a Platonic notion of structure. Structure is the pattern of decisions which remains evident when the work is the direct expression of energy in relation to a specific ground.[17]

III

If the various manifestations of immanence we have been examining are, in fact, the ground of postmodern poetics, we should now be able to see how that ground informs the features of the landscape. I want then to explore the "logical geography" (Gilbert Ryle's term) of postmodern poetry by showing how the basic ontology leads to characteristic positions on topics like the ego, language, history, and mythology.

For the postmoderns, modernist versions of the ego tend to one of two extremes—the Yeatsian equation of style and personality, the two unified by the artist's heroic desire to order, to form, and to individualize, and Eliot's Bradleyan and later his Christian despair concerning the existence of the ego and the corollary poetics of persona, tradition, and martyrdom. Even so immanentist a poet as Pound is accused by poets like Charles Olson or George Oppen of falling victim to "the nineteenth-century stance" of insistence on an ego system (SW, 82–84): "Pound's ego system, Pound's organization of the world around a character, a kind of masculine energy, is extremely foreign to me." And, as we have seen, confessional poetry marked the death-throes of the romantic self-transcending or totalizing individual.[18] The key term in the alternative conception is the *Bhagavad Gita*'s phrase "the ego as organ," with all its sexual connotations. The ego is a way man enters and registers "the condition of things" (SVH, 46, and Olson's discussion of negative capability). Thus W. S. Merwin reminds us that genuine *"experience"* is personal while *"activity"* is the mode of being for machines and men made the objects of others. Yet as organ, the ego has its own rhythm of expansion and contraction, and it has no separate existence; it is not a place to store experience but a *way* of experiencing. Consequently the postmodern poet need neither choose between role-playing and self-assertion nor turn the two into a dialectic. Personality now, as John Ashbery puts it, is no longer "bound to the permanent tug which used to be its notion of home" but is free "to branch out in all directions," as a centrality but not a center.[19]

Nonetheless a serious contradiction seems evident in postmodern treatments of the ego. In poets like Robert Creeley and Gary Snyder, there remains a strong autobiographical dimension, and these poets and others obviously use their platform personalities as witness and advertisement of their personal authority. One answer to this problem lies in the poet's resistance to the norms of his popular culture. Without an external referent for the validity and importance of his vision the only proof the poet can offer of the validity of his vision is its effect on his own life and his personal power. Furthermore, there is a strong anticontemplative bias in postmodern poetry or, at the least, an insistence that involvement in the poem should lead to action, that prehension is a way the subject makes use of what had initially been objective:

Wisdom is intuitive knowledge of the mind of love and clarity that lies beneath one's ego-driven anxieties and aggressions. Meditation is going into the mind to see this for yourself—over and over again, until it becomes the mind you live in. Morality is bringing it back out in the way you live, through personal example and responsible action.

(EHH, 92)

Autobiography then becomes a way of expressing in immanent terms how meaning takes form in and through actions, and how these actions become the essential means by which a ground is laid for authentic experience in the future. Finally, autobiography and its insistence on action as norm for truth becomes a valuable check on the speculative absurdities encouraged by academic easy chairs and a taste for metaphysical poetry.

Concepts of language, like those of the ego, are intimately connected with the way values are located and defined in human experience. In immanentist thinking, symbolist theories of language as the creation of forms for experience give way to doctrines stressing the way authentic language grows out of the world's vitality and gives expression to it. It is, in fact, a remarkable testimony to "logical geography" that so many postmodern thinkers have held to notions that language is directly linked with the experience of things in the teeth of the linguistic sciences' insistence that language is an arbitrary code imposed upon and now growing out of experience. The problematic task of justifying poetry as finding rather than making its words has inspired a long tradition in romantic poetics which distinguishes sharply between an essentially casual, artificial, social language and a language directly attuned to the dimensions of value emerging in natural events. Wordsworth's distinctions between artificial and natural speech begin a framework of oppositions adapted in various ways by thinkers as diverse as Emerson, T. E. Hulme, Heidegger, and Maurice Merleau-Ponty. (Even the New Critics' insistence on the radical differences between poetic and scientific discourse is a variant of that tradition.)[20] Hulme makes the epistemological and social implications of these oppositions most clear. He distinguishes sharply between on the one hand a "counter" language of everyday speech (or in Heidegger's terms "idle talk") where a word's energy is not referential but is used up in a pattern of action and response to action which never visualizes or contemplates the materials being manipulated and, on the other, the precise language or art which captures the real being of things and thus serves as a compromise for a language of intuition which would "hand over sensations bodily." For Hulme, however, poetic language ultimately serves to separate clearly rendered images from the confusions of the flux. He borrows vitalist strategies in the service of a faith in static, transcendent works of art. To come to the postmoderns we need to complement his meditative sense of poetic language with Fenellosa's vitalism; words must not freeze natural objects into nouns but capture their essential verbal qualities as transferences of force. Language reveals as an action within nature not an attack on it. We arrive then at Denise Levertov's reformulation of the Bergsonian ground:

> The poet's task is to hold in trust the knowledge that language, as Robert Duncan has declared, is not a set of counters to be manipulated, but a Power. And only in this knowledge does he arrive at music, at that quality of song within speech which is not the result of manipulations of euphonious parts but of an attention, at once to the organic relationships of experienced phenomena, and to the latent harmony and counterpoint of language itself as it is identified with those phenomena. Writing poetry is a process of discovery, revealing inherent music, the music of correspondences, the music of inscape.
>
> (OP, 238)

Language, like the lover's eye, is most true when most "transparent," and the poem in turn reinforces through its revelations the sense that consciousness is wedded to and fulfills natural being.

One cannot stress too strongly the importance of this second step: language is not only a process of discovering the world but also enables us to recognize man's place within it. The poet is not an independent self-conscious creator but an actor who becomes conscious of his situation and of the energies he shares with the world in the process of defining it:

> Definition is as much a part of the act as is sensation itself, in this sense, that life is preoccupation with itself, that conjecture about it is as much of it as its coming at us, its going on. In other words we are ourselves both the instrument of discovery and the instrument of definition.
>
> (SW, 53)

And because discovery and definition are simultaneous, we need alternative models to our old referential idea that truth is the property of statements about experience. One such model is provided by ordinary language philosophy: "The question of truth and falsehood does not turn only on what a sentence *is*, nor yet on what it *means*, but on, speaking very broadly, the circumstances in which it is uttered."[21] Although these philosophers base their work on that casual social language rejected by romantic poetics, statements like these point to language as a tool in use to extend our conscious participation in events. Moreover, in their meditations these philosophers call our attention to the multiplicity of *ways* consciousness in ordinary human situations takes account of and carefully distinguishes among the realities that matter to it. When Robert Creeley tells us "The use of words is a definition of words" (*QG*, 312), his action-oriented aesthetic has firm philosophical support. And Creeley's style, with its sparseness and "decreation" of ordinary syntax, is a way of exploring the dynamic energies of the contextual field in which a vital language has its true roots. When the syntactical connections fail to give us an adequate sense of what is being expressed we are forced to try to recreate the dramatic exchange of energies driving the speech.

Language can be a mode of transferring energy from culture to culture, as well as from nature to consciousness, so a poet's relation to the language of other cultures divorced from him in time or space can provide an interesting measure for his goals as a poet. The modernists harnessed the energies of the past primarily through the use of allusion or of traditional literary forms, but both seem to the postmoderns to smack too much of an intellectual distance from experience; both are conscious modes of mediating the immediate. Instead, the new generation, when they are historical, seek to recapture the original prehensive graspings of the world by focusing on etymology, for if poetry is a direct expression of being, we can find in the original treatments of a concept or experience an intuition of its essential meaning to human existence. The etymology of a word can preserve the initial prehension behind it and can restore for us a sense of what things meant to people less subject to the distortions and displacements of modern Western civilization and its categorizing habits of mind. The most important way, however, in which the postmoderns try to capture the prehensive energy of other cultures is through translation. It is true that modernist poets learned a good deal from the French, but rarely through their own translations; and the contrast between them and the extensive translating of the postmoderns cries out for explanation. It is not sufficient to point to perennial truths like young poets' disaffection from their culture and their need to find new possibilities of expression, because these conditions have been true for at least the past hundred and seventy years. More to the point here is that same contemporary distrust of mediation. Translation is a way of actually participating in and carrying over to one's own culture other dynamic modes of engaging the world. Translation, then, harnesses two modes of energy—the original and the process of engaging that original so as to make it comprehensible in one's own framework. It provides a good metaphor for an ideal relationship between the individual and his past.

The postmoderns' fear of mediation becomes most problematic, however, precisely when one notices how little attention they actually pay to the historical contexts which constitute their own past. Herbert Schneidau has argued powerfully that the arts no longer maintain the modernist's rich balance between fidelity to the flux and interpretative pattern, derived in large part from historical allusion and from the tradition of mythic universals popularized by Frazer. In his view the refusal to interpret experience deprives historical thinking of its utility and leaves the arts vacillating between apocalyptic radicalism and a quiescent resignation to the theme "whatever is, is right." Without some faith in history as a discipline for defining the present there are neither norms for controlled change nor criteria for defining what should and should not be accepted as necessary.[22]

There is a strong dose of truth in Schneidau's argument. He is, in fact, quite convincing with relation to cultural myths which developed in the sixties and to the more extreme avant-garde experiments by artists like John Cage and Andy Warhol. And he is not wrong about the poets, although we must look carefully at their reasons for rejecting conventional history and observe an incomplete but interesting alternative sense of history they have been developing. There are some good reasons for distrusting history as a frame for conceptual analysis and interpretation. We have seen Merwin speak of the "tyranny of history" and need look no further than apologists who claim historical necessity to justify the sorry state of present affairs to understand his nightmare. History so often means conservatism and seems to insist that we must remain with the hierarchies of Western analytical thinking which many see as the source of our ecological problems. Moreover, claims to the importance of historical thinking tend to beg the question of whose history—a question pertinent to both the subjects and objects of historical inquiry. Modern thinkers from Nietzsche to Lévi-Strauss have been demonstrating to us how history is a kind of myth which selects its details and its interpretations to fit some latent structure of desire. Theories of history make history more than they analyze it. Finally, history conceived as a study of change through time is essentially metonymic.[23] As Eliot's work so fully witnesses, a sense of history generates a continual feeling that the present moment is inadequate and incomplete: the present cries out for an absent framework if it is to be understood, and the man who relates the present to the past finds it difficult to avoid elegaic rhapsodies on the beauty of what cannot be repeated and the disorder of what remains. Whitehead's philosophy of emergent events indicates how what was can never adequately measure what is.

History, however, need not be primarily analytic and interpretive. The postmoderns (and indeed some of the moderns as well) look to history as a way of extending the energies of the present. Once we learn how to look the past can become a dimension of the present. The most obvious means for realizing this perspective on history is a concern with primitive cultures—not as romantic alternatives to the present or even as the locus for discovering eternal truths or archetypes acting in the present, but as a way of recovering modes of relating human and natural energies available to us. One could argue, in fact, that poets like Bly and Dickey in their attempts to capture primordial experience and preconscious links between man and nature are performing an essentially historical task. Similar attitudes are more elaborately developed by Snyder and Olson. Both see history as the presence of the past, and both look for concrete instances of that presence—Olson through Gloucester and Snyder through the traces of Indian and early American culture he finds in the Sierras and in folklore. Both cite as a model Carl Sauer's view of history as the successive exploration of environmental options available to a community:

It is the art of seeing how land and life have come to differ from one part of the earth to another. . . . It does not deal with land and life as separate things, but with a given land as lived in by a succession of peoples, who have appraised its resources for their times in terms of their capacities and needs, who have spread themselves through it as best suited their ends, and who have filled it with the works that expressed their particular way of life.[24]

History here is not a tale of adventure but a tracing of man's primary relations with natural process, and history in this sense lives on. We inhabit a landscape formed by the choices of our ancestors; time is quite literally manifested in space, in the way plants express the path of human settlement or tree growth reflects human use. History becomes one way of solving the dilemma posed by Heraclitus:

I see history as the one way to restore the familiar to us—to stop treating us cheap. Man is forever estranged to the degree that his stance towards reality disengages him from the familiar. And it has been the immense task of the last century and a half to get man back to what he knows. I repeat that phrase: *to what he knows*. For it turns out to coincide exactly with that other phrase: *to what he does*. What you do is precisely defined by what you know. Which is not reversible, and therein lies the reason why context is necessary to us.

(*SVH*, 29)

History grasped as process can perform some, though unfortunately not all, the ethical functions performed by conventional history. First of all, as Gary Snyder shows, the perception of the processes of primitive life might create for us ethical models and a profound reordering of our priorities. In an early version of his essay, "Poetry and the Primitive," Snyder cites several aspects of primitive culture which he feels we can incorporate into our world—mankind was one; culture was a "total social fabric" and permanent, not in flux; poetry was oral, communal, and religious; saner systems for sexual behavior and family structure existed; and finally there was an active sense of the interpenetration of man and nature.[25] Moreover, his poetry embodies the sense of reverence one gains from a perception of the endurance of the earth and of the many uses to which it can be put. And the fact that our fundamental concerns lead us to repeat actions done thousands of years ago produces a stabilizing assurance that the hectic pace and tensions of a society in "progress" are for the most part due to cultural illusions. To these reasons why history properly conceived need no longer be seen as a "nightmare," Charles Olson adds an explanation of how history can provide the "measure" lost in the death of God. History measures the intensity of the past by letting us see how past actions create energy for use by the present, and it measures the present in terms of its ability to use the options the past has made available. For the individual, a sense of history creates at once a sense of despair and the determined energy to persevere: because "what you do will stay inside what you know," because the possibilities are always limited, there will be "the content of despair for any man, therefore his need for courage." Courage in turn makes possible "the immediate rejoining of the struggle—to close the gap, to seek to make the thing . . . the equal of what one knows" (*SVH*, 30). Ultimately, the experience of man's historicity generates "the confi-

---

dence of limit," the mature confidence Olson calls arrogant (from *rogo*, I ask) humility.

The process view of history is incomplete without a correlative emphasis on mythology, for myth is the way man expresses the specifically human concerns that go into his use of environmental options. The postmodern poet tends to envision myth as "literally the activeness, the possible activeness and personalness of experiencing [Earth] as such" (*CM*, 9), and thus he explores it in ways very different from those of the modernists. T. S. Eliot's influential essay, "*Ulysses*, Order, and Myth" summarizes the modernist view of the way a poet should use myth. The essay's major purpose is to refute charges that Joyce was "a prophet of chaos"; Eliot claims that Joyce's love for multiple details enables him to meet the ultimate test of a writer—which is not only to order what he selects from life but the confusions and contradictions life demands we all take into consideration:

> In using the myth, in manipulating a continuous parallel between contemporaneity and antiquity, Mr. Joyce is pursuing a method which others must pursue after him. . . . It is simply a way of controlling, of ordering, of giving a shape and a significance to the immense panorama of futility and anarchy which is contemporary history. It is a method already adumbrated by Mr. Yeats, and of the need of which I believe Mr. Yeats to have been the first contemporary to be conscious. . . . Instead of a narrative method, we may now use the mythical method. It is, I seriously believe, a step toward making the modern world possible for art, toward that order and form which Mr. Aldington so earnestly desires.[26]

Eliot's statement expresses both modernist uses of myth—one employing anthropologists like Frazer and Jesse Weston to find and present universal spiritual dramas underlying cultural multiplicity and one on the Blakean romantic model seeking imaginative systems capable of holding "reality and justice in a single thought." The postmoderns, on the other hand, take myth as essentially a condition one lives in, a way of experiencing, and not as a way of ordering and comprehending experience. The sacramentalizing functions of myth, its powers of creating a numinous present, are far more important than its structural and structure creating properties, even though these may be the logical conditions for the desired effects. Denise Levertov, for example, devotes an entire essay to the theme that the poet ought not to think about myth as a frame for experience; he ought to think mythically, to relive the drama of the myth and participate in the psychic energies it is still capable of calling into play. And along the lines proposed by Olson in the quotation above (and picked up by Northrop Frye in his most recent work), Robert Duncan reminds us that "only the mythopoeic could reach the heart of the matter" where the energies of man and the world are intensely fused, a fusion he develops in the following metaphor:

> Our work is to arouse in a contemporary consciousness reverberations of old myth, to prepare the ground so that when we return to read we will see our modern texts charged with a plot that had already begun before the first signs and signatures we have found worked upon the walls of Altamira or Pech-Merle. *Mythos* Aristotle defined as the plot of the story. The plot we are to follow, the great myth or work, is the fiction of what Man is.[27]

The narrative method properly conceived is itself mythical and does not require the intellectual sifting of the ground by the mythical method. But in a skeptical society, the energies of man and the world are also in perpetual danger of drifting apart and the content of myth easily demythologized by discoveries of science. Harold Rosenberg's description of drip-painting catches an important tension in the postmodern quest: "Myth without myth content—a pure state. It joined painting to dance and to the inward act of prayer, as Cubism had joined it to architecture and city planning." The desire for myth as a way of making experience numinous runs the constant danger of finding the myth a pure state of process without content, and thus evanescent and easily dismissed as a fiction. Even worse, myth without viable content runs the risk of becoming self-indulgent aestheticism (anything will do so long as the sensation is there) or the madness of private myth.

IV

The best postmodern poetry is not without mythic content, but the fact that it must find its content in ways very different from those of its predecessors provides a vantage point for recognizing some of the pressures disturbing the poets and for briefly measuring its significance for our times. As I have suggested, the contemporaries find it impossible to accept the modernist quest for myths which will define and organize a culture's experiences. Not only do they distrust the form-creating imagination of a Yeats or Joyce, but in addition they find very little possibility for a valid mythology in American experience. The Falls at Paterson we might note have been replaced by a dam; the city is part of the problem, not the solution, and American Bridges now appear more an imperialistic than a poetic achievement. The war in Vietnam has made final the failures Williams and Crane encountered in making myths of American experience; now the city is symbol of pollution and decay— of death rather than life, the journey westward is the path of imperialism and traditional American individualism the source of our violence. Myth then cannot organize our experiences; nonetheless there are ways in which myth need not be a form for experience but a quality or dimension within it. It is to establish this second possibility that the poets turn to the poetry accompanying primitive rituals or to the traditions of wisdom poetry in primitive cultures (witness the popularity of Jerome Rothenberg's *Technicians of the Sacred* and translations by Merwin, Snyder, and others of wisdom poetry). For in many primitive cultures ritual seems to exist without a systematic mythical framework. Ritual is not a way of transcending or transforming particular experiences (as it is in the Mass) so much as a way of intensifying them, of making conscious the culture's unmediated numinous relationship with basic natural energies and desires. The poetry of primitive ritual derives its sense of the religious directly from experience, in fact from the fundamental experiences of human life like eating and making love, and does not require a mediating mythology. It thus fits our religious needs more completely than fully articulated religious systems which require faith in transcendental realities. Primitive poetry makes available for us the possibilities of a religion without mythology, a religion based precisely on the kind of intense perception of the familiar we now expect from our poets. So the primitive is not an alternative to contemporary experience but a model of ways we can view it and recover for domestic experience a sense of value impossible when we view the broader social scene.

This emphasis on a different kind of mythic content has freed poets from what might otherwise be a choice between impossible alternatives—between a return to propagandistic revolutionary poetry (a temptation not always resisted by poets as fine as Duncan, Levertov, and Snyder) and a surrender to the nausea and despair that so often accompanies the breakdown of public mythology (as we see so often in James

Wright). The sense of ritual possibilities in domestic experience first of all redeems the poet from the nausea Sartre showed us accompanies a sense of everyday objects alienated from all human concerns. Given the sense of a numinous energy latent in quotidian experience, the poet need not depend on society for his security; he is defined by the energies informing the particular ground on which he stands. And that ground can readily be seen as a common one—since we all share the same elementary desires and experiences, and thus all can experience the sense of the numinous revealed by the poet. Community exists through particularity; the poet can be at once public and private because we share the same processes he articulates for himself. At its most confident postmodern poetry can claim to be revolutionary without being abstract or based on arbitrary social myths, for it changes consciousness on the most primary levels.

Two problems, however, qualify and disturb the religious dimensions explored by these poets. First of all the poets define as source of value and basis for whatever ethical effects their poetry can have a numinous quality which is essentially natural. Now those more analytically inclined than the poets would be quick to point out that the natural is essentially premoral; fidelity to its numinous powers can be destructive as often as it is life-enhancing. In other words arguments for value based on nature, or for that matter on any prereflective qualities of experience, require an act of faith. And faith does not come easily today, a factor which may help explain why poetry plays such a small role in contemporary intellectual life.

The quest for the numinous not only separates poets from the society they want to save, but it also often separates them from themselves. Deprived of acceptable cultural frames of reference, they must place an enormous axiological burden on moments of immanence. Where ritual is an accepted part of a primitive life, it is only a momentary condition of insight for the contemporary and is thus as difficult as mystic experience to fit into one's ordinary existence. When it is precisely within this ordinary existence that one quests for the numinous, the contradictions grow almost unbearable. For one basic quality of the domestic in normal experience is its casual ordinariness. When we expect these aspects of our lives to be vital, to keep us in touch with the sources of being, we are calling up self-consciousness in those few areas of contemporary life where we can be free from it. The personal tragedies, the rootless-ness, the posturing of postmodern poets all witness how difficult it is to reconcile peace and intensity, to have the domestic fulfill demands traditionally satisfied by public aspects of one's life.

Postmodern poetry manifests a curious tension between public and private. Within the world of those who read poetry, it promises a mar-velous reconciliation of the two because the domestic, the ordinary, are universal circumstances through which we can realize the mode of con-sciousness that seems necessary now to the survival of the planet. The poets do reach depths of experience they share with others. But what this leaves us with is a pathetic band of the saved—a band united by perspec-tives it can find no way of mediating into the cultural mainstream and without a coherent public philosophy to combat the mainstream. Salva-tion, as we have lately seen manifested among our students, means psy-chically dropping out, and dropping out only furthers alienation. There are, of course, poets with significant public philosophies like Charles Olson and Gary Snyder, but Olson is too difficult and esoteric and Snyder perhaps too simplistic for public acceptance. Moreover, Snyder's critique of all forms of political action in Part IV of *The Back Country* indicates how oriented he is to individual consciousnesses and how far he remains from the actual choices to be made in the political arena. More com-mon in recent years than Snyder's and Olson's optimism that individual change can reform society, are visions like Denise Levertov's in *Relearn-ing the Alphabet*. Meditating on the gap between the public horrors of the war in Vietnam and her own vision of the value to be grasped by participating in numinous domestic experiences, she arrives at the pain-ful conclusion that her aesthetics of presence "is not enough." Yet she doesn't surrender; the burden of her suffering generates the magnificent experiment of "Relearning the Alphabet" which is an attempt to derive from domestic experience the germ of a simple public morality. Lever-tov's example, I think, provides a model for poetry in the seventies: at the least it will make of contradictions emerging within its value sys-tem, moving and illuminating poetry, and at its best it may actually help us create for America some kind of civilized and gentle *polis*.

Notes

1. The postmoderns I take as representative are those most often cited by their peers as breaking new ground and those most influential on younger poets. For decent summaries of directions in contemporary poetry, see A. Poulin Jr., "Contemporary American Poetry: The Radical Tradition" in Poulin, ed., *Contemporary American Poetry* (Boston: Houghton Mifflin, 1971), pp. 387–400; Paul Carroll, *The Poem in Its Skin* (Chicago: Follet, 1968), pp. 203–59; and Kenneth Rexroth, in *Assays* (Norfolk, Conn.: New Directions, 1961) and *The Alternate Society* (New York: Herder and Herder, 1970). For philosophical backgrounds, see Nathan S. Scott, *The Wild Prayer of Longing: Poetry and the Sacred* (New Haven: Yale, 1971); and for useful philosophical discussions of earlier immanentist poetics, see J. Hillis Miller's chapter on W. C. Williams in *Poets of Reality* (Cambridge, Mass: Harvard, 1965); Denis Donohue, *The Ordinary Universe: Soundings in Modern Poetry* (New York: Oxford, 1968); and L. S. Dembo, *Conceptions of Reality in Modern American Poetry* (Berkeley: University of California, 1966). I am not sure that anything done on contemporary poetics will be much more than a footnote to Miller's theoretical framework. And finally, for critiques of contemporary poetics, see Monroe Spears, *Dionysus and the City: Modernism in Twentieth-Century Poetry* (New York: Oxford, 1970), pp. 229–60; Frank Kermode, *Continuities* (New York: Random House, 1968), pp. 1–32; R. K. Meiners, *Everything to be Endured: An Essay on Robert Lowell and Modern Poetry* (Columbia, Missouri: University of Missouri, 1970); and Herbert Schneidau, "The Age of Interpretation and the Moment of Immediacy: Contemporary Art vs History," *ELH* 37 (1970): 287–313. Spears, Kermode, and Schneidau are also useful in contrasting modern and postmodern.

2. My definitions of value and fact derive from Northrop Frye's distinction between myths of concern and myths of freedom in *The Stubborn Structure* (London: Methuen, 1970), pp. 40–44.

3. R. L. Brett and A. R. Jones, eds., *Lyrical Ballads* (London: Methuen, 1963), pp. 249–50. On the different poetics of early and later Wordsworth, see James Heffernan, *Wordsworth's Theory of Poetry: The Transforming Imagination* (Ithaca: Cornell, 1969).

4. Because there are so many citations in this paper, I will use abbreviations for the following works and, for others, will cite page numbers in parentheses during the section in which the work is being discussed: Robert Bly, "The Dead World and the Live World," *The Sixties*, 8 (1966): 2–7, *DW*, and "A Wrong Turning in American Poetry," *Choice* 3 (1963): 33–47, *WT*; Robert Creeley, *A Quick Graph: Collected Notes and Essays* (San Francisco: Four Seasons Foundation, 1970), *QG*; James Dickey, *Babel to Byzantium: Poets and Poetry Now* (New York: Noonday, 1968), *BB*; Robert Duncan, "Notes on Grossinger's *Solar Journal:* Oecological Sections" (broadside published by Black Sparrow Press, 1970), *NG*, and *The Truth and Life of Myth* (New York: House of Books, 1968), *TL*; Denise Levertov, "Origins of a Poem," *Michigan Quarterly Review* 7 (1968), 233–38, *OP*; Howard Nemerov, ed., *Poets on Poetry* (New York: Basic Books, 1966), *PP*; Charles Olson, *Causal Mythology* (San Francisco: Four Seasons Foundation, 1969), *CM*, an *A Special View of History*, ed. Ann Charters (San Francisco: Oyez, 1970), *SVH*, and *Selected Writings*, ed. Robert Creeley (New York: New Directions, 1966), *SW*; Gary Snyder, *Earth House Hold* (New York: New Directions, 1969), *EHH*.

5. *The Wild Prayer of Longing*, p. 49. On the postmodern view of the gods see Denise Levertov, "A Personal Approach," in Tony Stonebruner, ed., *Parable, Myth and Languages* (Cambridge, Mass.: Church Society for College Work, 1967), pp. 30–31, and Jerome Rothenberg, ed., *Technicians of the Sacred* (Garden City: Doubleday, 1969), p. 393.

6. The dichotomy I'm dealing with between immanentist and symbolist thinking goes back beyond Wordsworth and Coleridge through "radical Puritan" and "conservative Anglican" to Augustine and Dante. We can note the following deep analogies between Puritan and contemporary thought: distrust of the mind's symbolic powers and the call for a plain style, sense of the cosmos as held together by a perpetually renewed act of creation which manifests itself as natural energy, alienation from the established culture, emphasis on art as life if it is to have any value, and constant attention to the dynamics of grace and conversion. The comparison becomes both obvious and exciting to anyone who, with the contemporaries in mind, reads Joan Weber, *The Eloquent I: Style and Self in Seventeenth-Century Prose* (Madison: University of Wisconsin, 1968), pp. 1–52, and Perry Miller, *The New England Mind: The Seventeenth Century* (Cambridge, Mass.: Harvard, 1967).

7. *The Primary Language of Poetry in the 1940s* (Berkeley: University of California, 1951), pp. 384, 408, 466.

8. Richard Wilbur, *The Poems of Richard Wilbur* (New York: Harcourt Brace, 1963), p. 117.

9. I elaborate this argument in my essay "Poetry in a Prose World: Robert Lowell's *Life Studies*," in Jerome Mazzaro, ed., *Profile of Robert Lowell* (Columbus, Ohio: Charles E. Merrill, 1971).

10. On Lowell's becoming a vehicle for experience, see John R. Reed, "Going Back: The Ironic Progress of Lowell's Poetry," in Mazzaro, ed., 81–96, and on the biological metaphor, see Philip Cooper, *The Autobiographical Myth of Robert Lowell* (Chapel Hill: University of North Carolina, 1970), pp. 61, 115, and *passim*. For moral criticism of Lowell's passivity, see Thomas Parkinson, "For the Union Dead," *Salamagundi* 1, 4 (1966–67): 87–95, and Patrick Cosgrave, *The Public Poetry of Robert Lowell* (London: Victor Gollancz, 1970). And for an influential argument different from mine on the confessional style as basic to postmodernism and as an elaboration of romantic treatments of the self-transcendent ego, see M. L. Rosenthal, *The New Poets* (New York: Oxford, 1967).

11. *Sickness Unto Death* (Garden City: Doubleday, 1954), p. 207.

12. For Oppen see "Interview with George Oppen," *Contemporary Literature*, 10 (1969): 163; Roethke, *The Poet and his Craft*, ed. Ralph Mills (Seattle: University of Washington, 1965), p. 122 and see p. 25; Duncan, *The Sweetness and Greatness of Dante's Divine Comedy* (San Francisco: Open Space, 1965); Kelley, in *The Sullen Art*, p. 37; and the poem is A. R. Ammons's "Corson's Inlet," in *Corson's Inlet* (Ithaca: Cornell, 1965). The whole poem makes a nice contrast with Wilbur's treatment of the world as locus of value and is an excellent expression of the ontology in contemporary poetics.

13. Rexroth, "Interview," *Contemporary Literature*, 10 (1969): 321. Martin Heidegger, *Introduction to Metaphysics*, trans. Ralph Manheim (Garden City: Doubleday, 1959), p. 2. For Heidegger I use the following abbreviations: *Introduction to Metaphysics, IM; Kant and the Problem of Metaphysics*, trans. James S. Churchill (Bloom-

ington: University of Indiana, 1962), *KPM*; and *Being and Time*, trans. John Macquarrie and Edward Robinson (New York: Harper and Row, 1962), *BT*.

14. "Letting-be" and the resulting sacralization of experience is Scott's basic theme in *The Wild Prayer of Longing*, where I find his Christian interpretation of Heidegger's paganism a serious distortion.

15. For Whitehead the following abbreviations are employed: *Process and Reality* (New York: MacMillan, 1969), *PR*; and *Science and the Modern World* (New York: MacMillan, 1967), *SMW*. Whitehead's philosophy is the deliberate opposite of the idealism on which so much of modernist thought is based. Thus he reminds us that for Kant, "the world emerges from the subject" while for him, "the subject emerges from the world" (*PR*, 106); objectivity and subjectivity are inverted just as he inverts Bradley's idealist and universalizing doctrine of actuality (*PR*, 231).

16. See Herbert Marcuse's discussion in *Eros and Civilization* (New York: Vintage, 1955), pp. 102–14 on the contrast between Hegel's teleological thinking and Nietzsche's Eros-inspired cult of the present. Also Jacques Derrida's affirmation of Nietzsche as a model for the man who rejects the nostalgia of absence for free play in a shifting world is relevant: see *"La Structure, Le Signe et le jeu dans le discours des sciences humains"* in his *L'ecriture et la differance* (Paris: Editions de Seuil, 1967).

17. See Harold Rosenberg, "The American Action Painters," in his *The Tradition of the New*, 2d ed. (New York: Horizon, 1959), especially pp. 28–33. Jerome Rothenberg, *Technicians of the Sacred*, p. 475, uses a Creeley poem to illustrate how the contemporary sense of structure as decisions in process is analogous to primitive poetics.

18. The quotation is from Oppen's "Interview," p. 170. On rejection of romantic individualism in the contemporary arts, see Allan Leepa, "Anti-art and Criticism," in Gregory Battock ed., *The New Art* (New York: E. P. Dutton, 1966), pp. 142–51; and for a philosophical-psychological rejection of the totalizing individual, see Marcuse's chapter cited above and the work of Jacques Lacan, particularly his essay in Richard Macksey and Eugenio Donato eds., *The Languages of Criticism and the Sciences of Man* (Baltimore: Johns Hopkins, 1969).

19. I found the phrase "ego-organ" cited by Clayton Eshleman, "Translating Cesar Vallejo: An Evolution," *Tri Quarterly Anthology of Contemporary Latin American Literature* (New York: E. P. Dutton, 1969), p. 41. For Merwin see his remarks in William J. Martz, ed., *The Distinctive Voice* (Glencoe, Ill.: MacMillan Free Press, 1966), p. 270. Ashberry is quoted from his poem "Definition of Blue," in *The Double Dream of Spring* (New York: E. P. Dutton, 1970), and the last phrase is taken from Ed Dorn, *What I See in the Maximus Poems* (Ventura, Cal.: A Migrant Pamphlet, 1960), pp. 11–13. Dorn's *Gunslinger: Book II* has a hilarious sequence where the character named "I" is killed and reborn with LSD provided by Cool Everything.

20. L. S. Dembo, *Conceptions of Reality in Modern American Poetry* (Berkeley: University of California, 1966) (especially in his "Introduction" and "Conclusion") presents an interesting attack on the modern and postmodern "mystifications of language" which derive from such a tradition. The phrase "transparent language" which I quote from below is taken from an interview with W. S. Merwin in the *Road Apple Review* 1, 2 (1969): 35. Stanley Burnshaw's thesis that poetry is the language of nature and is thus universal and opposed to cultural languages (see Part II of *The Seamless Web*) is an interesting variant of the two-language tradition which helps explain the

desire for transparence as opposed to artifice. For other helpful perspectives on the plain style in postmodern writing, see Roland Barthes, *Writing Degree Zero*, trans. Annette Lavers and Colin Smith (London: Jonathan Cape, 1967), pp. 80–93, and Paul Goodman, *Speaking and Language* (New York: Random House, 1967).

21. J. L. Austin, *Sense and Sensibilia* (New York: Oxford, 1962), p. 111. Several passages in Wittgenstein's *Philosophical Investigations* (London: Oxford, 1968) are also relevant, for example, pp. 224–26 and 175 where Wittgenstein uses the "way" metaphor in explaining that meaning can be equated with ways of using words.

22. "Age of Interpretation," *passim*.

23. Claude Lévi-Strauss' chapters "Time Regained" and "History and Dialectic" in *The Savage Mind* (Chicago: University of Chicago, 1966) provide a very suggestive contrast between spatial and temporal, metaphoric and metonymic ways of structuring experience.

24. Carl Ortwin Sauer, *Land and Life*, ed. John Leighly (Berkeley: University of California, 1967), p. 104; see also for my discussion below pp. 370 ff. Robert Duncan, in "Two Chapters from HD," *Tri Quarterly* 12 (1968): 67–98, tries to work out a more literary and artifact-oriented version of Sauer's methods, primarily by developing the metaphor of the palimpsest.

25. On tape from the 1965 Berkeley Poetry Conference. For Snyder, the sense of interpenetration was active because dramatized in ritual.

26. Eliot's essay is reprinted in Richard Ellmann and Charles Feidelson, eds., *The Modern Tradition* (New York: Oxford, 1965), pp. 679–81. For a more extreme praise of postmodernist treatments of myth, see Richard Wasson, "Notes on a New Sensibility," *Partisan Review* 36 (1969): 460–77.

27. "Two Chapters of HD," p. 67; see also *NG*. For the quotation below see *Artworks and Packages* (New York: Horizon Press, 1969), p. 58.

Charles Olson

Preliminary Images

Charles Olson, at his most irritating, is like a computer overloaded with modern thought and ancient culture. He simply spews out citations, translations, and beliefs. That unruly habit helps breed the charge that his wordscapes are jagged and impenetrable. Such contortions are matters of surface only. The totality of the work suggests a deep coherence though the later poems look different. If the earlier poems tend to be columns of lines the later ones are blocks of lines, fragments thrown on the page. If the early poet is a man of vision, the later one is a visionary. Yet the writing, prose and poetry, has a radical continuity.

I offer a preliminary image of that work: a gyroscope. Picture three rings, on three planes, set within each other: the poet, in theory and practice; the historian; and the cosmographer. The last devises a mythology, a set of figures, and a cosmography, a map of the heavens and the earth which they inhabit. The wheel within which the rings are set is the poet's ego; the structure of the self. The rings interlock. For example, the poet hammers out the intuitions of the historian and of the cosmographer. Such a figure even figures in Olson's poem, "The Binnacle," written around 1957:

> . . . The gy-
> res-
> copes (a
>   continuously driven, whose
> spinning is,
> so that the earth's

```
causes it (us) to
point
        (a wheel or disk mounted
        but also free to,

and to any torque which
would try

us.
```

(*AM*, 273)

Unhappily, the work also reveals a domineering patriarchal bias. From time to time, his tone is ugly, hard-hat. To be sure, the poetry is often delicate and generous about women. Some of it is a moving discourse with the beloved, given a profane grace. Some gives women a sacred power. Some, like "The Cause, the Cause," apparently dramatizes the Jungian theory of animus and anima, in which the man must recognize the feminine, the anima, within himself, and she the animus, or masculine, within herself. The elegant "For Sappho, Back" even claims for a woman the virtues of the poet and the virtuous man: an eye, or vision; a "thickness of . . . blood," or acceptance of death and fragmentation; "objective, scrupulous attention," or the sense of the idiosyncratic thinginess of each thing; impeccable, limpid "rhythm," a life that has the fluid coherence of music.

Yet the most sweeping tributes to women are conventional, to their procreative powers and their sexuality. Olson dislikes American cheerleaders and girls in cute Capri pants, but he apparently fails to imagine women who act other than as mothers or lovers, be it in a conjugal or cosmic setting. In his copy of *The Secret of the Golden Flower: A Chinese Book of Life*, he underlined a sentence in Richard Wilhelm's commentary: "The *animus* dwells in the eyes, the *anima* in the abdomen." He also slashed exclamation marks into the margin.[1] The poems of tribute also emerge from a context in which the grand line of poets is thought to be a masculine dynasty, father to son. Even the critics and academic scholars whom he despised, and whose life he rejected, are men. In a moment of roar and outburst, he writes:

And my anger is—the anger of all men who write from their own suffering, that, you can't put us down with *schemas*—you can't wag yr fingers—yr weak cocks—in our faces: we do what we are obliged to do: measure us by what you have done with what you've had to do with, brother: we say that to them. And if they once faced that, dealt with that, intead of what their light heads take off our work (like peeling our skin) they'd stop such shit—and find out, that HOW A THING IS SAID is as important as WHAT IS SAID, that is *WHAT IS SAID.*

(LO, 93)

My reading is an exercise in ambivalence, caught as I am between admiration for craft and energy and a weary suspicion of the place I would be assigned, often between those craftful, energetic lines.

The Poet

Olson's obsession with time—how to grasp it, graph it, defy it—is consistent with his obsession with his time in particular. He embodies the dilemma and promise of postmodern America. He believes that the world did change a few decades before he was born in 1910. His personal list of great modernists—Melville, Dostoevsky, Rimbaud, Lawrence, Williams, Pound—were "men who engaged themselves with modern reality in such fierceness and pity as to be of real use to any of us who want to take on the postmodern." The relics and reminders of their struggle are sacred texts for the men who claim to be their heirs, the most succinct concept of which is probably found in "Equal, That Is, to the Real Itself." The title is a paradigmatic example of the Olson style: commas deployed to enforce caesuras; caesuras deployed to enforce attention.

All things did come in again, in the 19th century. An idea shook loose, and energy and motion became as important a structure of things as that they are plural, and, by matter, mass. It was even shown that in the infinitely small the older concepts of space ceased to be valid at all. Quantity—the measurable and numberable—was suddenly as shafted in, to any thing, as it was also, as had been obvious, the striking character of the external world, that all things do extend out. Nothing was now inert fact, all things were there for feeling, to promote it, and be felt; and man, in the midst of it, knowing well how he was folded in, as well as how suddenly and strikingly he could extend himself, spring or, without even moving, go, to far, the farthest—he was suddenly possessed or repossessed of a character of being, a thing among things, which I shall call his physicality. It made a re-entry of or to the universe. Reality was without interruption, and we are still in the business of finding out how all action, and thought, have to be refounded.

(HU, 118–19)

The price of quantity is the perception of a chaos as pervasive as that at the beginning of time, which the mythical goddess Tiamat once personified.

Olson's trust in language distinguishes him from many postmodernists. The poetic medium is neither net nor blindfold, but one of man's "proudest" acts. It may engage, grasp, and surmount Tiamat. Poets must throw out—not speech, but an obsolete mode of speech: the infamous old discourse. Its tools are logic, which substitutes patterns of thought for reality, and classification, which substitutes categories of things for the things themselves—the effect of this old discourse is a total substitution of a linguistic world for a phenomenal one.

As ardently as Olson sweeps the old discourse off the stage of history, he introduces the new. The new discourse accepts, even demands, the marriage of sign and sound as linguistic gesture. The necessary condition for such a gesture seems to be a collapse of distance between kinetic events and their description. He also labels the new discourse "logography." A logographer writes as if "each word is physical and . . . objects as originally motivating." He may manipulate a distinction between "logos" and "shout" or "tongue." Logos is "the act of thought about the instant," shout "the act of the instant." Both are immediate acts. Only the artist, after all, is on time. Since each man creates speech anew, each event will be its own name; since each poem flashes its own tongue,

> There may be no more names than there are objects
> There can be no more verbs than there are actions.
>
> (M, 36)

Yet Olson believes that language is an incremental racial history. In "A Syllabary for a Dancer," he writes:

sign, in language and in dance, is that force of representation which holds in itself always the fables of the objects . . . important enough to give a name to, and the motion of those signs (what a verb does or in dance, the movement of the mobiles of the body) holds in itself all the wills which man has made himself capable of—or has seen other things capable of.[2]

Language even has the power to reveal religious visions. In "The Advantage of Literacy," he says:

I . . . believe that the discourse which makes it [logography] possible can also itself be defined as the mythological, and that this in its turn can be specified, so that gesture and action, born of the earth, may in turn join heaven and hell, can be called proprioception.[3]

The theory of language is no longer innovative, but deeply traditional. Olson yearns to transform words into the Word. At first, the new discourse is apparently a formula for using language simultaneously as a mirror and medium for the flow of energy. It grows to become a way into a divininely charged and ordered world. The postmodernist, as he reads the sacred texts, as he consolidates the heroic experiments of their engravers, as he extends the new discourse, serves as a bridge to such a world. One of Olson's self-images is that of the Hanged Man, Key 12 of the major arcana of the Tarot, who hangs head-down from the Tree of Life, between two realms. The sign of the Hanged Man (⚧) is the same as the alchemical sign for sulphur, the principle of combustibility, the transforming and awakening fire Olson mentions so commonly.

So mentioning, Olson assigns the struggle for the new discourse and a revealed world an ethical weight. His sense of the premodern, modern, and postmodern world has the *chiaroscuro* of a morality play. The moral pressure upon the poet, romantic in ancestry, is relentless. His vocabulary of the poet's engagement, pity, and fierceness, of the poem as hammer or ax, is pugnacious. Those who construed the old world, those who ignore the vision of the new, are enemies. His primal villains are Athenians. They invented logic and classification. Like Nietzsche in *The Birth of Tragedy*, Olson blames Socrates for abandoning the sensuous apprehension of the concrete in favor of the rational pursuit of the abstract. The moral code of the old discourse is the old humanism, which arrogantly declares man the center of an anthropocentric universe. Those who assent to the new vision of the universe are heroic. Their moral code is the new humanism; which modestly declares man but one "object in field of force declaring self as force" (*SW*, 112).

The structure of Olson's assertions rests on two axioms: the value of the particular, including the particular physiology of the poet's body, and the value of process, including that body in motion. The particular, of course, is in perpetual process. A remarkable feature of Olson's own poetry is its absence of periods. The absence of the punctuation mark, a syntactical device, reminds us that the poem, a high-energy construct, is transferring force from a particular, through a particular (the poet), to an object. Courageously reconciling modern science and postmodern literature, Olson describes that transfer as if it obeyed the laws of the conservation of energy:

There is a rule: a thing ought to take off, and put down, and travel at all the varying speeds in between, precisely equal in amount and behavior to the thing it sets out from or seeks. Or if it multiplies it only multiplies by changing that thing.

(*HU*, 93)

Then, once released, a poem assumed a degree of active autonomy. A thing among things, it must

stand on its own feet as, a force, in, the fields of force which surround everyone of us, of which we, too, are forces: to stand FORTH.

(*LO*, 50)

Olson is neither brute materialist nor wild nominalist. The flow of force among things, poets, poems, and people is like the flow of the universe itself. The man whom Whitehead so deeply influenced proclaims that reality is "process in the space-time continuum . . . all creation . . . is . . . motion." Concomitantly, only through process, flow and resistance, can "a man come . . . to core." As the poem, "Maximus at Tyre and at Boston," concludes:

> we are only
> as we find out we are.
>   (*M*, 95)

Moreover, its parts are continuous. In Part I of "Concerning Exaggeration, or/How, Properly, to Heap Up," Olson writes:

I am not my parts. I am one system,
affect all others, act, and express myself as such, wild
or indifferent.

(*AM*, 103)

That universe of interweaving and reflecting elements has significance. Olson declares that the root meaning of breath is *pneuma*, or spirit. The famous phrase about writing poetry, "composition by field," takes on quadruple meanings. The field is the page upon which the poet, at his typewriter, scores his poem: the soil of a place, the sand, dirt, and "fishermans field" of Gloucester, which the poet explores; the physical state of space of which the poet is a part; and the metaphorical ground where the Tree of Life may grow.

The process which each field reveals, then, is purposeful. A dance emerges from those bodies in space. From Olson's scattered remarks about form, I extract four senses: (1) form is the seizure of the moment, a Mayan mask, a poem; (2) form is the structure of each organism as it has evolved, the body's arrangement of bones and brains and organs, or the city's arrangement of its economy and politics and ethics; (3) form is a pattern of reoccurring events—birth, sexual struggles, death, even cannibalism; (4) form is the structure of character, which archetypal figures reveal, and of the cosmos.

Olson, whose masters include neo-Platonists, celebrates love as the desire for the good and for form. The historical Maximus of Tyre (125–85), the controlling voice of the *Maximus Poems*, was a follower of Plato. He announces:

> love is form, and cannot be without
> important substance (the weight
> say, 58 carats each one of us, perforce
> our goldsmith's scale
>
> feather to feather added.
> (*M*, 1)

Form, however, means limits, an exclusion of some material. The lover, then, may be reticent. In "Love," Olson writes, perhaps wryly:

> There are only
> two ways:
> create the situation
> (and this is love)
> or avoid it.
> (*AM*, 215)

Olson's poetics are clearly derivative. He borrows both concepts and phrases. He acknowledges some debts—to Robert Creeley, to Edward Dahlberg. He cheerfully spends, without credit, large dividends from others—Fenollosa, Pound, Williams, Dewey. The theory of language itself is coarse and questionable. It strives to be at once descriptive (a fable about the evolution of language) and prescriptive (a statement of the burdens language should bear). Nor does Olson explain how an intellectual process as disreputable as the old discourse could produce the very theories he uses to attack it (e.g. quantum theory). The value of poetics never springs from its intellectual neatness and symmetry, but

---

from its catalytic force in liberating specific poetic energies. To put the matter gracefully: Olson found the past of use. So used, the past met a critical test of his. The poetics, the poetry, and the sense of human process feed each other. For Olson, to have one without the others would be neither human nor poetic.

Some of the most haunting poems, which act out the poetics, show poetry and life pulling in and out of each other. Take, for example, the eight verse paragraphs of "A Discrete Gloss." The speaker, in a Mexican fishing port, addresses "you." "You" may be Olson himself, you, me, or any inhabitant of the human universe. The speaker may also be encountering a mysterious "he"—Giotto perhaps, an artist, some magister. Each citizen, the speaker asserts, is novel. Though novelty is defined, not by itself, but in contrast to nature, to pure intellect, to created others, the events outside are surprisingly like events within. They are often bizarre, grotesque, vile, violent, animal.

> The tide, the number 9 and creation
> whatever sits outside you is
> by what difference what
> you also are: this church
> or this slaughter house behind it, both
> under palms alongside the mud-flats the sea leaves
> in front of this three-time city
>
> In what sense is
> what happens before the eye
> so very different from
> what actually goes on within: this man
> letting a fat whore hug him in the bus
> as it goes counter to the eastering earth,
> and I stare, until both of us turn away
> as the bus stops and she goes behind it to piss
>
> (AM, 101)

The poem teaches us about the field in which we live. Olson also teaches a way in which to grasp that field: the eye, the organ of immediate vision, not speech, the structure of reflective thought, gives us scenes. The poem offers a phenomenology that threatens to abrogate a medium of poetry.

> Man is no creature of his own discourse
> here on this beach made by the tide which passed

and dragged away old guts (or the birds
had it before the fish fed) and he turned, I turned away,
where nine madereros left a politician cut and stoned for dead
(where she pissed), it can be seen
that these boats dry in colours only he
had an eye for. And it says, it says here
in the face of everything it says
this, is the more exact

(AM, 101)

The dignity and seriousness of the poem itself restore linguistic powers. Olson's control of the line, the central unit, is impeccable. Lines are at once self-sufficient and part of a process: look at "what happens before the eye." As interjection, it praises objects and things. As part of a rhetorical question, it wonders about objects and things. As predicate it is part of a statement about the world of objects and things. The end of each paragraph is simply white space, the visual equivalent of expelled breath. The intelligence, however, is free to move within the space, within the stillness. It must pick over, not simply the given number of syllables and scene, but the field to which the poem alludes. The number 9, for example, may refer to the Ninth Key of the major arcana of the Tarot. (Olson often plays such games; "The Moon Is the Number 18" uses the Tarot.) That card is the Hermit, who holds the lamp of Wisdom, waiting for initiates. That card also represents intellect and discretion. Olson's occult wit, his shuffling of the Tarot deck, hints at a belief in forces beyond nature, forces that transform process into pattern, "the force / of force where force forever is."

The Historian

The last words of the *Mayan Letters* puzzle me. "The trouble is, it is very difficult, to be both poet and, an historian." Does he mean that they are incompatible activities? That one could no more be both poet and historian than both space traveler and coal miner? Surely not. Olson is at his most impressive as he reconciles the job of the poet (to write down poems) and of the historian (to write up the past). Constructing them as like figures aids the task. The past presses the historian as the present does the poet. The historian must respond to its frequencies and weights as energetically, as wholly, as vitally, as the poet does to his field. The model historian responds to his presentness as the poet responds to his: as an eyewitness. Herodotus, Olson repeatedly declares, exemplifies the root meaning of historian; to look for one's self, to note for one's self the skulls of the dead in the desert, to listen for one's self to the voices of the survivors. Time past itself is like time present: constellations of events, animal, natural, human.

Olson, however, is interested in more than simple analogies between the poet and the historian, poetry and history. In several theories, in frequent practice, he collapses them. History becomes the activity of present life: the willfullness, the innate voluntarism of the verb to live. The poet, simply because he breathes, is history. Simply to know himself he must be an historian. If history is also the memory of time, the poet/historian remembers, not because he is scholarly or clever, but because the process of time—at once random and creative—has imprinted itself in the pattern of his organism, and perhaps all organisms to come.

The influence of Whitehead is as pervasive as sound in a thunderclap. In "A Later Note on Letter #15," in *Maximus IV, V, VI,* dated January 15, 1962, Olson writes:

> the dream being
> self-action with Whitehead's important corollary: that
> no event
>
> is not penetrated, in intersection or collision with, an eternal
> event
>
> The poetics of such a situation
> are yet to be found out.
>
> *(M-IV, 79)*

"Letter 15" itself, from Maximus to Gloucester, which revises a sea story in "Letter 2," illuminates the nexus of past and present, historian and poet. When the Maximus poems are all public, a structural principle may be discovered: the attempt to discover the "poetics of such a situation." Sequence itself may embody Olson's notion of the order and generative power of the universe. Similar events will not be casual parallelisms, but those that have partaken of an eternal event. Similar characters may also share a deep resemblance, a common "signature." Olson himself looks back to John Smith to see both ideal and image. As he writes, in "Maximus, at Tyre and at Boston,"

> we who throw down hierarchy,
> who say the history of weeds
> is a history of man,
>
> do not fail to keep
> a sort of company.

(M, 94)

In effect, then, the responsible historian uses materials that will throw history into the realm of myth. When Olson permits historical figures to speak for themselves, when he inserts actual documents, he both authenticates his vision of the past and assembles a mythology for the present.

While Olson's theory of history often leaps grandly between the thing and the Kosmos, between the single flower and the Golden Flower, he prides himself on his grasp of modern society. He claims that he knows more about economic realities than Pound, more about the industrial city than Williams. A notion that may prove to be either bold insight or bald chauvinism proclaims the most modern of societies to be America. "In Place; & Names," he states, "I've been absorbed by the subject of America all of my life." Olson's America matters because it stands at the edge of history. It now confronts the chaos of quantity. Not only is it pushing into the future, for good or evil, but it represents the end of one push of history: the questing navigators, the oceanic explorers. Ulysses of Homer mapped the Mediterranean. The Ulysses of Dante the Atlantic. Ahab the Pacific. Symbolically, Ahab died childless. In *Call Me Ishmael*, Olson theorizes:

The third and final odyssey was Ahab's. The Atlantic crossed, the new land America known, the dream's death lay around the Horn, where West returned to East. The Pacific is the end of the UNKNOWN which Homer's and Dante's Ulysses opened men's eyes to. END of individual responsible only to himself. Ahab is full stop.

(CMI, 118–19)

In "Proprioception," he muses about the strength of America's inherited ideology:

a secularization which not only loses nothing of the divine but by seeing process in reality redeems all idealism fr (sic) theocracy or mobocracy, whether it is rational or superstitious, whether it is democratic or socialism.

$$(P, 9)$$

The speech of "the last first people"—their common idioms—will invigorate poetry. The *parole* of the new people, the spontaneous tongue, will energize literature. Towns in America, Gloucester in particular, have the promise—or once did—to become the small, interdependent, just community: the "polis." Olson, who apparently equates the just citizen and the cultured man, attributes to the residents of the polis the rectitude of the poet. In "Letter 6," Maximus says, "polis is / eyes." Even in some of the earliest of Olson's published work, a distrust of the larger state is clear. Despite his praise of "man's individual spirit," he is no romantic anarchist. He seeks the golden mean between that and colossal collectivities.

Yet, crankily, passionately, Olson denounces contemporary American reality. He is yet another postmodern in exile in his own land. Some of his most comic, but savage, invectives berate Gloucester's urban renewal. He opposes the polis to the "Metropolis," gigantic bureaucracies of New York, Washington, or Europe, and to the "pejorocracy." The attacks on pejorocracy, which denotes a diminution of promise, a lessening, go back to "The Kingfishers," dated 1949:

what pudor pejorocracy affronts
how awe, night-rest and neighborhood can rot
what breed where dirtiness is law
what crawls
below

(AM, 48)

Some of the crimes of pejorocracy are economic. Capitalists and their functionaries have replaced laborers, visionaries, and explorers. Miles Standish replaced John Smith as the navigator of the Puritans. Among those capitalists were, of course, the slavetraders. Some crimes are those of the imperious, flaunted will. Even Ahab was manic in his ego-centeredness. Other crimes are cultural. Instead of poetry there is flaccid, imitative verse, television, advertising copy. Olson uses the neologistic pun "mu-sick" as early as the "ABC" poems to summarize them. The mouth (the Greek root of mouth is "mu")—the organ of speech, of song, one source of sexual pleasure—is sick. America has become violent. Marrying will and technology, it has dropped the atomic bomb and threatens to drop the hydrogen bomb. His jeremiads about America synthesize, interestingly, the critique of the contemporary radical left (the hatred of capitalism, excessive consumption, racism) and of the contemporary radical right (the accusation that the work ethic has been lost).

Disappointment with America's present is consistent with the glamorization of America's past: some of the first white men (e.g., John Winthrop) and the indigenous Indians. Olson's nationalism, if profound, is insufficient for his purposes. His backward-flowing quest goes past the storm-swept shores on which John Smith landed; past the Greeks; to the early cultures of the Near East. He finds there a place of coherence in which society had once come to core. Its traces, present in "primitive" peoples such as the Maya, reveal themselves to the genuine scholar. There, too, the poet may discover the origins of language, the first uttered syllables. The leap backward in time will purge contemporary language. It will cleanse the syllable and the sentence of the crust in which an aberrant historical process has enfolded them. An ethnopoetics will vivify postmodern literature as Wordsworth thought rural diction might the literature of his time.

The vision of Sumer, as Olson imagined it in the early 1950s, is of the exemplary society that emerged from the deep past only to be submerged before Greek civilization, a glory Olson dates from 3378 B.C. to 2500 B.C. As he describes Sumer, it becomes more and more colored by that golden harmony that others have attributed to the Garden of Eden. For Sumer enacted an ethic, a science of ideal human behavior, "primordial and phallic." Its leaders were heroes who refused "to overthrow or dominate external reality." The exercise of power was protective, not oppressive; conservative, not exploitative. Through the gates of the center flowed a culture that fertilized the land around it. In "The Gate and the Center" Olson declares

this one people held such exact and superior force that all peoples around them were sustained by it, nourished, increased, advanced, that a city was a coherence which, for the first time since the ice, gave man the chance to join knowledge to culture and, with this weapon, shape dignities of economics and value sufficient to make daily life itself a dignity and a sufficiency.

(HU, 19)

Seeking the vision of Sumer is more than an escape into the exotic. For Olson believes that its citizens are forces now working in the present. They might be models for a new polis, "an IMAGE of possibilities," and the source of our archetypes. The archaeologist of the unconscious, as he strips back the hidden layers of the interior landscape, may find these figures, striding, largely. A self-confessed euhemerist, he suggests that these archaic, exceptional men were inflated into the gods of pagan faiths, the seeds of the "grrONd stories."

Olson's quest into the past refuses to stop at Sumer. He drifts back to Gondwanaland, our primal land mass; back to the original chaos, Tiamat; back to an original cell—the monogene, the monocyte, the Primal Androgyne. In *Maximus IV, V, VI* he commands:

brang that thing out,
the Monogene

the original unit
survives in the salt.
        (*M-IV,* 72)

In fable, parable, and commentary, Olson imagines what the primal sexual act might have been. Was it, for example, a rape by Oceanus? As the poet abandons history for creation myths, he abandons Herodotus for Hesiod, whose theogony, he surmises, might have been the end of a line of archaic speculation.

Sadly, the restless daring fails to disguise the benign authoritarianism of his morally charged political vision and theory of archetypes. A center is to culture as sun to sky: a radiant, vital, dominating presence. The temptation toward worship is compelling. It cuts against the apparent egalitarianism of Olson's field theory. In the field we are all objects of more or less equal weight—dogs, cats, stones, birds, and the Mother of Christ. Emotional ambiguities also cloud the vision. On the one hand, Olson drives into the remote, not simply out of curiosity, but out of despair. On the other hand, he emanates what one might vulgarly call an American optimism. I have found an opening anecdote in the *Mayan Letters* revealing and appealing. Olson and his wife have seen some boys stone a frigate bird. Though nearly dead, the bird flies again—after Olson and his wife help it. The story is simply a story, but it is also a tribute to the powers of endurance and revival. Olson implies that even if the Metropolis is beyond redemption, Gloucester is not. In "Letter 27 [withheld]," *Maximus IV, V, VI*, Maximus says:

                    I have this sense,

    that I am one

    with my skin
                        Plus this—plus this:
    that forever the geography
    which leans in
    on me I compell
    backwards I compell Gloucester
    to yield, to
    change
                            Polis
    is this.

                        (*M-IV*, 15)

The Cosmographer

The poet picturing the process of history gestures toward the pictures that will become a cosmography. Understanding history, the footprints of the temporal, is a step toward understanding a cosmography, a print of the atemporal. The poetry even promises that a belief in it will help redeem those mired in history. Since Olson's vision of the dispensation of the heavens and the earth is incomplete until all the poems are absorbed, I will only guess that another structural principle of the Maximus poems may be an attempt to reconcile the philosophy of Whitehead and the teachings of the *Secret of the Golden Flower* with its commentary by Jung. In brief, a modern American cosmology; an ancient Chinese cosmology; and a modern European psychology. If so, the poems should integrate the poet's consciousness, unconscious, collective unconscious, and a cosmic consciousness. One picture of the final, ineffable harmony might be Key XXI of the Tarot, the image of the world, the *Anima Mundi*; another picture of the sun.

What can now be said about the cosmography with some certainty? For one thing, the poet wants to assassinate time, to transubstantiate history into ahistory. In "Across Space and Time," Olson, in lines so spread

---

out across the page that they seem to drag language and rhythm toward the edge of stillness, compares himself to the serpent who symbolizes eternity:

If the great outside system—species and stars—proceeds successfully across great time, and curves to return to stations it was once in before, and the belt of the ecliptic slides like her cestus in months of a great year taking 25,725.6 years, what wonder that any one of us may be inflamed with love at birth and spend a lifetime seeking to take the tail into one's mouth.

(AM, 266)

He also assumes the role of a cosmographer. In *Maximus IV, V, VI* the letter/note of November 12, 1961, he writes: "I am making a map-pemunde. It is to include my being" (*M-IV*, 87). Olson graphs the self; his place, Gloucester; his world, the "mundi," "The earth with a city in her hair/entangled of trees;" and the heavens. Dramatically, he peoples his map with figures from his life, Gloucester, world history, and a compendium of mythologies. As several of them appear and reappear, they become patterns of character and behavior. Take, for example, John Watts, who stole salt from Ten Pound Island in 1622, a settler Olson praises. Salt, in later alchemical traditions, was a principle of fixity.

The vision of Maximus itself expands. He first stands offshore, by islands hidden in the blood, at once animal and miracle. At the end of *Maximus IV, V, VI*, he, like Ishmael, begins a journey that hints at both death and resurrection:

I set out now
in a box upon the sea.
(*M-IV*, 203)

In between he animates more and more bodies, at once Orphic and metamorphic. Though masculine, he even becomes feminine. Maximus, in the letter of "November 12, 1961," says:

Maximus is a whelping mother, giving birth
With the crunch of his own pelvis.
(*M-IV*, 87)

As he takes on more and more identities, he speaks more and more languages. He generates a vast range of voices: lyricist, priest, sage, navigator, even nature itself. Olson gives the oceans letters enough to roar.

The poet, who once sought to rebarbarize language through a return to its tribal roots, now seeks to sacralize language through a conjecture of what even deeper roots might be. Simultaneously, the poetry as a whole strains to become a universal tongue, to which all tongues have contributed, the linguistic analogy of a cosmic consciousness, perhaps a guide to it.

As the cosmographer imagines the divine, he stubbornly rejects the notion of God as either an Unmoved Mover or a Christian father. Nor does he respect bureaucracies that nurture such repellent notions. In *The Special View of History* he writes, proudly:

We were able, I take it, to establish a cosmology *without letting God* in as creator in the old sense, in the old static sense of the universe. I believe we are equally enabled today to establish a mythology *without letting God in* as a primordial nature in the old static sense, but only an image of Primordial Nature in the prospective sense of the absolute as that which is included in the relative.

(SVH, 55)

"Letter 19 (A Pastoral Letter)" tells of Maximus's disdain when a minister or priest tries to minister to him. The poem juxtaposes the scene against two images. The first, apparently a real hallucinatory experience, at once snarls at the Christian God and accepts the possibility of religious visions:

> I have known the face
> of God.
> And turned away,
> turned,
> as He did,
> his backside.
> (M, 88)

The next pictures the unity among the human, the natural, and the supernatural: the blaspheming poet's daughter, naked on a porch on a cloudy Sunday, singing to a bird, cheerful, spontaneous, innocent. Olson is the man who took Melville as prophet until Melville got "balled up" with Christ.

The scene of singing child and winging bird helps to correct the notion of a static cosmos that the image of a map might give. Olson seems to leave increasingly less of the cosmos to chance, but no matter how fixed the cosmos, it still moves. Such process has the inevitability of an inertial system. Some patterns—the cycle of the seasons, the orbit of the planets—are natural and fixed, and, as a result, predictable. Other patterns are human. That we will follow them is predictable if we wish to live with the intensity and passion necessary for illumination.

One such pattern is descent—an exploration of the unconscious, and if the inner and outer have the awesome similarity that Olson came to believe they had, of the cosmos as well. Such explorations, since they demand a confrontation with the dead, often take the cosmographer to the underworld or into hell. Fire, in the poems about the dead, like "An Ode to Nativity," a wonderful thing that rises like a hot star, is that heat which represents the price extracted for the light of illumination. Strikingly, the ghosts that prey upon us are often those of women, especially mothers. Olson, bitterly, personalizes that great scene which Olson's mentors—Pound, Homer—have already dramatized: the descent of Odysseus into the underworld, where he must face, among other terrors, the ghost of his mother. It is often hard to tell if the ghosts in the poetry are metaphors for demons that must be exorcised or something more, something palpable. Olson may be literalizing a supernatural cosmos that Jung wrote about in the "European Commentary" to *The Secret of the Golden Flower*:

The *anima*, called *p'o*, and written with the character for "white," and that for "daemon," that is, "white ghost," belongs to the lower, earth-bound, bodily soul, partakes of the *yin* principle, and is therefore feminine. After death, it sinks and becomes *kuei* (daemon), often explained as the "one who returns" (i.e., to earth), a *revenant*, a ghost.[4]

The perilous descent, a form of death, promises rebirth. In a homologous pattern, the bear, to which Olson often alludes, hibernates and then, in spring, emerges. The box in which Maximus sets out is like that of the Egyptian god, Osiris, in which he floated, after his brother Seth (or Typhon, a monster of the Maximus poems) put him there, in which his sister/wife Isis found him. Death is inseparable from the created world. Maximus says:

When a man's coffin is the sea
the whole creation shall come to his funeral,

it turns out; the globe
is below, all lapis.

(*M,* 153)

The reborn man sees that world as naked, newborn. Having the fresh vision of the child is not the same thing as having the weakness of a baby. For Olson, at his most exalted, renders inseparable the strenuous glory of a rebirth of the poet, the city, and the earth.

Olson, who plays with as much mythic material as he can, also explores the pattern of ascent. For example, lecturing in Wisconsin, in 1968, he discussed a notoriously vague triad of terms he had mentioned in the letter to Elaine Feinstein in 1959: *topos*, landscape, place, habitation, the Gloucester that is the starting point to the whole of creation; *typos*, things in themselves and type, a word to be inked upon a page; and *tropos*, "the management . . . the maneuver . . . the ourselves." That maneuver is the descent into and the ascent from the dark cave of the self, during which we discover the sun within and the sun without. The process both finds and shapes what is there. Olson suggests that such descent and ascent may be perpetual. Descent always leads to ascent; ascent always to descent. In "La Torre," he alludes to the Heraclitean cosmology that universalizes such kinesis:

> To destroy
> is to start again, is a factor of
> sun, fire is
> when the sun is out, dowsed
> (*AM*, 76)

In *The Special View of History*, borrowing from Heraclitus and Jung, he announces that *Enantiodromia* ("running the other way") is a law of the "Universe of Opposites." Opposites flow out of each other—in the self, in history, in the cosmos. Living and dying are like gliding and turning forever over the surfaces of a Moebius strip, a figure Olson sought to describe as early as 1946 in "The Moebius Strip."

As the sweep of his vision widens the poet elevates Gloucester, if not America. Some poems simply imply that the culture from the center of the Near East has reached Gloucester. In "Bk ii chapter 37," in *Maximus IV, V, VI*, he writes:

> there is another
> place near the river where there is a seated
> wooden image of Demeter. The city's own
> wooden image of the goddess is on a hill
> along the next ridge above Middle Street

between the two towers of a church called
the Lady of Good Voyage.

(M-IV, 84)

Others, which Carl O. Sauer seemingly influences, imply that Gloucester itself might represent that center. As a port, it may bridge the
past of the Age of Pisces and the future of the Age of Aquarius. As a
port, Gloucester is also on land. Olson, though he distrusts symbolism,
charges that fact with meaning. The poet uses the act of carving wood,
which grows in land, as a metaphor for the act of creating poetry. The
historian, who celebrates the peaceful city, believes that the good citizen cultivates his fields. He uses, but does not abuse, nature's bounty.
The good citizen also taps the sexual forces of nature. Maximus, significantly, in "Letter 7," summons up the memory of a carpenter who came
to Gloucester to build boats:

> That carpenter is much on my mind:
> I think he was the first Maximus
>
> Anyhow, he was the first to make things,
> not just live off nature
>
> And he displays,
> in the record, some of those traits
> goes with that difference, traits present circumstances
> keep my eye on.

(M, 31)

The poet, however, does more than suggest that his home, an image
analogous to the image of a possible center of the past, might become the
center of the future. A late poem, its address 28 Ft. Square, Gloucester,
its season, the day before the winter solstice, implies that Gloucester is
the center of the moving forces of the cosmos.

> If I twist West I curl into the tightest Rose, if right
> into the Color of the East, and North and South are
> then the Sun's half-handling of the Earth. These aspects
> annular Eternal—the rightest Rose is the World, the vision
>
> is the Face of God—in this aspect the Nation turns now
> to its Perfection.[5]

The seeing poet is a seer. For the cosmographer, the field of Gloucester
is a garden in which the Tree of Life grows, on which the sun of heaven
shines.

The Ego

Perhaps it is paradoxical, even nonsensical, to say that the texts of Olson and the world of texts takes real unity from the ego, Olson's singular self. In theory, Olson passionately denounces the ego. An early essay, "This is Yeats Speaking," a defense of Pound in 1946, reviles the language of a false self-esteem: crowing over, bragging about a triumph over mere personal incoherence. Such false triumphs are mere lyrical self-indulgence, flabby Bohemianism, vanity. One purpose of "Projective Verse" is to endorse its contrary: objectism. A cultural effect of objectism would be anonymous art. The name of the creator would disappear as utterly as those tribal bards who were the oral poets of preliteracy. A literary effect would be the shape of the long poem. In writing to Creeley, Olson suggests that one might use the method of the *Cantos*, transforming time into a space field, but only "WITH THE ALTERNATIVE TO THE EGO-POSITION." A psychological effect would be taking Keats's man of achievement—the person of negative capability, whose method is to be in uncertainties, doubts, mysteries—as a model for the poet. Olson deplores, as his master Keats did, the man of decided character, whose literary equivalent is "the egotistical sublime."

Much of Olson's work has sturdy impersonality. He deploys general statements. He uses the impersonal "one" or the collective "we" as the subject of his sentences. He works through masks or *personae:* Apollonius of Tyana, whom Pound praises; Maximus of Tyre. Even the most personal poems have some distancing devices. His various schemes for the structure of the self, such as the single intelligence, a totality of being, tend to have at least one element that fuses the self, perceiving and receiving, acting and acted upon, with a larger reality. The poet might even be said to abandon the self, to destroy alienation through immersion in the swarm of phenomena and the structure of creation. Like the Melville Olson prefers, the poet is underwater, looking up, eyes bloodshot, even blind until the moment of vision.

Yet, Olson also passionately praises the function of the poet. That figure is the unacknowledged legislator of the world. He will "restate" man, revivify through the intermediary of immediate language his place in the world of things and of the cosmos. Moreover, he practices the "only social art worth any interchange with another human being"—

expression. Not only is the artist a "violet," "sweetening" revolutionary figure, but in the world a proper revolution will bring, art as expression will replace politics and economics as the system of brokerage among objects. The American poet is the great prophet of revolution, because of America's current ability to drag the rest of the world after it, for better or worse. As Robert Duncan once told Ann Charters, Olson had

an essentially magic view of the poem. Not magic in the sense of doing something you mean to do in the end, but in the sense of causing things to happen. . . . Charles wanted to produce a new and redeemed man. This is actually Charles' alchemy.

(*SVH*, 11)

One meaning of projective, after all, is the casting of the powder of the philosopher's stone upon metal to transmute it into gold or silver. The rhetoric in which such notions are thrown out to the world is often so muscular, salvationistic, that the endorsements of negative capability often make it seem less a sweet drift into reality than a hard, fast salute.

The self-assertion the poetics takes away, morality restores. Olson's poetry and prose themselves are confidently dogmatic. Like the real Apollonius and Maximus, he is a wandering teacher. Maximus lectures Gloucester. Indeed, Olson, referring to the first Maximus poem, wrote "it is like an epistle of an apostle fr Rome to the Ephesians when it takes its place in yr pages!" The letter form, which structures many of the *Maximus* poems, traditionally preaches and witnesses as well as conveying facts and gossip. (I am unsure whether Olson, who once actually carried mail in Gloucester, is making an autobiographical joke or not.) As he pictures, for his reader, the world of the unconscious, the preconscious, the subconscious, and cosmic consciousness, he is also taking on the task of a tribal shaman.

The ego establishes itself through a device other than making the poet a self-appointed guardian and messiah. Olson is too ambitious and apparently too committed to a metaphysic of unity to create collages, "the dramatic juxtaposition of disparate materials without commitment to explicit syntactical relations between elements" (to use a phrase of David Antin's). He provides a syntax: the kinesis of his body, the process of his mind. During the *Maximus* poems, the speaker/etcher of language becomes bolder about the substitution of private consciousness for public and cosmic event. *Maximus IV, V, VI* inverts Olson's earlier maxim about history as the memory of time to:

> my memory is
> the history of time.
>   (*M-IV,* 86)

The ego then swells to erect itself to become both the recording and the record of universal mind as it goes forth to the end of the world, to the end of time, to a new beginning.

But what, one might ask, if the structure of the poet's fully rendered self, the unconscious willfully rendered conscious, were like the structure of cosmos? What if those structures were correspondences in interlocking motion? Then to say that the poet is arrogantly prophetic and the poetry circumscribed within the poet's ego would be a damnable misreading. Such questions shift the subject of discourse from poetry to faith. I suspect that Olson might call that a fine and obedient response to life's demands.

Notes

1. Trans. by Richard Wilhelm, with commentary by C. G. Jung (London, 1945), p. 15. Olson made an exclamation mark in the right margin. I am grateful to Olson Archives, Special Collections, University of Connecticut, Storrs, for permission to examine the book.

2. *Maps,* no. 4 (1971): 10.

3. "The Advantage of Literacy," *Coyote's Journal 1* (1956): 56.

4. *The Secret of the Golden Flower,* p. 114.

5. "The Winter the GEN. STARKS (*sic*) was stuck" (Cleveland: Asphodel Bookshop Catalogue 13, 1966). In the Rare Book Room of the New York Public Library, the help of which I gratefully acknowledge.

The Dialectics of Literary Tradition

Emerson chose three mottos for his most influential essay, "Self-Reliance"; the first, from the *Satires* of Persius: "Do not seek yourself outside yourself." The second, from Beaumont and Fletcher:

> Man is his own star; and the soul that can
> Render an honest and a perfect man,
> Commands all light, all influence, all fate;
> Nothing to him falls early or too late.

The third, one of Emerson's own gnomic verses, is prophetic of much contemporary shamanism:

> Cast the bantling on the rocks,
> Suckle him with the she-wolf's teat,
> Wintered with the hawk and fox,
> Power and speed be hands and feet.

Like the fierce, rhapsodic essay they precede, these mottos are addressed to young Americans, men and women, of 1840, who badly needed to be told that they were not latecomers. But we *are* latecomers (as indeed they were), and we are better off for consciously knowing it, at least right now. Emerson's single aim was to awaken his auditors to a sense of their own potential *power of making*. To serve his tradition now, we need to counsel a *power of conserving*.

"The hint of the dialectic is more valuable than the dialectic itself," Emerson once remarked, but I intend to contradict him on that also and to sketch some aspects of the dialectics of literary tradition. Modernism in literature has not passed; rather, it has been exposed as never having been there. Gossip grows old and becomes myth; myth grows older, and becomes dogma. Wyndham Lewis, Eliot, and Pound gossiped with one another; the New Criticism aged them into a myth of modernism; now the antiquarian Hugh Kenner has dogmatized this myth into the Pound Era, a canon of accepted titans. Pretenders to godhood Kenner roughly reduces to their mortality; the grand triumph of Kenner is his judgment that Wallace Stevens represented the culmination of the poetics of Edward Lear.

Yet this is already dogma grown antique: postmodernism also has its canons and its canonizers; and I find myself surrounded by living classics, in recently dead poets of strong ambition and hysterical intensity, and in hyperactive novelist non-novelists, who are I suppose the proper seers for their armies of student non-students. I discover it does little good these days to remind literary students that Cowley, Cleveland, Denham, and Waller were for generations considered great poets, or that much of the best contemporary opinion preferred Campbell, Moore, and Rogers to John Keats. And I would fear to tell students that while I judge Ruskin to have been the best critic of the nineteenth century, he did proclaim *Aurora Leigh* by Mrs. Browning to be the best long poem of the nineteenth century. Great critics nod, and entire generations go wrong in judging their own achievements. Without what Shelley called a being washed in the blood of the Great Redeemer, Time, literary tradition appears powerless to justify its own selectivities. Yet if tradition cannot establish its own centrality, it becomes something other than the liberation from time's chaos it implicitly promised to be. Like all convention, it moves from an idealized function to a stifling or blocking tendency.

I intend here to reverse Emerson (though I revere him) and to assert for literary tradition its currently pragmatic as opposed to idealized function: it is now valuable precisely because it partly blocks, because it stifles the weak, because it represses even the strong. To study literary tradition today is to achieve a dangerous but enabling act of the mind that works against all ease in fresh "creation." Kierkegaard could afford to believe that he became great in proportion to greatness that he strove against, but we come later. Nietzsche insisted that nothing was more pernicious than the sense of being a latecomer, but I want to insist upon the contrary: nothing is now more salutary than such a sense. Without it, we cannot distinguish between the energy of humanistic performance and merely organic energy, which never alas needs to be saved from itself.

I remember, as a young man setting out on a professional training to be a university teacher, how afflicted I was by my sense of uselessness, my not exactly vitalizing fear that my chosen profession reduced to an incoherent blend of antiquarianism and culture-mongering. I recall also that I would solace myself by thinking that while a scholar-teacher of literature could do no good, at least he could do no harm, or anyway not to others, whatever he did to himself. But that was at the very start of the decade of the fifties, and after more than twenty years I have come to understand that I underrated my profession, as much in its capacity for doing harm as in its potential for good works. Even our treasons, our betrayals of our implicit trusts, are treasons of something more than of the intellectuals, and most directly damage our immediate students, our Oedipal sons, and daughters. Our profession is not genuinely akin any longer to that of the historians or the philosophers. Without willing the change, our theoretical critics have become negative theologians, our practical critics are close to being Agaddic commentators, and all of our teachers, of whatever generation, teach how to live, what to do, in order to avoid the damnation of death-in-life. I do not believe that I am talking about an ideology, nor am I acknowledging any shade whatsoever of the recent Marxist critiques of our profession. Whatever the academic profession of letters now is on the Continent (shall we say an anthropology half-Marxist, half-Buddhist?) or in Britain (shall we say a middle-class amateurism displacing an aristocratic amateurism?), it is currently in America a wholly Emersonian phenomenon. Emerson abandoned his church to become a secular orator, rightly trusting that the lecture, rather than the sermon, was the luminous melody of proper sound for Americans. We have institutionalized Emerson's procedures, while abandoning (understandably) his aims, for the burden of his prophecy is already carried by our auditors.

Northrop Frye, who increasingly looks like the Proclus or Iamblichus of our day, has pseudo-platonized the dialectics of tradition, its relation to fresh creation, into what he calls the Myth of Concern, which turns out to be a Low Church version of T. S. Eliot's Anglo-Catholic myth of Tradition and the Individual Talent. In Frye's reduction, the student discovers that he becomes something, and thus uncovers or demystifies himself by first being persuaded that tradition is inclusive rather than exclusive, and so makes a place for him. The student is a cultural assimilator who *thinks* because he has *joined* a larger body of thought. Freedom, for Frye as for Eliot, is the change, however slight, that any genuine single consciousness brings about in the order of literature simply by joining the simultaneity of such order. I confess that I no longer understand this simultaneity, except as a fiction that Frye, like Eliot, passes upon himself. This fiction is a noble idealization, and as a lie against time will go the way of every other noble idealization. Such positive thinking served many purposes during the sixties, when continuities, of any kind, badly required to be summoned, even if they did not come to our call. Wherever we are bound, our dialectical development now seems invested in the interplay of repetition and discontinuity and needs a very different sense of what our stance is in regard to literary tradition.

All of us now have been preempted, as I think we are all quite uneasily aware. We are rueful that we are asked ("compelled" might be more accurate) to pay for the discontents not only of the civilization we enjoy, but of the civilization of all previous generations from whom we have inherited. Literary tradition, once we even contemplate entering its academies, now insists upon being our "family history," and inducts us into its "family romance" in the unfortunate role prefigured by Browning's Childe Roland, a candidate for heroism who aspired only to fail at least as miserably as his precursors failed. There are no longer any archetypes to displace; we have been ejected from the imperial palace whence we came, and any attempt to find a substitute for it will not be a benign displacement but only another culpable trespass, neither more nor less desperate than any Oedipal return to origins. For us, creative emulation of literary tradition leads to images of inversion, incest, sado-masochistic parody, of which the great, gloriously self-defeating master is Pynchon, whose *Gravity's Rainbow* is a perfect text for the sixties, Age of Frye and Borges, but already deliberately belated for the seventies. Substitute-gratifications and myths-of-displacement turn out to be an identity in Pynchon's book.

Gershom Scholem has an essay on "Tradition and New Creation in the Ritual of the Kabbalists" that reads like a prescription for Pynchon's novel, and I suspect Pynchon found another source in it. The magical formula of the Kabbalistic view of ritual, according to Scholem, is as follows: "everything not only *is in* everything else but also *acts upon* everything else." Remind yourself that Kabbalah literally means "tradition," that which has been received, and reflect on the extraordinary overdetermination and stupefying overorganization that a Kabbalistic book like *Gravity's Rainbow* is condemned to manifest. I will mention Kabbalism and its overrelevances again at the close of this discourse, but need first to demythologize and de-esotericize my own view of literary tradition. The proper starting point for any demystification has to be a return to the commonal. Let me ask then: what is literary tradition? What is a classic? What is a canonical view of tradition? How are canons of accepted classics formed, and how are they unformed? I think that all these quite traditional questions can take one simplistic but still dialectical question as their summing-up: do we choose a tradition or does it choose us, and why is it necessary that a choosing take place, or a being chosen? What happens if one tries to write, or to teach, or to think, or even to read without the sense of a tradition?

Why, nothing at all happens, just nothing. You cannot write or teach or think or even read, without imitation, and what you imitate is what another person has done, that person's writing or teaching or thinking or reading. Your relation to what informs that person *is* tradition, for tradition is influence that extends past one generation, a carrying-over of influence. Tradition, the Latin *traditio*, is etymologically a handing-over or a giving-over, a delivery, a giving-up and so even a surrender or a betrayal. *Traditio* in our sense is Latin only in language; the concept deeply derives from the Hebraic *Mishnah*, an oral handing-over, or transmission of oral precedents, of what has been found to work, of what has been instructed successfully. Tradition is good teaching, where "good" means pragmatic, instrumental, fecund. But how primal is teaching, in comparison to writing? Necessarily, the question is rhetorical; whether or not the psychic Primal Scene is the one where we were begotten, and whether or not the societal Primal Scene is the murder of a Sacred Father by rival sons, I would venture that the artistic Primal Scene *is* the trespass of teaching. What Jacques Derrida calls the Scene of Writing itself depends upon a Scene of Teaching, and poetry is crucially pedagogical in its origins and function. Literary tradition begins when a fresh author is simultaneously cognizant not only of his own struggle against the forms and presence of a precursor, but is compelled also to a sense of the precursor's place in regard to what came before *him*.

Ernst Robert Curtius, in the best study of literary tradition I have ever read, his definitive *European Literature and the Latin Middle Ages* (1948), concluded that "like all life, tradition is a vast passing away and renewal." But even Curtius, who could accept his own wisdom, cautioned us that Western literary tradition could be apprehended clearly "only" for the twenty-five centuries from Homer to Goethe; for the two centuries after Goethe we still could not know what was canonical or not. The later Enlightenment, Romanticism, Modernism, Postmodernism; all these, by implication, are one phenomenon, and we still cannot know precisely whether or not that phenomenon possesses continuity rather than primarily discontinuity in regard to the tradition between Homer and Goethe. Nor are there Muses, nymphs who *know*, still available to tell us the secrets of continuity, for the nymphs certainly are now departing. I prophesy though that the first break with literary continuity will be brought about in generations to come, if the burgeoning religion of Liberated Woman spreads from its clusters of enthusiasts to dominate the West. Homer will cease to be the inevitable precursor, and the rhetoric and forms or our literature then may break at last from tradition.

It remains not arbitrary nor even accidental to say that everyone who now reads and writes in the West, of whatever racial background, sex, or ideological camp, is still a son or daughter of Homer. As a teacher of literature who prefers the morality of the Hebrew Bible to that of Homer, indeed who prefers the Bible aesthetically to Homer, I am no happier about this dark truth than you are, if you happen to agree with William Blake when he passionately cries aloud that it is Homer and Virgil, the Classics, and not the Goths and Vandals that fill Europe with wars. But how did this truth, whether dark or not, impose itself upon us?

All continuities possess the paradox of being absolutely arbitrary in their origins, and absolutely inescapable in their teleologies. You know this so vividly from what we all of us oxymoronically call our love lives that its literary counterparts need little demonstration for you. Though each generation of critics rightly reaffirms the aesthetic supremacy of Homer, he is so much part of the aesthetic *given* for them (and us) that the reaffirmation is a redundancy. What we call "literature" is inescapably connected to education by a continuity of twenty-five hundred years, a continuity that began in the sixth century B.C., when Homer first became a schoolbook for the Greeks, or as Curtius says simply and definitively: "Homer, for them was the 'tradition.'" When Homer became a schoolbook, literature became a school subject quite permanently. Again, Curtius makes the central formulation: "Education becomes the medium of the literary tradition: a fact which is characteristic of Europe, but which is not necessarily so in the nature of things."

This formulation is worth considerable dialectical investigation, particularly in a time as educationally confused as ours recently has been. Nothing in the literary world even sounds quite so silly to me as the passionate declarations that poetry must be liberated from the academy, declarations that would be absurd at any time, but peculiarly so some twenty-five hundred years after Homer and the academy first became indistinguishable. For the answer to the question "What is literature?" must begin with the word "literature," based on Quintilian's word *litteratura* which was his translation of the Greek *grammatike*, the art of reading and writing, conceived as a dual enterprise. Literature, and the study of literature, were in their origins a single, unified concept. When Hesiod and Pindar invoke the Muses, they do so *as students*, so as to enable themselves to *teach their readers*. When the first literary scholars wholly distinct from poets, created their philology in Alexandria, they began by classifying and then selecting authors, canonizing according to secular principles clearly ancestral in relation to our own. The question we go on asking—"What is a classic?"—they first answered for us, by reducing the tragedians initially to five, and later to three. Curtius informs us that the name *classicus* first appears very late, under the Antonine emperors, meaning literary citizens of the first class, but the concept of classification was itself Alexandrian. We are Alexandrians still, and we may as well be proud of it, for it is central to our profession. Even "Modernism," a shibboleth many of us think we may have invented, is necessarily an Alexandrian inheritance also. The scholar Aristarchus, working at the Museion in Alexandria, first contrasted the *neoteroi* or "moderns" with Homer, in defense of a latecomer poet like Callimachus. *Modernus*, based on the word *modo*, for "now," first came into use in the sixth century A.D., and it is worth remembering that "Modernism" always means "For Now."

Alexandria, which thus founded our scholarship, permanently set the literary tradition of the school and introduced the secularized notion of the canon, though the actual term of canon for "catalog" of authors was not used until the eighteenth century. Curtius, in his wonderfully comprehensive researches, ascribes the first canon formation in a modern vernacular, secular literature to the sixteenth-century Italians. The French in the seventeenth century followed, establishing their permanent version of classicism, a version that the English Augustans bravely but vainly tried to emulate before they were flooded out by that great English renaissance of the English Renaissance we now call the Age of Sensibility or the Sublime, and date fairly confidently from the mid-1740s. This renaissance of the Renaissance was and is romanticism, which is of course the tradition of the last two centuries. Canon-formation, for us, has become a part of romantic tradition, and our still-current educational crisis in the West is rather clearly only another romantic epicycle, part of the continuity of upheaval that began with revolution in the West Indies and America, spread to France and through her to the Continent, and thence to Russia, Asia, and Africa in our time. Just as romanticism and revolution became one composite form, so the dialectic of fresh canon-formation joining itself to a gradual ideological reversal endures into this current decade.

But romantic tradition differs vitally from earlier forms of tradition, and I think this difference can be reduced to a useful formula. Romantic tradition is *consciously late,* and romantic literary psychology is therefore necessarily a *psychology of belatedness.* The romance-of-trespass, of violating a sacred or daemonic ground, is a central form in modern literature, from Coleridge and Wordsworth to the present. Whitman follows Emerson by insisting that he strikes up for a new world, yet the guilt of belatedness haunts him and all of his American literary descendants. Yeats was early driven into Gnostic evasions of nature by a parallel guilt, and even the apocalyptic Lawrence is most persuasive when he follows his own analyses of Melville and Whitman to trumpet the doom of what he oddly insisted upon calling blood-consciousness. Romanticism, more than any other tradition, is appalled by its own overt continuities, and vainly but perpetually fantasizes some end to repetitions.

This romantic psychology of belatedness, from which Emerson failed to save us, his American descendants, is the cause, in my judgment, of the excessively volatile senses-of-tradition that have made canon-formation so uncertain a process during the last two centuries, and particularly during the last twenty years. Take some contemporary examples. A quick way to start a quarrel with any current group of critics would be to express my conviction that Robert Lowell is anything but a permanent poet, that he has been mostly a maker of period-pieces from his origins until now. Similarly, as violent a quarrel would ensue if I expressed my judgment that Norman Mailer is so flawed a writer that his current enshrinement among academics is the largest single index to our current sense of belatedness. Lowell and Mailer, however I rate them, are at least conspicuous literary energies. It would lead to something more intense than quarrels if I expressed my bedazzlement at what now passes for "Black poetry," or the "literature of Woman's Liberation." But our mutual sense of canonical standards has undergone a remarkable dimming, a fading into the light of a common garishness. Revisionism, always a romantic energizer, has become so much a norm that even rhetorical standards seem to have lost their efficacy. Literary tradition has become the captive of the revisionary impulse, and I think we must go past viewing-with-alarm if we are to understand this quite inescapable phenomenon, the subsuming of tradition by belatedness.

The revisionary impulse, in writing and in reading, has a directly inverse relationship to our psychological confidence in what I've already called the Scene of Instruction. Milton's Satan, who remains the greatest really modern or post-Enlightenment poet in the language, can give us a paradigm of this inverse relationship. The ultimate Scene of Instruction is described by Raphael in Book V of *Paradise Lost*, where God proclaims to the Angels that: "This day I have begot whom I declare/ My only son," and provocatively warns that: "him who disobeys/Mee disobeys . . ./and . . . falls/into utter darkness." We can describe this as an imposition of the psychology of belatedness and Satan, like any strong poet, declines to be merely a latecomer. His way of returning to origins, of making the Oedipal trespass, is to become a rival creator to God-as-creator. He embraces Sin as his Muse, and begets upon her the highly original poem of Death, the only poem that God will permit him to write.

Let me reduce my own allegory, or my allegorical interpretation of Satan, by invoking a wonderful poem of Emily Dickinson's, "The Bible is an antique Volume—" (no. 1545), in which she calls Eden "the ancient Homestead," Satan "the Brigadier," and Sin "a distinguished Precipice/ Others must resist." As a heretic whose orthodoxy was Emersonianism, Dickinson recognized in Satan a distinguished precursor gallantly battling against the psychology of belatedness. But then, Dickinson and Emerson wrote in an America that needed, for a while, to battle against the European exhaustions of history. I am temperamentally a natural revisionist, and I respond to Satan's speeches more strongly than to any other poetry I know, so it causes some anguish in me to counsel that currently we need Milton's sense of tradition much more than Emerson's revisionary tradition. Indeed, the counsel of necessity must be taken further: most simply, we need Milton, and not the romantic return of the repressed Milton, but the Milton who made his great poem identical with the process of repression that is vital to literary tradition. But a resistance even in myself is set up by my counsel of necessity, because even I want to know: what do I mean by "we"? Teachers? Students? Writers? Readers?

I do not believe that these are separate categories, nor do I believe that sex, race, social class can narrow this "we" down. If we are human, then we depend upon a Scene of Instruction, which is necessarily also a scene of authority and of priority. If you will not have one instructor or another, then precisely by rejecting all instructors, you will condemn yourself to the earliest Scene of Instruction that imposed itself upon you. The clearest analogue is necessarily Oedipal; reject your parents vehemently enough, and you will become a belated version of them, but compound with their reality, and you may partly free yourself. Milton's Satan failed, particularly as poet, after making a most distinguished beginning, because he became only a parody of the bleakest aspects of Milton's God. I greatly prefer Pynchon to Mailer as a writer because a voluntary parody is more impressive than an involuntary one, but I wonder if our aesthetic possibilities need to be reduced now to just such a choice. Do the dialectics of literary tradition condemn us, at this time, either to an affirmation of belatedness, via Kabbalistic inversion, or to a mock-vitalistic lie-against-time, via an emphasis upon the self-as-performer?

I cannot answer this hard question, because I am uneasy with the current alternatives to the ways of Pynchon and of Mailer, at least in fictional or quasi-fictional prose. Saul Bellow, with all his literary virtues, clearly shows the primal exhaustions of being a latecomer rather more strenuously in his way than Pynchon or Mailer do in theirs. I honestly don't enjoy Bellow more, and I would hesitate to find anything universal in such enjoyment even if I had it. Contemporary American poetry seems healthier to me and provides alternatives to the voluntary parodies that Lowell has given us, or the involuntary parodies at which Ginsberg is so prominent. Yet even the poets I most admire, John Ashbery and A. R. Ammons, are rendered somewhat problematic by a cultural situation of such belatedness that literary survival itself seems fairly questionable. As Pynchon says in the closing pages of his uncanny book: "You've got much older. . . . Fathers are carriers of the virus of Death, and sons are the infected." And he adds a little further on in his Gospel of sado-anarchism that this time we *will* arrive, my God, too late."

I am aware that this must seem a Gospel of Gloom, and no one ought to be asked to welcome a kakangelist, a bearer of ill-tidings. But I cannot see that evasions of Necessity benefit anyone, and least of all benefit educationally. The teacher of literature now in America, far more than the teacher of history or philosophy or religion, is condemned to teach the presentness of the past, because history, philosophy, and religion have withdrawn as agents from the Scene of Instruction, leaving the bewildered teacher of literature alone at the altar, terrifiedly wondering whether he is to be sacrifice or priest. If he evades his burden by attempting to teach only the supposed presence of the present, he will find himself teaching only some simplistic, partial reduction that wholly obliterates the present in the name of one or another historicizing formula, or past injustice, or dead faith, whether secular or not. Yet how is he to teach a tradition now grown so wealthy and so heavy that to accommodate it demands more strength than any single consciousness can provide, short of the parodistic Kabbalism of a Pynchon?

All literary tradition has been necessarily elitist, in every period, if only because the Scene of Instruction always depends upon a primal choosing and a being chosen which is what "elite" means. Teaching, as Plato knew, is necessarily a branch of erotics, in the wide sense of desiring what we have not got, of redressing our poverty, of compounding with our fantasies. No teacher, however impartial he or she attempts to be, can avoid choosing among students, or being chosen by them, for this is the very nature of teaching. Literary teaching is precisely like literature itself; no strong writer can choose his precursors until first he is chosen by them, and no strong student can fail to be chosen by his teachers. Strong students, like strong writers, will rise in the most unexpected places and times, to wrestle with the internalized violence pressed upon them by their teachers and precursors.

Yet our immediate concern, as I am aware, is hardly with the strong, but with the myriads of the many, as Emersonian democracy seeks to make its promises a little less deceptive than they have been. Do the dialectics of literary tradition yield us no wisdom that can help with the final burden of the latecomer, which is the extension of the literary franchise? What is the particular inescapability of literary tradition for the teacher who must go out to find himself as a voice in the wilderness? Is he to teach *Paradise Lost* in preference to the Imamu Amiri Baraka?

I think these questions are self-answering, or rather will be, with the passage of only a few more years. For the literary teacher, more than ever, will find he is teaching *Paradise Lost* and the other central classics of Western literary tradition, whether he is teaching them overtly or not. The psychology of belatedness is unsparing, and the Scene of Instruction becomes ever more primal as our society sags around us. Instruction, in our late phase, becomes an antithetical process almost in spite of itself, and for antithetical teaching you require antithetical texts, that is to say, texts antithetical to your students as well as to yourself and to other texts. Milton's Satan may stand as representative of the entire canon when he challenges us to challenge Heaven with him, and he will provide the truest handbook for all those, of whatever origin, who as he says "with ambitious mind/Will covet more." Any teacher of the dispossessed, of those who assert *they* are the insulted and injured, will serve the deepest needs of his students when he gives them possession of Satan's grand opening of the Debate in Hell, which I cite now to close this introduction to the dialectics of tradition:

> With this advantage then
> To union, and firm Faith, and firm accord,
> More than can be in Heav'n, we now return
> To claim our just inheritance of old,
> Surer to prosper than prosperity
> Could have assur'd us; and by what best way,
> Whether of open War or covert guile,
> We now debate; who can advise, may speak.

Hélène Cixous, translated by Carol Bové

At Circe's, or, The Self-Opener

Bloom passes in the street which passes into Bloom. He opens the door which opens him and enters the brothel which prostitutes him. Who touches thinks speaks here? Where is "I"? Am I the one who was me? The Self-Opener theater which is gaping in Circe not only replays all parts of *Ulysses* in one scene but, by decompartmentalization and by depersonalization, decomposes each and everyone into his several selves, breaks the real into fragments, and calls on the multiplicity of entire pieces to speak, without distinction of object, of subject, of interiority or of exteriority, of property. Isolated voices float and call, each speaks toward the exterior. Persons decompose, partial objects are personalized; hoary voices resound; everything becomes detached and stands in suspension; sudden apparitions enter things into the general dislocation. The scene gives a start. All at once someone is there. At that very instant an object is no longer there. The approach no longer exists. But the sudden appearance, the brutal reversal: there/not-there, without transition, without withdrawal.

Between powerlessness and complete power, uncertain selves violently oscillate, between greatest passivity and liveliest affirmation. Somewhere some of them cancel each other out, or abort, nonworlds, bungled entrances, impeded births, *Circe*, schizotext: the ascendancy of the Other, of the Other Sow.[1] On all fours the pigs! Bloom, prepared to crawl, arrives at the brothel door hallucinating with additional paws in his pocket: a pig's foot and a sheep's foot. He who enters here casts aside the interiority of the body and of thought, the self's unity and integrity in space, continuity in time, to be pushed to the limit of suffering by the logic of the Delirium which produces this overall absurdity. Here things are other things. Everything is endlessly transformed. You can be someone else because each is always no one. The self is without a core of identity. Certain things jump out at you; the caps prepare you; there are imperative signs which come from another world. Are you sure of not being what you are not? Whatever your name you can be someone else: half man half woman for example, Bloom, or each in turn. The Other Sow who commands can do everything: she takes ideas from your head and puts hers in their place. Since your body has windowpanes everyone can see you. The Other Sow manages by modern "pornosophic" means to break you and to bugger you even at a distance. Everything operates, and in fact, this machine produces machines in abundance, but it's the Other Sow who makes it go. Even your physiological functions belong to her: you piss when she wants to. Your skin is in a way turned inside out like the world's skin and what was outside in now inside. You yourself are a stage where you meet yourself among many others through whom flash the thoughts of anyone-like-you. What is implicit is explicit. What is mute speaks. What is transparent opacifies. Your body's opacity is transferred to the world whose diffuse clarity flashes through your body. You belong to all the world, make use of it while it has room for any-self.

This chapter opens like an opera out of gear: you perceive (read-see-hear) that it takes place on a kind of below-stage, a substage, where "the human" no longer means anything, but where things are stirring somehow or other in the quarters of a nonhuman, of a below. Somewhere, there is still a bit of code, but very little, just barely some points which prick the text on the great backdrop of culture—a signifier whose source is Wagner, but so isolated that it nearly says nothing ("Nothung!" Sigmund's sword which I cannot help taking for Nothing!). The immense debacle of representation which bursts all logical chains, divisions, differences, frees a mass of fantasies: as if Western imagination, memory banks, cult treasures, the ideological membrane, the great ontological structures had collapsed, then it's the great pell-mell unburdening, ancestors the dead descendants men children insects, walking sticks, the old-fashioned the progressive, located objects, lost beings, sexes, all that mixes interpenetrates lights up changes is diluted, contaminated, permeation without limits, the unconscious communicate, it's the feast day of the repressed! All that was forbidden surges forth, guilt revels in all possible infractions, masochism satisfies its most torturing desires, amazochism wrenches itself free, superegos vie in their tyranny, all the Sades who sleep in the dungeons of souls frolic about in every corner justine-izing to their asses' content mounts are split into vulvae long restrained, a vaginal wind blows on the visitors, a veterinarian's arm is needed to bring forth the new mammals, a heavenly soap shoots forth its rays, the procuress fans herself and becomes a procurer,[2] organs fly, kisses blow, finally hemimirrors knock off those who, confronting them, behold new faces, a deluge of events mutates the stage at an imperceptible speed, History masturbates and spits out a shower of myths, fetuses, full terms, and ends of the world, somorrhe godome, extremes touch and penetrate each other, beyond cause effects no longer account for anything what is is and there is some for everybody.

It's the end of metaphors: figures work themselves out, allusions are no longer in play, the returning repetition stops short and erects a different stage. The banal is aroused to the point of the grotesque. Mask, bestiary, temptation, mystery, Walpurgis Night, masses and countermasses, coronations, elections, prevolutions, phallucinations. Sing the *Introit*, you are Stephen, you enter the quarter of tolerance walking stick raised and the carnival beings. Totter, fall seven times: you are Bloom on the verge of being Booloohoom and Company. Imagine an episodic mirror which doesn't succeed in erasing the worst of what it imagines.[3] Stephen and Bloom contemplate each other in it: but there is no longer any reflection in its depths other than the one which contorted it in a primitive version: "the face of William Shakespeare, beardless, appears there, rigid in facial paralysis, crowned by the reflection of the reindeer antlered hatrack in the hall,"[4] Shakespeare, the innumerable, the one who resembles everybody.

Circe, fifteenth episode of *Ulysses* (Correspondences: Scene: the brothel; Time: midnight; Organ: locomotor apparatus; Art: magic; Symbol: whore; Technique: hallucination). Fragments of dialogue cut by long stage directions, a system of plays and parentheses comprise the monstrous text. Pieces, tableaux settle for an instant, the time to record a passage, a bit of face; a syntax is produced, by nonlogical connection, by heterogenous links related through a few references: suspicious subjects who assemble their states under the names of Bloom, Stephen, prostitutes, the madam, names, moreover, which are unstable.

As a first step, consider the following opening tableaux: first tableau:

consisting of stage directions: the entrance through Mabbot Street; second tableau: a phantasmagoric court of miracles, the invalids' museum; third tableau: two exchanges of answers frame the introduction of an idiot; fourth tableau: Cissy Caffrey's song and the arrival of the two soldiers.

From one tableau to another and within the same tableau, supralogical signifying connections (or signifying connections of another logic) are superimposed upon the simulacrum of rational organization. All details are signs which open. The real is gaping. Upon what?

The Mabbot street entrance of nighttown, before which stretches an uncobbled transiding set with skeleton tracks, red and green will-o'-the-wisps and danger signals. Rows of flimsy houses with gaping doors. Rare lamps with faint rainbow fans. Round Rabaiotti's halted ice gondola stunted men and women squabble. They grab wafers between which are wedged lumps of coal and copper snow. Sucking, they scatter slowly. Children. The swancomb of the gondola, highreared, forges on through the murk, white and blue under a lighthouse. Whistles call and answer, etc. (pp. 429–30)

First tableau. It's a decor, installed, centered, marked out with danger signals, the entrance, the straight stretch of tracks, the channeled text. In this decor: a "stage": the ice gondola which halts; men, women, or children? around. At the end the *stage moves*, the gondola departs. What happened, the little which happened, to all appearances, was produced elsewhere, on a stage which this stage displaces to such an extent that it is quasi-unrecognizable. One does not yet indicate the relation to the other except by the unusual presence of a common but distorted element. When the gondola moves on, with its swancomb, you have the cloudy feeling of attending the opening of a sick opera, a choleric Wagner. Precise descriptive elements are at work, so charged that they make the description vibrate like a hallucination or a description of a hallucination. The perversion of the description seems to be of a magical nature. The deformed rules. A general threat weighs upon the stage, extends from Street to stretches, distends Stretch–street–set–side–Tram-Tracks–layers–strata; on all sides the signifier does its obscure work of insistence, but undecipherable. It inserts itself and lingers without your being able to assign a sense to it; there is "s," "t," the formless in this suspicious scene. A system of relations is established at the level of the line, investing the senses, the ear, the eye through intense strokes. Perhaps it's the contamination of "skeleton," mark of the danger introduced into the text or production of the textual malaise: someone already "interprets" the visible, unless it's the visible which produces its own disguises directly. A world which the text forces back springs up and pierces it. Imagine the underside of the text, where discourse becomes detached and fantasies imprint their anxiety. And, "danger signals," text signal, makes the text the echo of another text which it is as well.

The text posits: "Row houses, . . . rare lamps, . . . round Rabaiotti's . . . ," rows of objects, inventory of passivity, from row to lengthening. Doors are gaping: the entrance is reiterated, modulated by danger. As soon as it enters the hatch, it rushes in. The "r" anaphorizes and sets off the "s," which "flimsy," "skeleton," "wisps," whisper. It's the contestation of a solidity of the world. All of that is fake, false houses, chains of deserted objects. Contestation of the real in the real: that which holds, links, transmits, lacks substance. "Rare," "faint," vocalic sweeping: "rare lamps with faint rainbow fans:" faint "a's," run aground, wiped out by soft "r's," "w's." Signs: objects: sidetrack framework—presage?

Of what? Will-o-the-wisps, eyes? Flimsy houses, illusory? Paper partitions: a surface which splits from a blow. And if this weren't theater? Doors are gaping, with a gape opening onto nothing, absolute. The gondola lets the incongruous pass sweeping along the distant city, an italy of which only ice remains. The elsewhere of the sad quarter is this aberrant element which condenses all the desires of underdeveloped beings. The characters: stunted, rachitic men and women, unwelcome, as if they had emerged from the sidetrack framework. Animals, they squabble over frightful goodies, mouthfuls of coal and copper. Regressions: "s-s-s," sucking, they disperse. The text advances a signifier cut up *by everything:* between two periods: ".Children." Without predicates. A signifier without solidity, plural, indefinite, indistinct, appears and disappears. Only the text says them. They disperse. The gondola with a rigid neck, only sign capable of rising toward a height, "highreared," departs. Noises: exchange of whistles—which are only mentioned: effacement of origins and of ends.

Second tableau. What speaks? Calls call. Answers: isolated voices float, detached far from the persons who utter. The dialogue functions without a subject, by anonymous, general structures. "Wait, my love, and I'll be with you": the sentence, in several voices, says the mother, the lover, the whore, who knows? "Round behind the stable" does not directly answer the call, but an unformulated "where?" Someone understands and projects a resounding, enigmatic dialogue, someone from the outside. Unless the dialogue is searching, with its voices, for buying subjects? A call and an answer for everybody? The idiot, in relation to this generality, is a particular (*idios*). In relation to the calls, he is deaf; in relation to the answers, he is mute. The St. Vitus dance corresponds to the rachitis of the others. The uncoordinated shakes the text: a disorder which does not liberate. His goggle-eyes make a sign to the will-o'-the-wisps, danger signals, gas lamps. The idiot is the convulsive embodiment of the setting. A chain of children's hands encircle him: detached hands, like the voices. Ends of children. Left-handed! continues the inscription of motor troubles, the arm is paralyzed, the language afflicted. In his verbal deformations, the idiot does, on the level of the role allotted him, what the inscription of the deformed does to all of the signifiers of the text.

"Where's the great light?" Which one? The definite takes on the value of mystery here, in the absence of referents. The one who knows is not known: sentences emerge suddenly, like the objects and the limbs of the body, from a background of fog.

Third tableau. What is bound one minute is unbound the next. Released, the idiot jerks on. The unformed and the infirm spring up, a pygmy, a form, a gnome, a crone, a bandy child. A pile of outcasts. These scraps of being have movements which show up their stilted, nonhuman, discordant aspect: the entire body of the text is anguished, brusque, good-for-nothing. Stunted growth, sinking, reduce these failures to the limit of the species, vague limit, equally uncertain: the form in a heap against the dustbin no longer has the strength to affirm a genus, it flops down into a neutral. Broken rhythms take up in a more extreme form the jerking of the idiot: the lurching of the drunk navvy, the swinging of the pygmy, stumbling, limping, sidling, toward animality: disconnection which not even the pair of bobbies resists. The real crumbles. All that is perceived is "subject" in this neurotic grammar. Oaths, whistles, arms, plate, woman, chap, take their posts and the initiative by an indefinite personalization.

Fourth tableau. From the noise to the face, the voice summons the body which lets it escape, woman's shrill voice which sings the verses of an apparently innocuous song, actually obscene, and containing a whole series of signifiers which bring about, by allusion, designation, or phonic or semantic contiguity the free play of a certain number of Ulysses or sexual code signs. The duck leg, injected into the song by the club and the height of the policemen, is reinjected into the soldiers' whip, tight in their oxters, while at the same time announcing the ash stick, Stephen's magic instrument, of which the inscription, the activity, and the deconstructive and remarkable effects are innumerable in all the density of the text. As if nothing had happened, belly and phallus enter through the song, and for an instant the text unveils what it is, stage of the unconscious, but also system of partitions and passages, of thresholds and of lips, brothel and sheath thoroughly agitated by intruders, and shaken by spasms. Circe is herself the sex which sets traps.

Bloom is a Maid of All Work: Flower's Worst Style

"Bloom, (Bows.) 'Master! Mistress! Mantamer!' (He lifts his arms. His bangle bracelets fall.) Bello, (Satirically.) 'By day you will souse and bat out smelling underclothes, also when we ladies are unwell, and swab out latrines with dress pinned up and a dishclout tied to your tail. Won't that be nice?' (He places a ruby ring on her finger.)," etc., (pp. 538–39). He's entered, bothered, tripping, Hungarian Jew half Jewish neither Jewish nor Hungarian Leopold Bloom Virag's[5] son, very like Sacher-Masoch who penetrates him and lives in him through his first name, conjugated with Shakespeare by a common horned headdress, ready for everybody, broken, introjected, turned inside out like a glove by the monstrous Bella mistress of several genuses and of all powers busty mustachioed who turns into Bello when Bloom is seized by the desire to be a sow, driven toward the virago's altar by the need to act out his fantasies, to push impotence to the extreme, to the point where no one appropriates his own acts any longer for Bloom. He is abandoned to influences; absolute executant, his body hesitates, mutates, materializes inconceivable possibilities, falls, turns, forks, slots itself, perversifies itself: all that he cannot be invades him. His tongue is timid, but his body speaks all languages, and pours out provocations, manifestations, inventions, aggressions, of which its parts are the letter and the spirit. Almost dog when he enters sniffing burdened with aborted sins of uncommitted crimes, Bloom passes from one state to another through repeated falls, collisions, and fascinations, projected everywhere, then withdrawing, and reprojecting himself, backward-buggering, defiguring metaphorical productions by sudden actualizations, undifferentiating the imaginary, the symbolic, the real, what is said is done, what is feared is executed " 'So that gesture, not music, nor odours, would be a universal language, the gift of tongues rendering visible not the lay sense but the first entelechy, the structural rhythm.' [Stephen] Lynch, 'Pornosophical philotheology!' " (p. 432) they say; desire does not argue, it pays language back in its own coin; Bloom collects, real piggy bank for the forbidden; all imaginable follies and filth fall into his body through the slot. Saying and seeing go together like the keyhole and the eye: one passes through the other and effects it instantaneously. In this world of disconnected forces, all object-beings, machines, are individualized and invested with an absolute but ephemeral power. Machines do not have themselves "recognized" following the normal process of approaching identity. They jump out at you, directly and immediately and impose themselves. There is no appearance but quantities of pure identities. A general disconnection of codes has taken place, followed by an authoritative redistribution of signifiers which seize the signified like parasites: the real has a totalitarian aspect—a group of absolute but tiny and unstable principalities let loose, a rowdy pandemonium. It's the end of the implicit and the silent: everything which is inside is outside, intellectual functions are televised, physical functions are exposed, Bloom decompartmentalizes, identifies himself with a cohort of subblooms, flowers, superblooms, successive booloohooms. In acting itself out, each fantasy modifies him; he can be that which passes through "Circe's" mind. The mind itself is not fixed: everything happens, and everyone happens by, "Circe" designating this great thinking dreaming delirious vagina which produces sheaves of very powerful signs, and organizes and disorganizes sexuality while playing at pushing taboos to the limit of genitality: what is important on this stage overrun by simulacra of tyrants, employers, *Venus im Pelz*, booted superegos and pork butcher divinities, during the feast of submission, is, after all, disobedience and indecision. No one remains the slave of anything, neither of a difference, nor of a repetition, everyone talks in turn.

Noteworthy in this regard is the "piped" inscription of Bloom's worst style: his passage through a whore's skin (symbol of the episode: the whore) is in the mode of an initiation to the female condition of which the rites reproduce all the violence of sexual rivalry, redoubled by the exchange and the transposition. But it is a brutal initiation without mystery: it is not an unveiling, it is quasi-military instruction, a violent manual written in all the catechistic codes which the desire to be obeyed can invent. Raped, appraised, marked down, Bloom takes her place among Bella-Bello's equally bastard boarders: Zoe (life), Kitty (kitten), Flora (vegetable). Brothel blossom, she uncovers a pistil. In a way Bloom is overcome, punished, castrated by the mother-father in a great pregenital clearing of the decks, repression being for the moment repressed: all of the suddenly liberated impulsive tendencies hurl themselves upon the available body, it's the sadistic, anal, urethral orgy, while however a part of the subject which is on the castrator's side gradually confiscates the pleasures of the same subject. Ambivalence retrieves the libido on all sides at once, in the absence of the taboo of contradiction: Bloom is at once guilty and punished, curious and anguished, frustrated, satisfied, emutilated, pre-Oedipalized, and, moreover, intense objective and subjective castration desire. In relation to the femininity phase, he is threatened as a girl and as a boy by the mother and father which he eventually is. The brothel scene falls back upon all the scenes which it condemns and parodies: there is Bellabello in every mother and in every piggy a trace of Circe; inversely, and at the same level of desire, prostitutes are mutated little boys. Bloom and Bello have more than one letter in common: "b," "l," "o."

The paragraph revolves around the "maid of all work." Bloom is made woman, and what is worse, housemaid, many-layered humiliation. Woman is subservient to her own physiological functions. The maid's functions are perverted in regard to what they are in reality, the relation to the employers' bed, a relation which is always repressed. The maid is therefore twice subservient: to her employers and to their sex. The intolerable accumulates. Domestic of a multiplied master, woman Bloom is in the bargain subservient to those who are themselves subservient. In relation to the prostitute's role, she is removed and inferior. Greater degradation cannot be imagined.

Moreover the passage is situated between two drinks filled to the brim. Everything is good, the piss in the pots is also a chic beverage: the call of the piss makes all the fantasies of nourishing liquids spring forth. There is femininity with malodorous periods and good milkmaid femininity. Better yet, from cow to bull, you go back, in the following paragraph, to the legendary, primordial penis, the one which gives "whole milk." In this way, from urine to semen, by a reversal of the excremental which turns out to be re-injected into pure pleasure, wastes are sublimated—or subloomated. "You will make the beds, . . ."

It's a passage through recipients: "bed," "tub," "pot" (you will go from pot to chamber pots to Flower's vagina); with the future of command, and the "including" of the clause, the latter is an additional humiliation (humiliation, like piss, has inexhaustable resources), since it subordinates Bloom to a subordinate of subordinates. Champagne! The text continues along a double track: rinsing—in the sense of cleaning—the chamber pots, emptying these filled-up hollows, and lapping up. It's the second track that Bello pursues. The association can at any time overturn, noble champagne is for drinking vulgarly. It is gulped down. The mouth joins in this way the pot of piss in swallowing what another mouth pours, or will pour into the third receptacle which is the pot. The piss is to the champagne what Bella is to Bello or Bloom to Flower, its reversal, the champagne itself.

Seven supervises its transferral from one receptacle to another, sacred numeral which drums out a measure (uninterpretable however) repeated in Circe: the just will fall seven times (Circe was rewritten seven times by Joyce), seven pots, seven swords, seven days, or Bello-beard's seven women. Flux from pot piss to champagne flute, flux of significance, from pipe to flute, to reed. "Drink me piping hot" says the urine, creating its piplicity in the course of the text, "piping hot"—boiling, calls up all the plays on flute (to pipe = to play the flute, to whistle a command). "We have piped unto you and ye have not danced" (Luke, VII, 32) calls the reticent through Saint Luke's voice, those who do not know how to be aroused, we have played the flute and you have not danced, flux of flutes which make Flower dance, and the overdetermined, manipulated text jump, "Hop! You will dance attendance or I'll lecture you," none of that with Bello, here when they whistle for you, you obey. Drink me, orders Bello-the-urine, Bello-made-piss or worse, offering himself to be drunk. With "dance" the error (the lack) which sprung from the hollow of the pot, from the hollow of the sexual organ, is made precise, comes to light, "your misdeeds." The correction, through Luke and the lecture, is religious, little indecent mixture topped off by Miss Ruby's bot bared for a spanking. A current flows from the negative (Bloom) toward the positive pole (Bello) which acquires bloomesque "electrons" of structure. Sometimes the charges are reversed. Bloom is then a kind of hole in the general structure which Bello's ero-tricity penetrates, but a nonnegative hole, antiparsicle. This positive "hole" is attracted by the minus pole; the scene functioning through the application of semiconductor "pots," like a transistor. Hop! In the same way the upper and lower portions of the body are exchanged in the structure: the hair brush on the back-side assimilates the ass and the head, and the name Miss Ruby makes both ass and face shine like jewels. The spanking sends the maid of all work back to a sadistic nursery. "You'll be taught the error of your ways" slips the text between two meanings: "Your errors will be pointed out to you," "that will teach you"—to commit them, you will know how to do what shouldn't be done.

"At night . . ." Reversal? After the thrashing, the anointing: all the women's creams, pastes and powders and perfumes, sublime excrements, will thoroughly oil erogenous hands. And in the Ruby's subsequent stage, the hands are turned over to bracelets. The dressing up, the fondling, the gratification are carried out in a manner which resembles repression: not less than forty-three buttons, parceled, bound up, partial objects reduced to powerlessness, rendered passive, all of that opposing the naked bottom. Nudity, underlined by the excess of the opening, is carried to the point of the indecent. There is a play on sheaths (glove, sheath, vagina); the glove takes over for the preceding hollow objects, "bed," "tub," "pot," "pipe." With the glove knights in the time of courtly love were trapped. A completely out of place lordly figure is drawn, from the universe of tokens and trials: in the chain of the subservient, here is someone who comes upon an incongruous post. Chuckling. The knights raised up by Circe fall, thrown down, in her quarters: those "called up" are "voluntary" in the brothel. From knight to colonel, from voluntary enlistment to draftees, the parody becomes detached while turning around: who parodies whom? In which way? in which way? the code thus functions for hardly the time of a sequence, only to snag, to stumble: the current flows, from negative to positive and vice-versa, following the "rectifier's" intervention. If Miss Ruby is "lady-like" and the "knight" is colonel, she becomes a lady at the moment that he degrades himself.

"My new attraction" calls to mind the circus or the traveling theater. Bello always has something of the trainer about him (in this capacity he is also "Venus in furs"), something of the lord, by the *droit du seigneur*: "First I'll have a go at you myself." A very short go because the current flows quickly and already the demand precipitates the offer.

"A man I know on the turf named Charles Alberta Marsh (I was in bed with him just now and another gentleman out of the Hanaper and Petty Bag office) is on the lookout for a maid of all work at a short knock. Swell the bust" (p. 539). Another possibility: the auction. After all it's only a different kind of exposure of a business going under several names. Illustrated history of a commodity: the woman as a girl, as a lady, as a white slave, to be trafficked like a dog: "For that lot trained by owner to fetch and carry, basket in mouth." The muzzle opens, the hollow returns, everywhere, violently. The mouth is a hole which offers itself to the filling, but soon the hole is everywhere: on a string, in a series, all the openings are an opening. You enter . . . "in the mouth (*He bares his arm and plunges it elbowdeep in Bloom's vulva.*) There's fine depth for you! What, boys? That give you a hardon?" (p. 539). In so far as Flower Bloom has more than one calyx, the feminization is exuberant, the phantasmic body fecunt on all sides. One organ does not suffice: Flower exposes himself everywhere, the hole spreads: in this way the fiction which vulvas him brings to light his shameful desire. The most deeply buried manages to expose itself. You see this depth, that of the text itself, which thrusts itself and grows hollow without resistance: "(He shoves his arm in a bidder's face)." Lap it up and wet your whistle. The equivalence vulva-face emerges from the repetition of the gesture. But the bidder's face is turned around to the receptacle, opens like a taster's mouth waiting for the liquid. "Here, wet the deck and wipe it round," cuts the current; the paragraph returns to its beginning, wiping up everything that has flowed forth.

Notes

1. The French for "the ascendancy of the Other, of the Other Sow" is "l'emprise de l'Autrui, de l'Autre Truie." The pun is lost in English.

2. The French "maquerelle" (madam) and "maquereau" (pimp) have a fish connotation which the English translations do not.

3. The original sentence names an imaginary "piroir" which puns on "pire" (worst) and begins a series of rhyming words: "Imaginez un piroir: c'est un miroir à tiroirs; il n'arrive pas à effacer ce qu'il imagine de pire." Plays on "pire" continue in the second half of the essay where the title "Le pire-style de Fleur," ("Flower's Worst Style") alludes to the "pistil" which Flower Bloom uncovers.

4. James Joyce, *Ulysses* (New York: Random House, 1961), p. 567. Following page references are from this edition.–translator

5. Bloom's father, Rudolf Virag, a Hungarian Jew whose suicide is coupled with the death of Bloom's son Rudy, had his name translated into English: Virag = Bloom (flower). Translation affects, patronymic loss and recoveries abound in *Ulysses*.

Postmodern Oral Poetry
Buckminster Fuller, John Cage, and David Antin

David Antin's entrance into the "primitive" realm of oral poetry synthesizes the advances of his immediate predecessors and progresses quite a bit further. He acknowledges the work of Albert Lord, a professor at Harvard who went into the field in search of a contemporary analogue for the oral culture which nurtured Homer. Lord, whose manner Antin must have found sympathetic, even underwent a learning exercise commonly employed by young Yugoslavian singers in attempting to master an epic song. By studying a living oral tradition, one of the few that's left, Lord thought he would get a sense of what it was that Homer did and how it got down in a form that we are able to read. And for Antin, the only way to really understand an experience is to "simply" enter its domain and its processes—have a firsthand experience of an art form that's not within your realm or, if you're a professional examiner or relator of various art forms, work with actual art possibilities in that area you don't understand. The firsthand experience is the finest mode for elucidating what someone else is doing. So that's why I'm talking on tape in an attempt to apprehend individuals who really are at their intellectual and artistic best when talking. That's how they best understand reality, that's how they best transform reality, and speculatively that's how a "postmodern critic" might achieve and simulate an "inside view" of contemporary oral poetry.

It took David Antin quite a while to get to his current and most striking art process; that is, the oral delivery of what he alternatively terms "poem-raps" or "talking" or "talks" or most recently, "thoughts." I was amused by a change Antin made in the published notation of a piece he performed, as it were, for my check ("talking at the boundaries"): the oral "publisher for these talks" became the printed "publisher for thoughts." But that is more accurate because what you're really getting is the mind thinking in synchronization with the mouth articulating words and phrases. For Antin talking and thinking are rather similar processes, or perhaps the way that the process can be presented and preserved in a manner that another can attempt to encounter. When you're talking—at least when Antin's talking—the pace is faster than a normative human pace, one step ahead. He's had a reputation for being very smart; his suspicious detractors would probably use the term "smart-alec." Before I met him, those of his contemporaries still living in New York City would tell me that he'd be perfect for an interview: he's a good talker, they'd say. In an interview I did with Jerome Rothenberg, Rothenberg mentioned that it's no accident Antin is now talking his poems because during their undergraduate days Antin would dominate the conversation. They'd sit up nights and Antin would be the one who'd carry on—Rothenberg would do most of the listening. But he needed an audience: the earlier situation was of course more informal than his present procedure. When thinking about his early poems, Antin claims that the speed with which he apprehended reality was "delayed" by the syrupy transition between images characteristic of the sequential image poetry that Rothenberg, Kelly, Schwerner, Wakoski, and others were writing in the early sixties. So he really didn't want to be thought of in that context, as a writer of image, or more commonly, "deep image" poetry, because even at that early stage he must have aspired to the speed of his oral transmissions. Getting language onto paper was a drag, because the conventional vanguard possibilities weren't suited to his manner of thinking. He held back most of what he wrote at the time and never subsequently gathered together a book of "deep image" poetry.

In addition, Antin had endured arduous training in preparation for a novelistic career and had published one highly finished Flaubertian story, "The Balanced Aquarium," in the *Kenyon Review* (of all places). He went into retreat in order to write a novel provisionally entitled *The Stigmata*, which finally had too much transition for his blood. Even prose, which I think at this time he may have considered closer to talking than the poetic possibilities available in the late fifties and early sixties, was not quite right and he abandoned the novel, though I suspect some of the life experience which may have been incorporated in *The Stigmata* has surfaced in his recent "talks."

Unfortunately, Antin didn't see the potential usefulness of the work of Buckminster Fuller, but of course at that time few did. From my perspective, there is a certain amount of similarity between their work. Both I think feel that the proper way to "realize" what's outside yourself is the immediate act of talking about what you're observing. Apprehending and talking in the same instant, as well as enlarging the confines of the known universe. Fuller doesn't bother at all with Wittgenstein as far as I can determine, while Antin uses the *Philosophic Investigations* to support his contention that an utterance is an image of reality and that any language act (and it doesn't always have to be verbal) is the way an animate being represents reality. Getting up on his feet and talking is Antin's ideal *and* practical embodiment of human intellectual activity.

Fuller seems to operate in a similar manner, but he doesn't term the activity "poetry." The talks which Fuller gives are transcribed into blocks of prose which Hugh Kenner claims are "studied" for their visual quality: each line is broken in an appropriate manner. My experience of reading Fuller's prose, however, is quite like reading thick, justified poetry. Similarly, David Antin regards his own prose as "concrete poetry with justified margins" though when I read such works in literary and art journals the I B M composer seems to have done away with Antin's spatial specifications. The scores for his improvised oral poems evade technological standards more successfully. Fuller is responsible for linguistic items obviously resembling "poems" visually but often labeled "ventilated prose," in which each unit (if one is to believe the anecdote) was an intuitively measured "dose" any businessman could understand. The rather exotic, somewhat cranky language was impossible as a continuous progression of prose, but when broken up into segments resembling poetic lines even the readers of *Fortune* magazine might be able to follow Fuller's thought. This encompassing of "poetry" as part of his domain occurred in 1940, when Fuller was working for the Luce conglomerate. The business world prodded Buckminster Fuller into acts of poetic lucidity; that is, his written prose was shown to an editor who literally couldn't understand the progress of the argument (and therefore anticipated the difficulties of the reading audience). This editor asked Fuller whether he could alleviate the confusion. When Fuller countered by reading aloud what he had written, the relation between breath-units and thought-units, as it were, became transparent. That year, 1940, was a veritable watershed for Buckminster Fuller the poet: he quarried no less than two quite considerable poems by "ventilating" the prose he had written. Indeed, the business world accidentally legitimized the ontological status of the earliest of these works—two nameless poets whom Fuller's employer had over for dinner one day were shown what Fuller had done and pronounced it "poetry." Fuller of course denied the crime because he knew that most of the potential readers of his writing wouldn't look at it if it were labeled "poetry." But, speaking for myself, the experience of "No More Secondhand God" and "Machine Tools" resembles the experience of poetry.

Fuller's subsequent writing has been done mainly on his feet. A prophetic and utopian stylist, he travels from one public speaking engagement to another brimming over with ideas which he wants to get across to a human audience. In his wonderful book *Bucky*, Hugh Kenner argues adjectivally that Fuller is a poet. The tone of the talks is rhapsodic—energy mounts, words can't come quite as fast as his ecstatic mental apprehension of reality, and by the fourth hour. . . . Unfortunately, I've never been in attendance during one of Fuller's talks, but for Kenner (who is an eminent authority in such matters), Fuller's activity during these pieces is that of a poet. Oddly enough, these talks are transcribed into justified rather than ventilated prose. Even an artist as devoted to Buckminster Fuller's ideas as John Cage has been recently, admits to never having read the talks as prose: he learned through personal conversation. David Antin has little to say about Fuller. He's never made a reference in print, but when I asked Antin about Fuller on the phone he singled out Bucky's vernacular American antiformalism.

I think that they share a rapid-fire oral articulation of their understanding of the universe. Everyone, they would agree, has a particular representation of reality—some paint it, some write it, and so forth—but they talk it. Fuller attempts to proselytize a construct of reality, but Antin's intentions are more subtle. Does Fuller want to bring you over to his view of reality by convincing you that it is *the* view or does he, like John Cage, want you to come to your own realization and the articulation of it via an undirected presentation that will shock you into a realization of what you should realize for yourself? It seems to me that Fuller does try to teach in a more traditional way. There's a lot of time spent on the transcripts—his office claims that they go through seven versions on their path to typeset prose in the belief that readers will take them more seriously in that form and read them as they would most other intellectual writing, with the further hope that his readership will act in a manner which will help to realize Fuller's aims. Which is a curious way of going about it, from my perspective. A fair number of individuals become enthralled by Fuller (as by any attractive messiah) and subsequently fall by the wayside. Fuller knows that he's making a personal construct of reality but to a greater degree than either Cage or Antin he would attempt to convince humans that his construct is in fact the way things are. Though in fact Fuller admits that everyone has the potential to realize this construct for themselves. So that his activities are in some sense a model for others—not merely learning instructions, or programmed learning. A variant of Zen teaching, by example.

In the sixties Fuller had been writing what he terms "poems." Five of them appear in *Intuition*. They're somewhat unusual linguistic entities written (during a period of years when his most obvious public activity was talking) in an attempt to get his thoughts down on paper when in their first surfacing they weren't oral. They weren't talking, taped, and transcribed. Instead, they were words he observed going through his mind but they didn't come out of his mouth because his personal situation at the time of observation was not one in which talking on tape was convenient or natural. I think that they came to him when he was in one way or other isolated. He didn't have a live audience in front of him; therefore, these poems emerged not as oral poetry but rather as what might be called "dictated oral," with a blank sheet of paper as fill-in for a scribe or tape-recorder. Albert Lord uses this term in his account of the process by which Homer's oral composition was preserved. There was a man named Homer who was reciting poems and finally via the influence of surrounding cultures, Greece decided to begin preserving cultural attributes. "Let's preserve Homer's work." And for someone without a tape-recorder (they hadn't been invented yet) to get down a version of what is being said requires that the speaker operate in an unaccustomed manner—he'll have to talk slower and hesitate at moments appropriate for the scribe rather than the talker. It would be impossible to proceed at the mind's pace because the scribe couldn't follow. Now

Antin can talk as fast as he can perceive and not worry about it because a visual translation of the oral occasion will soon be available. The tape-recorder saves the day.

To get back to Fuller's recent poetry, it seems that he's able to record mental activity with his pen or pencil on ordinary paper. I was particularly interested in the process by which he thought through "The Lord's Prayer" twice and wrote down two rather divergent texts, divergent from each other and from the established written text that he was originally thinking through. Remnants of the established version remain, but Fuller has made it his own, has made it new. In other words, he worked with a written text, which Albert Lord argues would weaken the possibility for oral poetry. That is, when writing enters an oral culture eventually the texts take on such authority that individuals simply memorize rather than intuitively picking up bits and pieces and finally mastering on their own a whole oral process. Fuller probably had memorized "The Lord's Prayer" during elementary school but at this point in his life the sacred text evolved into a *topoi* for improvisation.

David Antin occasionally engages in similar procedures, though it's doubtful whether Fuller's example is the primary one. For example, Antin published what purported to be a prose article on Jean Tinguely in *Art News*. He pointed to this piece as a significant symptom of a disease commonly labeled art. Ostensibly it was a review-essay by an art critic; however, the "critic" *used* the occasion of a Tinguely sculpture being exhibited at the Museum of Modern Art for his own artistic purposes. Antin invented a machine—Tinguely had not put together the machine that David Antin the art critic *described*. The essay might be described (in a phrase toward which Antin would be hostile) as "a flight of fancy." Antin does not explicate and/or evaluate the Tinguely sculpture as a given object (and appropriately so because Tinguely's objects are usually self-destroying). Antin's piece exists halfway between objective criticism and art works which use up what's at hand.

The precise manner in which Fuller's recent lengthy poems ("Intuition: Metaphysical Mosaic" and "Brain and Mind") came to exist is not exactly clear, though I suspect they were improvised on paper during a number of sittings. The two versions of "The Lord's Prayer" were more striking formally because their origins and the means by which they evolved are relatively unambiguous. They're probably not that satisfying from a New Critical examination of the text proper, but I don't care. I'm interested in what Fuller would certainly call his content, and I prefer reading his poems to his heavily revised prose transcripts. But the sheer quantity of "coinage" distracts me. Still, Fuller's work is more useful than the poetry of say Dylan Thomas, John Berryman, Sylvia Plath, and Anne Sexton in that it does intend to lead you somewhere. Fuller's vision is sanely optimistic as is his personal example—he's seventy-nine and still going. He didn't drink himself to death, nor did he asphyxiate himself. For most of his life he's discovered and participated in the excitement of the universe. He's part of a synergistic system rather than an entropic one. When, in the twenties, things weren't going well for him, he contemplated suicide, but he was able to circumvent that possibility because he realized that he didn't want to rid the world of that useful body of experience. At this mythic moment in 1928, he decided that he really hadn't been doing enough with his given abilities, that he hadn't shaped them in a pronounced way, and therefore he took a vow of silence for two years. Ezra Pound made a similar vow *after* he had done his work, but as Fuller tells us, his own silent period came *before*. He wouldn't talk until he knew what he was going to talk about. That is, he allowed himself a literal period of time in which to think out his ideas. Presumably then, any one of his public talks is a unique embodiment of intellectual and emotional material given its basic confines during that vow of silence. Each time Fuller talks he recycles parts of the fifty-five hours of material he claims he owns. 385,000 words. The precise quantification is peculiar, but Fuller's claim is not unlike Pound's continual quoting of T. E. Hulme's adage, "All a man ever thought would go onto a half sheet of notepaper. The rest is application and elaboration."

David Antin has a similar potential. His expertise in a number of intellectual and aesthetic disciplines provides him with an extraordinary amount of material to recycle. I doubt that he's calculated mathematically the quantity he has at hand—that would be scientifically inhuman in his terms. And what, in fact, would be the measuring rod? Thus Albert Lord's notion of the "formulaic"—that an oral poet must have a stock of formulas at hand (not quite clichés as Lord has it, though I suspect they really are) in order to proceed—would strike Antin as overly mechanical. "It's just slang," he might say. Every human simply has "material" to which they can add or subtract bits and pieces while experiencing or even representing their reality. You might formalize it as human speech if you have certain things you intend, the occasion arises, and your mind's able enough. Each situation necessitates a drawing together of different aspects to yield a unique linguistic entity. Antin's early interest in translating Breton's poems suggests that he learned how important one's opening was if one were to continue: the structure of simulated oral rhetoric depended very heavily on the first line. The image poetry that he wrote in his own voice at the same time wasn't as appropriate to his latent artistic possibilities. He must have intuited this as, at about the same time, Ian Hamilton Finlay sensed that writing poetry in lines and stanzas was, for him, simply an unnatural language act. But like Buckminster Fuller, David Antin sat it out for a while, the intention being that he would complete a novel. He left New York City for upstate New York and when he returned (having abandoned the novel) he was in a different place.

Antin soon began laying the intellectual groundwork for a deliberate change. In late 1963 or 1964 he began defining things for himself publicly. The breakaway poem "Definitions for Mendy" was begun, apparently drawing partly upon life experience that had occurred much earlier. A new magazine *SOME/THING* (coedited with Jerome Rothenberg) presented a number of works by other poets very much concerned with defining first principles. Antin apparently wanted to articulate the metaphysics of his present situation before or as he was making art from that position. A piece entitled "SILENCE/NOISE" functioning as Antin's editorial statement in the first *SOME/THING* suggests that a reading of John Cage's *Silence* had been useful in establishing his own ground. There are some local parodies of Cage's manner but the typography is particularly interesting in terms of Antin's later development. He avoids punctuation for the most part and substitutes triple-spacing for periods and commas, although in this instance the left margin is held in respect. Cage's deployment of various typefaces within a single piece has also been noted, though Antin's insistent capitalization may derive from the "Landsend" section of Hubert Selby Jr.'s novel *Last Exit to Brooklyn* which appeared in 1964. Selby's characters shout at each other continuously and Selby renders this quality of speech by continuous capital letters. Antin is shouting because it's the only way to be heard over the noise. Noise being defined as imprecise understandings of reality which block out speech, the possibility Antin is concerned to preserve. It's a variant of the orthodox Cagean position. Antin now considers Cage's presence at that time as "a kind of major & beautiful obstacle in the path." Finally, that is, for Antin (being the kind of oral genius he is—a good talker who can get his points across) the act of telling another human something in a discursive fashion is an option he'd like to have. While regarding interactive art as a profound idea, Antin argues that the grounds on which the interaction is to occur must be carefully considered by the artist. There are silent intervals in "SILENCE/NOISE" apparently intended to push a reader from his accustomed path and perhaps to a partial self-realization. I suspect Antin deliberately eschews interactive possibilities within his recent improvised oral poetry. He casually invents throwaway phrases to occupy the potential silence while he turns the cassette over. While he's talking, Antin apparently doesn't want to make it easy for the listening consciousness to drift into its own progression of thought. He seems to want his talk to dominate consciousness like the unstoppable sequence of cinematic images on a screen in front of a viewer. Or, as the composer Philip Corner states, "His mind is in our mind, and it is music."

Within "SILENCE/NOISE" there are some mimetic counters to help persuade the reader. The noise of a bell literally intruding on one passage is, however, a bit too reminiscent of the recording of "Indeterminacy" made in 1959 by John Cage and David Tudor, though Antin's tone toward Cage's attempt to read each one of his ninety written stories in periods of one minute each, no matter the number of words, and simultaneously with portions of the Fontana mix and improvised sounds by Tudor, may be ironic. He directly objects to Cage's insistence that there's no such thing as absolute silence, though on my reading Antin isn't very convincing. "SILENCE/NOISE" concludes with a direct rejection of the premises of deep image poetry: "STATEMENT: I CAN CALL SPIRITS FROM THE VASTY DEEP QUESTION: BUT WILL THEY COME." I imagine Antin may have "socially" concurred in the confidence that profound things could be dredged up, but at bottom he was probably suspicious all along. The concluding sentences of this piece make his terrain quite clear:

THE FEELING THAT SOME/THING LIES OUT THERE THAT WE CANNOT LAY HOLD OF IS THE FEELING OF THE INADEQUACY OF THE EXISTING

ORDER IT IS THE DEMAND FOR A DIFFERENT ORDER THE CONDITION
OF POETRY THE NEED TO GAIN GROUND

"SILENCE/NOISE" was not that unlike two pieces titled "autobiography" and "autobiography 2." All three were written, just as Cage had written the ninety stories that constituted "Indeterminacy." However, Antin's works were much more distant from his ostensible life than Cage's stories, which apparently were the literary examples closest at hand. Antin, like Cage, claims for his autobiographical domain the experience of others which happens to intersect his own life but is not quite an integral part of it until articulated on paper. Indeed certain oblique references to real people in Antin's autobiographies are made much more identifiable when the source material arises for recycling in his recent talks. But the life experience infringing on these early autobiographical works is very condensed and abbreviated. There's a biographical statement on the last page of "autobiography" which is even more distant than the sections proper. He does use "I" within the text, though it's unclear if it's his "I." Antin's presence in the biographical statement is represented by a "he."

The Jamesian germs for his recent improvised talks were certainly in the air during the middle sixties. Antin might have witnessed some of the "happenings" that were performed in New York City. Setting a place and time for determinate and indeterminate events might have seemed a likely possibility for his own work. Judson Dance Theatre, which thrived during this period and to which Antin was attracted, allowed for improvisation and "normal" movement within a structure. But Antin took his first deliberate step toward the art of orally improvised talk because of the Boston Museum's interest in reviving the lecture format. If you teach, you might eventually be forced to lecture in order to get material across efficiently. But it's a hopelessly useless straight-jacket unless you contemplate exactly what you want to do with the inherited structure and how to deal with the audience. This early talk was entitled "In Place of a Lecture" and was recorded in 1968. His wife, Eleanor Antin, collaborated with him by reading a psychological case study about a man who divines water. There are three roles, each (after Cage) having its own typeface: the reading of the case study plus improvised commentary by David Antin and by Eleanor Antin. Apparently, the particular Cagean example in mind was the lecture-poem "Where Are We Going?

and What Are We Doing?" consisting of four different vocal lines which progress discontinuously. The tone of "In Place of a Lecture" is conversational—though it was rehearsed, takes were rejected, and so forth. The intention, unlike Cage's, is not to exemplify the overlapping or simultaneous quality of life experience but rather to articulate a discursive position, though at least partly by embodying the intention in process. Antin always displays an ego wrestling with an intellectual and emotional problem, rather than the ego's struggles to eliminate itself and to come into as close a relation to nature as humanly possible. Cage facetiously refers to a "will of the wisp concern for lucidity" in his lecture, but it would have been difficult to apprehend this concern in any of the moments when simultaneity of two or more voices was realized. Members of the audience often walked out, but Cage didn't particularly mind. As he states in the Foreword to *Silence*, "I don't give these lectures to surprise people, but out of a need for poetry."

David Antin would not have been as blasé—after all an educational lecturer originally intends to interest his audience in the subject toward which he takes an attitude. Instead of disrupting consciousness by simultaneous occurrences of speech, Antin wishes to create a continuous experience on three different planes. The particular case study has been carefully chosen—the Antins make use of a text (rather than an art-object in its own right as in the case of the "essay" on Jean Tinguely) for an art experience which is also a lecture. Within the overall structure, David Antin exemplifies a local instance of Lord's conjecture about the power a written text can have over an artist's consciousness. He asks his wife to substitute real names for the textual usage "the doctor" and "the diviner." Eventually she slips back into the original terms because of the printed text's overpowering presence while in front of her eyes. The chosen text has an intrinsic thematic relevance as well: the subject for scientific investigation is a diviner, whose processes are as intuitive and unfathomable as any artist. The distance and scientific objectivity of the investigator won't help if there is such an activity as divining. In addition, the Antins can't help but be sympathetic to activity occurring in what Buckminster Fuller would term the outlaw area, since the structure they themselves are working in is beyond the boundaries established for poetry by properly distanced and objective literary critics. The diviner, simply because he recognizes that his abilities are beyond the pale, feels that he has to come in for treatment of his symptoms, which David Antin must have thought analogous to the condition of artists in the present social structure.

Before committing himself to solo numbers, David Antin tried another collaborative piece with his wife, "The London March." It's the closest he ever comes to "domestic" poetry, and it doesn't hold up very well. The referents and the tone in which they're addressed date badly— the 1968 political campaign, Vietnam, and so forth. Antin is clearly attempting to be outrageous, but the statements he makes seem uttered because of their shock value. Unlike Cage, in this instance David Antin is not being usefully outrageous. I'm struck by the merely silly political radicalism. However, the ostensible text has an ultimately undefinable, shall we say artistic, character. David and Eleanor Antin are playing solitaire and that, in this piece, is the subject or topic. Using a card game as a prop seems only natural; when Buckminster Fuller began improvising orally in front of an audience he relied to a certain extent on physical models that he brought along with him. It's obviously difficult to revive oral poetry within a literate culture; the workers in the field need as much help as they can get. Albert Lord thought that it was impossible for a literate individual who expressed himself in writing to become an oral poet. David Antin is certainly trying to prove that Lord's premise (based on actual anthropological fieldwork) doesn't hold. I believe that to be one of the casually unstated motives for Antin's recent work.

Also, as David Antin becomes a more experienced oral poet, he gradually gives up the props that were necessary to extricate himself from the usual creative possibilities which, although natural for most of his contemporaries, began to feel more and more unnatural to him: writing or typing poems directly onto paper. At first, he must depend on a text established in advance, the knowledge that a take can be rejected if it doesn't satisfy him, and his wife as actress and audience. "The London March" advances beyond "In Place of a Lecture" on the path toward postmodern oral poetry in that the fixed text is given up. Though the chosen deck of cards also resists their encroachments upon it. They've physically used it up and it's about ready for their son, Blaise, who would tear it to pieces. But the deck of cards, like a piece of art, retains its unviolable presence. It might cooperate with human intentions, but only under certain conditions explored later on in this piece. Thus these two exploratory moves into the domain of oral poetry share a local intention to exemplify the implacable, unworldly, undefinable, inexplicable quality of art. As an "image," the deck of cards advances beyond the fifties' stereotype of the alienated artist retained in the "sick" diviner. In fact within "The London March" there's a considerable amount of domestic discussion about their personal situation during the fifties. If one was able to survive those bad times, it might be possible to achieve a positive attitude in one's art and life as the cultural situation improved in the sixties. David and Eleanor Antin purge the fifties within "The London March," although they aren't able to discard the ostensible prop within the piece itself and substitute self-initiated art activity. In fact, that may be the subtle point about their experience of the fifties—that pure acts of original genius are literally impossible as well as incapacitating when thought of as an ideal. Postmodern art requires props.

"In Place of a Lecture" and "The London March" were slightly theatrical, collaborative improvisations. David Antin stresses another occasion as if it were the true *figura* for the solo improvised talks which will constitute his forthcoming New Directions book *talking at the boundaries.* That is, the art critic Dore Ashton asked him to talk at Cooper Union. Antin deliberately concocted a bizarre title, "The Metaphysics of Expectation: The Real Meaning of Genre," to assist Ashton in publicizing the talk. He also entered the lecture hall at the appointed time without any notes or books, because he had in the interim realized that he could talk just as well about a set topic (a prop) without any additional materials at hand. In fact, the title had delimited a domain which he was investigating during that period of his life.

The Cooper Union "lecture" hasn't been published but in 1972 the structure was identified and labeled. That is, Eleanor Antin was directly responsible for his decision to claim these talks as poems and to devote himself almost solely to extending the possibilities of oral poetry in our time. After improvising a solo talk at Pomona, David Antin drove back to Solana Beach. He and his wife listened to the tape recording of his talk on the way. Eleanor Antin said, "My god, it's a poem." David Antin realized she was right. He had been talking as an artist for most of his life, but hadn't accorded this activity the status of art, possibly because it had seemed difficult to "fix" as an art object. Talking was the way he utilized his "artistic ability"; he was a "talking artist," not a "hunger artist." Now he could synthesize his training or preparation in a number of fields by speaking freely (as he always could) on appropriate topics. And by labeling these talks "poems" he might have a useful effect on those readers or listeners who were ready to be loosened up while perhaps shocking the more conservative in an ultimately beneficial way by the sheer quality of the intellectual "content" in these outlandish looking "poems." I mean, how do you define a poem if these "things" are poems? And that's the point. On the simplest level, perhaps carried to its extreme by Else von Freytag-Loringhoven, once one declares oneself a poet, any activity that one cares to label poetry (or more expansively, art) carries a certain kind of (personal) authority. Antin of course could point to the lines and stanzas with titles collected in books published by publishers of poetry as a secondary authority.

At this point, David Antin prefers to formalize occasions on which he's going to talk and call the talking "poetry." He doesn't keep tape recorders going continuously in hopes of expanding his "poetic output." Rather, he arranges for talks in front of a particular audience in a particular place on a topic usually chosen in advance of the actual occasion. Sometimes Antin does not choose to consider a formalized talking situation as a poetic activity—this is particularly the case of the question and answer period following his improvised solo performance. He taped that session after his Cooper Union talk and finally decided that the format was too clichéd for anything interesting to occur within it. That obvious an interchange was not art activity. John Cage had debunked this possibility in the late forties by preparing six answers in advance for any questions that might occur to an audience after hearing his "Lecture on Nothing." Antin was certainly aware of Cage's precedent, though his own procedure in a question and answer period is rather different. Cage wants a listener to explore things for himself. Antin will try to clarify a point for someone who asks a question, he will argue for what he believes at the present moment. And present moment is accurate—although Antin often seems to be shifting his grounds, he is actually arguing by example that no one with any sort of mental life thinks the same thoughts all the time. Improvised talks are not unlike venturing out on the ocean on an open raft; question and answer periods can be as stagey as a Jewish comedian on a luxury liner. Though not necessarily. Antin has recently been considering the radio talk-show format. During the summer of 1974 he improvised a talk on radio and then answered questions that the listeners phoned in. In this case he had a vague sense of audience, though since it was listener-supported radio Antin could make a few basic assumptions. The kind of questions which were phoned in suggested that listeners to this radio station had very short attention spans. Typically, one might listen to KPFA-Berkeley while cooking a five-minute egg. The monthly calendar didn't foster deliberate listening habits, on the basis of Antin's casual sampling. As a result of this experience, Antin intended to shorten the talk and expand the question and answer period when he performed on KPFA's sister station in Los Angeles.

When Antin transposes aural sounds on tape to carbon marks on paper, the question and answer period can suggest aspects of the orally improvised piece that weren't successful simply in argumentative terms and that might be extended or polished while transcribing. If one compares a finished transcript with the original tape, the specialized artistry of the process of transcription becomes evident. Transcribing isn't merely a mechanical act for Antin—a secretary couldn't produce the final form. Intuitive artistic decisions are made throughout the act of transcribing. The process by which Antin transcribes is certainly analogous to the way he "writes" poems or prose. The tape isn't inviolable, though an attempt is made to retain and strengthen what Antin terms its "striking force." Slang, his natural substitute for Lord's mechanical notion of the formulaic, is not cut out. Certain supporting details that he may have inadvertently forgotten during the original talk are inserted where appropriate. This is especially the case with regard to the stories or anecdotes which constitute a large percentage of the talks. Finally, he wishes to provide a reader who wasn't in attendance at the talk itself with a sense of the verification and fullness that the speaker's live presence yields, while at the same time compensating for the difference in the way the piece will be perceived when it can be read a number of times instead of heard only once.

Antin's tone toward his improvised talks is remarkable. I detect a casual challenge. One could listen to a talk as it was being articulated, read and reread it later in its printed form, trace the derivations of the form, put oneself through a similar process, or simply ignore the whole activity by cordoning it off in the visual arts and concerning yourself with "poetry, *proper.*" Antin has recrossed the boundary between two related forms of artistic activity in order to loosen up restricted definitions of poetry via the metaphysical drive of minimal and conceptual art while at the same time bringing back the sober intellectualism of the literary world at its best to the often vacuous and faddish world of the visual arts. He immediately raises the question: is what this man is doing "art"? The numerous "alienated" writers would certainly jump on his procedure in order to defend their techniques: certainly "writing" is a more arduous and agonizing activity than *this.* What you do is too *easy!* Of course they wouldn't think of extrapolating from Antin's practice themselves. And discovering how difficult it is.

As a reader of Cage, David Antin can't help but be amused by the financial arrangements associated with his improvised oral poems. All he needs is a formalized date, place, and topic, but he's paid as well. He begins "talking at the boundaries" by amusing himself with these topics, most especially the fact that his subject arrived on a voucher. It must have reminded him of Cage's marvelous story:

> One day while I was composing, the telephone rang. A lady's voice said, "Is this John Cage, the percussion composer?" I said, "Yes." She said, "This is the J. Walter Thompson Company." I didn't know what that was, but she explained that their business was advertising. She said, "Hold on. One of our directors wants to speak to you." During a pause my mind went back to my composition. Then suddenly a man's voice said, "Mr. Cage, are you willing to prostitute your art?" I said, "Yes." He said, "Well, bring us some samples Friday at two." I did. After hearing a few recordings, one of the directors said to me, "Wait a minute." Then seven directors formed what looked like a football huddle. From this one of them finally emerged, came over to me, and said, "You're too good for us. We're going to save you for Robinson Crusoe."

Commercial intrusions on the making of art in this culture are so transparent that it's useful to adopt a casually sardonic attitude toward such crassness. Though Cage's artistic procedures are much more rigorously formal than those of Antin, the younger man acknowledges Cage along with Gertrude Stein as the major innovators in twentieth-century literature, *for him.* The "Lecture on Nothing" and the "Lecture on Something," delivered in the late forties at the Artists' Club in New York City, are clearly very important for Antin's artistic evolution, even though they were written out and then read. Within "Lecture on Nothing" Cage indicates that he continues to talk in hopes that an idea will surface of its own accord, though the fact that he has written out his talk in advance eliminates this possibility for him. Antin has enough confidence in his "preparation" to assume that his ideas will literally surface as Cage suggests. Oddly enough, one might compare the formal relation between Antin and Cage to Pound's consideration of Whitman in "A Pact": "It was you that broke the new wood,/Now is a time for carving."

Within the "Lecture on Nothing" and the "Lecture on Something," Cage does offer local discussions of particular topics. Indeed, he later decided that the subject of the "Lecture on Something" was the work of Morton Feldman and the piece was published in an appropriate context. The one instance I know of in which Cage chose oral improvisation and documented the results in print is very curious. It's titled "Talk 1," and it was included in *A Year from Monday* which appeared in 1967. I'm reminded a bit of the methodology of "In Place of a Lecture" and "The London March." It's conceivable that David and Eleanor Antin might have paid a certain amount of attention to Cage's first venture into oral improvisation before moving in that direction themselves. Very simply, John Cage asked members of the Once Group in Ann Arbor to arrange for impromptu conversations with him during the public performance time they had set. Microphones would pick up the conversations (Cage had written out a long list of possible topics in advance) and disseminate them to the audience. However, the microphones were set in such a way (with Cage's approval) that the sound of the conversations was distorted and barely a few actual words could be heard. Mostly there was electronic "noise," or "music." Cage describes the occasion and documents the topics of conversation, arranging those topics visually as he remembered the original random arrangements of chairs. He has said he admired Fuller's improvised oral talks; it's curious that Cage has never seriously extrapolated from the precedent. I can't really account for his motives in obscuring improvised conversations on topics set in advance. Perhaps the mere act of formally improvised art is too egoistic for his blood. But in any case, Cage accepted the sounds of the environment as natural interference and even introduced deliberate interference in order to emphasize his point. Antin prefers to clear a space in which language can exist and potentially reach other users of language.

Preparation is a central issue for contemporary oral poetry. It looks easy but it needs a lot of practice. I lost my way a number of times in improvising this piece, though I had researched the subject thoroughly. Can you learn appropriate skills by going to art school and/or a writers' workshop? I doubt that there's any systematic way to prepare to be an artist of any sort. David Antin casually chanced upon improvised oral poetry; he had prepared to be a novelist and that was an alienating experience. It seems crucial to take into account innate abilities; Antin knew he was a good talker and finally was able to "capitalize" artistically on his knack for talking. There was a long gestation period, concluded by the bringing to consciousness of the artistic possibilities for talk. Antin isn't the only poet who has been experimenting with oral poetry during the sixties and seventies. Charles Olson's well-known *Reading at Berkeley* was a proto-performance piece, although Antin feels that Olson stumbled on the possibility and didn't really know what he was doing. Instead of merely reading his poems, Olson reacts to events and presences in the lecture hall, talks around his poems, and in the process articulates a political thesis about his position in the world and in the world of poetry. Herbert Kenny's interview, recently published in George Butterick's magazine *Olson*, suggests that Charles Olson gradually began to realize that a taped interview (rather than writing at a desk) might be an appropriate way for him to document his ideas. Who knows how far Olson might have gone in this direction had he lived on into the seventies. As it is, much of Olson's published work other than his poems consists of informal, semi-improvised acts like letters, lectures, lecture notes, and so forth. His former colleague at Black Mountain College, Robert Creeley, has been giving what listeners often term "campy" readings recently. After reading aloud ten or so times a poem that he's written, Creeley naturally gets tired of the simple act of reading in front of still another live audience. So he interrupts himself to comment on what he's read, comment on his situation, and so forth. One's attention shifts to Robert Creeley rather than to the "certified art-objects" he's made: to the body of work, rather than just the work. There's also the example of the Southwestern poet Larry Goodell who became very bored with the usual poetry readings he witnessed and decided to invent a theatrical structure for his own readings, incorporating costume changes and something resembling a ritual plot. Though Goodell apparently reads poems written beforehand (hence allowing little opportunity for verbal improvisation), his "act" requires a formal performance situation in order to exist, both for itself and for an audience, though the latter could make do with a videotape.

The ontology of Antin's improvised oral poetry is unusual, to say the least. A talk first exists as it is being articulated live by David Antin. The original aural experience can be simulated by listening to a tape recording of the talk proper. Since one can listen to any part or the whole talk any number of times, the audiotape is not merely a canned substitute for the original experience. It has an unfixed temporal existence of its own. Antin hasn't yet arranged, as far as I know, to have one of his improvised performances videotaped. Since he's worked with videotape before, I'm not clear about his reasons. The videotape would share certain possibilities inherent in the audiotape and at the same time compensate more adequately for the absence of Antin's human presence in the poem. The printed version is the most distant from the original act, but it's the most convenient in terms of the present distributional system for "art." Though Antin insists on unjustifying the "sacred" left margin and eliminating punctuation and capitalization in order to locate his oral poems in an unprecedented typographical domain, distinct from that of prose and poetry. But the printed "score" is almost as difficult to "retain" in one's mind as the other means of reproduction of the original talk. Oral poetry insists on the sequential quality of language in time—it never presents the illusion of being at all points instantaneously accessible to an audience. Each page of the typed transcript may present a unique spatial image, but each poem consists of a sequence of these spatial images whose primary insistence is not their spatial quality. The process has been delayed in print. Delayed, not fixed or frozen, just as Antin delayed his public appearance in print while the oral possibilities were being thought through. It wasn't a bad decision since to my mind he's about to emerge as the major poet of the seventies.

Joseph N. Riddel

From Heidegger to Derrida to Chance
Doubling and (Poetic) Language

"You have a quarrel on hand, I see," said I, "with some of the algebraists of Paris; but proceed."—Edgar Allan Poe, "The Purloined Letter"

I

American criticism has come to Heidegger, or he to it, very late, and for the most part by indirection. The detour produces a certain, inevitable distortion, like the itinerary of a translation, though it may be no more than the inevitable misinterpretation already posited in the Heideggerean hermeneutic. On the other hand, this lateness circumvents not a few historical distractions. While our philosophers have had to confront the politics as well as the "language" of Heidegger, literary criticism has been able to ignore the kind of resistances which, according to Jacques Derrida, mark in one way or another almost every "reading" of Heidegger in Europe—the political resistances which conceal deeper resistances, and reciprocally. Derrida remarks in various places upon the apparent obligation to begin a consideration of Heidegger with a kind of apologetics for the political and/or ideological contaminations that threaten his readers. We have been spared this for the most part, only perhaps because we have been spared a direct Heideggereanism.

But we have not been spared the problems of a certain historical seam-liness. What historians of modern thought have come to distinguish as two Heideggers (the existentialist-phenomenologist destroyer of metaphysics and the celebrant of poetic "dwelling"), we have received in a more or less single package of transcriptions which tend to suppress the difference, or at least to remove it as a primary concern for literary criticism. Beyond that question, however, another one arises. Presuming two Heideggers, even if one is continuous with the other, do the two lend themselves to a unified hermeneutical method? It is not my concern here to take up the question of this historical placing of an early and late Heidegger, and certainly not to consider the sameness and difference in any "evolution" of his thought.

The task here is much more modest—to remark the "place" of Heidegger in certain "projects" of literary criticism. But for this purpose, one cannot ignore that the commercial (Heidegger might say, technological) chance of his translation into English texts has provided his thought with a kind of interpretive framing—the appearance in the early fifties of parts of the Hölderlin book, combined with the more recent translations of Heidegger on language and poesis, bookending the earliest and basic text, *Being and Time.* Setting this historical dislocation aside, there is the other fact that whatever impact Heidegger has had on literary criticism comes not so much directly from his own critical writings, via comparatist critics alert to the intellectual dialogue in Europe, as by another indirection: the absorption of the Heideggerean hermeneutic into various European criticisms, from existentialism to the "criticism of consciousness" to structuralism. In particular, one would have to say that the so-called Geneva School, which has had an indelible impact on American criticism, again by a certain indirection, is situated in a critique of "consciousness" and "place" which is at the same time undergirded and undermined by Heidegger's early writing. But at the very moment that a "criticism of consciousness," with its phenomenological orientation, had begun to offer a fruitful alternative to American formalist and thematic criticism, another kind of formalism known as structuralism and directed explicitly at the "ground" of phenomenology, the priority of consciousness, had begun to be translated into a variety of American methodologies.

What has been missing from the American debate, however, except in the work of a few critics with deep continental roots, is the considerable history of hermeneutical thinking which has crisscrossed Europe in the last hundred years. At the center of that thinking has been the Heideggerean destruction of metaphysics, but no less the retrieval and reinterpretation of Hegelian and Nietzschean thought, the appropriation of psychoanalysis by philosophy, and the centering of criticism on the problematics of language opened up by the new linguistics. The history is familiar enough in its broader outlines, though for the most part the American critic's awareness of the dialogue between phenomenology and structuralism has been so foreshortened (condensed largely within the past decade) that the intellectual consequences of the confrontation have been repressed. The dialogue has come so late to the American academy that, with certain powerful exceptions, we find ourselves in a "poststructuralist" period without having suffered the rites of initiation into that which it has displaced. This can lead to superficial jokes about the abbreviated half-life of the Parisian element of ideas. It is disconcerting, after all, to be reminded that within a singular deployment of a hermeneutical method derived in part from Heidegger (and from Nietzsche and Freud), translated as a "destruction," or more precisely, "deconstruction" of metaphysics, we may find lumped into one grand "metaphysical" heap: not only Platonic idealism and Aristotelian formalism but all of the varieties of subjectivism from Descartes through Hegel and Nietzsche as well, which we recognize in one form or other of romanticism or dialectical thought; not to say phenomenology (which thought to escape the subject-object problem), existentialism, and even structuralism itself; and finally, even the deconstructors themselves (especially Heidegger). In short, all of Western (Heidegger called it onto-theological) thought, including even the thinking of the thinkers who have tried to "overthrow" metaphysics, are combined into a "deconstruction," as in the Derridean analysis, that only reveals the historical "net" of "white mythology."

Every "move" of this (non-)history of ideas surpasses and displaces a previous move which it appropriates, surpasses and displaces that which has no history itself, since it is coexistent not only with the history of the West but with the history of history (that is, the history of meaning) itself. In a succession of "moves" that now reveal something more like a game of chess (Derrida says, somewhere, played upon a multileveled board without bottom) than an advance, we experience the foreshortened history of ideas which culminate in a variety of attempts to "close" metaphysics and "overthrow" it, appropriate it, or, more radically, step outside it: Nietzsche's naming of Hegel as the end of metaphysics;

Husserl's dream to write its closure; Heidegger's reading of Nietzsche's will to power as the ultimate subjectivism; and the revival of the Nietzschean question of interpretation in the recent work of Michel Foucault, Gilles Deleuze, and, in a certain "advanced" sense, Jacques Derrida. Derrida, in fact, in an essay entitled "Les Fins de l'homme," calls this latest overthrow by the name of "France" or "French thought" (in contrast, obviously, to the closures of German thought, particularly Heidegger's).[1] Have we, in and through these names, arrived at the "end of philosophy" which Heidegger long since announced as Nietzsche's *capital* achievement? Have we, that is, arrived there by the disruption achieved in the Derridean deconstruction of Heidegger's destruction? The question, which could be made portentous, is obviously beyond our asking here. But a more modest question can be posed. Translated over into a more limited field, what does this "deconstruction of metaphysics," or what does deconstruction as a method, portend for literary criticism which in one way or another has to embrace all the assumptions of an "aesthetic" that is part and parcel metaphysical, an aesthetic which assumes the indissoluble relation between poetry and truth, and thus privileges form, consciousness, and even "poetic language" itself? In one way or another, as Derrida has indicated in a series of essays,[2] literature is considered a metaphor (for) (of) truth, of meaning or sense, or is inflated into the kerygmatic utterance of the single "word" which all metaphysical thinking in one way or the other pursues as its lost origin.

Geoffrey Hartman has recently posed the desperate question (or is it a plea?) for the humanist "crisis" of our time: "Is it too late, or can our age, like every previous one, protect the concept of art?"[3] (One deploys "crisis" in quotation marks, mindful of Paul de Man's alignment of the terms "crisis" and "criticism" as nearly interchangeable.)[4] Art, of course, is a "concept" and *as such* takes its meaning within the horizon of the very metaphysics which is under attack by those who would save art from metaphysics. The fact that Hartman's question (rhetorical) is posed most desperately in the face of the "baroquely elaborated asceticism of the School of Derrida" is revealing, for it is a plea (almost certain to have a rippling or doubling effect) to maintain the fiction of "self-presencing" even in the face of a questioning which forces his recognition that the fiction is only itself a simulacrum. Hartman's plea may sound Heideggerean in urging a return to "wonder" and therefore to an "authentic" art which will preserve us against an inauthentic (ascetic) (deconstructive) thought. And it may well share something with the early Heidegger, though with a difference which is of no point here. Heidegger surely does make a last, late defense of the "concept" of art, displacing as it were the classical conception of representation (which Hartman, following his master Auerbach, has reappropriated) with another (presencing), but in no way moving beyond the implication of art in the concept presence, as Derrida has repeatedly shown. Is Derrida, then, the great disenchanter, who in making a game of the concept has placed the concept *hors jeu?* that is, declared it offside? Has Derrida's disruption of the "play of language," which Heidegger so eloquently proclaims as "bound to the hidden rule"[5] that commands the reciprocal difference of poetry and thinking and thus governs *aletheia*—has Derrida's "play," by revealing the "hidden rule" as the law of all metaphoricity, destroyed the concept of art and perhaps given us back "literature" (again, in quotation marks)? In a way (not Heideggerean) this essay will concern itself with the different paths broken by this figure of language's "play" in Heidegger and Derrida, since it is within the parentheses of these names that the future of the metaphor "(poetic) language" (as an illusion?) turns (tropes).

II

Even for the literary critic, the basic Heidegger text remains *Being and Time*,[6] appropriately incomplete, almost a pre-text to a writing that would appear in another, fragmentary form, primarily as "lectures" or "essays." *Being and Time* is, in a sense, a clearing of obstacles (classical ontology) in a path that will lead "to" language—a methodology which destroys by overcoming, that is, reappropriating. But it has turned up in literary criticism in a number of ways in-different to its methodology: as an existential analytic, as a text of modern "thematics," with its identification of care, anxiety, fallenness, being-toward-death, being-in-the-world, and so on, the themes, in short, of a phenomenology. Its method, however, has tended to undermine "thematics," which is always tied to the ontology against which the book was directed. Thus Heidegger begins with a hermeneutic already situated within a "tradition" of conceptualization and proposes to clear that "history" as a way of gaining "access" to the "primordial 'sources' from which the categories and concepts handed down to us have been in part genuinely drawn" (BT, 43). His delineation of a method which will "destroy the traditional content of ancient ontology" (BT, 44) proceeds through the matrix of a philosophical metaphoricity which presents itself as a "content." It is an exercise in language, in "translation," an etymological unweaving which finally comes to the point of declaring its own theme as the problematics of "language." (The English version of the text thus might appear as the translation of a text on translation, a text composed originally in the "possibilities for thought" Heidegger finds inherent in the German language. Heidegger thus employs this "power" to unveil the same originating "spirit" and "power" of the Greek language, long obscured and dulled in the metaphysical translation of pre-Socratic concepts.)[7]

As he protested in later texts, the "destructive" hermeneutic was easily misinterpreted, as a kind of etymological retreat in search of the archaic origin of conceptuality and even for the origin of language (see OB, 93—where he says that, despite hostile misinterpretations, the "destruction" did not "desire to win back the original experiences of metaphysics"). The clearing projected a reappropriation, not a philological archaism. The development of what would later become the poetics of Being, of the metaphysical forgetting of Being as the unconcealed, of *logos* as the reciprocal difference of *physis*, of the Same that marks the difference between thinking and saying, does seem implicit in the "destruction." Certainly the figure of "breaking" a "path," of opening the "way" to language, and therefore of achieving an "authentic" language or "articulating" the "proximity" of Being and being, is anticipated by a destruction which no more advocates a return to some ideal or primordial philosophizing than it suggests a full recuperation of some lost essence or truth. Heidegger's early discourse on his method locates his search clearly within the temporal horizon of *Dasein*, and thus within the "limits" of interpretation.

The "theme" of language emerges rather late in the first section of *Being and Time*, and then as language in general, or more accurately, as the speech or discourse of "interpretation" through which *Dasein* discloses itself. The interpretation of Greek ontology uncovers the "definition" of *Dasein* as that "living thing whose Being is essentially determined by the potentiality for discourse" (BT, 47). Language as such becomes the relation of the temporal unfolding of the Being of *Dasein*. Thus when Heidegger finally arrives at language as "theme" (*BT*, 203), he must preoccupy himself largely with a "destruction" of the concept language as the "deposited" understanding of historical knowledge (*Gerede* or "idle talk"), but reserves the privileged concept of speech or discourse as the "structure" of *Dasein*. As Derrida reveals in a "reading" of Heidegger's famous footnote on time (see *BT*, 500), this early Heideggerean separation of the authentic and inauthentic, of the primordial and the derivative, of discourse as the structure of the Being of *Dasein* and "idle talk," of *Verfallen* as the passage from one temporality to the other, constitutes a reappropriation of metaphysics: "Is there not at least some Platonism in the notion of *Verfallen?*"[8] If the "destruction" suspends nostalgia, as Derrida indicates elsewhere, and repudiates the dream of some recovery of archaic concepts, it produces on the other side of nostalgia the figure of the potential return of presence, a figure that always effaces itself, producing in Heidegger a kind of metaphysical "hope," the "quest for the proper word and the unique name."[9]

The "destructive" method of *Being and Time* employs a hermeneutical violence or a systematic interrogation of the onto-theological concepts which reside within and govern the structure of Western thought: particularly the concepts that define the relation between Being and beings. Thus the crucial concept of "time." This interrogation differs from "understanding," as Heidegger presents it in Section 32 of *Being and Time* (pp. 188 ff.), in the sense of a "development" that overthrows the concept understanding. The development is disruptive—a disruption of any significance that may be presumed to inhere in the already interpreted (the present-at-hand), and thus disruptive of the habit of imposing significance upon the present as if that significance were immanent in the thing. Interpretation as reappropriation is grounded in understanding, but always goes beyond it, breaking the interpreted free from its circumspect context of involvements. Interpretation always involves a putting in question, the assumption of a point of view (not in this case subjective); the displacement effected in interpretation is a kind of "articulation," an assertion that communicates, and thus a "re-telling" that is shared with Others (sometimes viewed as a theory of intersubjectivity). Interpretation is therefore grounded in what Heidegger calls "fore-having" (*Vorhabe*, or "what is before us" or "what we have in advance"), "fore-sight" (*Vorsicht*, or "what we see in advance"), and "fore-conception" (*Vorgriff*, or anticipation, "what we grasp in advance"). This Heideggerean foreplay as anticipation disrupts the concept of the a priori. It presents the present-at-hand to be interpreted as the already interpreted, as already appropriated in the structure of discourse that is at the same time originary and fore-structured. Language is always involved in interpretation, in an always incomplete disclosure.

For literary criticism this projection of the "fore-knowledge" may be the literary text itself, as Paul de Man has argued—and thus what de Man interprets as authentic or literary language is that language which has already achieved the highest form of "self-understanding" or the fullest possible interpretation (a kind of totalized understanding).[10] This "text" is situated in a "context," a language within language, a text which is at the same time concealed and unconcealed, an interpretation demanding interpretation. Every interpretation already presumes a meaning (or "operates in the forestructure," as Heidegger writes), but more significantly, it presumes a point (a proximity) between the concealed knowledge of the text and that knowledge which interpretation can disclose: "Any interpretation which is to contribute understanding, must already have understood what is to be interpreted" (*BT*, 194).

Heidegger's hermeneutic circle, however, is not a vicious circle, not closed. It is a circle which in its approximation of closure allows the text to become fully disclosed, though such an ideal disclosure would also lead to a disappearance or effacement of the text as a fore-structure.[11] Thus the hermeneutic circle, though inescapable, is liberating. It embraces the limitations of the "existential constitution of Dasein" (*BT*, 195). "What is decisive," Heidegger writes, "is not to get out of the circle but to come into it the right way," by a deliberate process of determining the fore-structure; for once the circle is defined as the potential for interpretation, we discover that it hides within itself a "positive possibility of the most primordial kind of knowing" (*BT*, 195). But as de Man further indicates, the possibility of a full disclosure, or an ideal commentary, is already denied. Interpretation bears within its structure an always deferred end.

At the point in *Being and Time* where assertion as predication and communication become the way of "methodological foresight," Heidegger introduces language as his "theme *for the first time*" (*BT*, 203), language "which already hides in itself a developed way of conceiving"

(*BT*, 199). Language here is the structure of *Dasein*, and not yet, as it will become, the "house of Being," poetic language. But even here, language as discourse is identified with the presencing of speech and not the secondariness of writing: "*The existential-ontological foundation of language is discourse or talk*" (*BT*, 203). Talk as communication is always about something, but this something is not simply a thing explained or defined: "What the discourse is about is a structural item that it necessarily possesses, and its own structure is modelled upon this basic state of Dasein" (*BT*, 205). Language is the structure of Man.[12] (At this point in the text, page 202, Heidegger projects the full development of the question of Being in a later section, which he did not write, except in the sense of the later fragments, essays, lectures on language as the "house of Being.") But language is not the ontological structure of man as subject. As Heidegger indicates in the "Letter on Humanism," the "proximity" of man and language confirms the proximity (nearness) of man and Being, not in the sense of two existences but in the sense of their sharing the same structure of presencing. In *Being and Time*, however, the particular nature of poetic language is defined as a very special form of communication: "In 'poetical' discourse, the communication of the existential possibilities of one's state-of-mind can become an aim in itself, and this amounts to a disclosing of existence" (*BT*, 205).

The seeds of a phenomenological poetics lies within this kind of "possibility," though "state-of-mind" here is not pure consciousness or cogito, but a consciousness of consciousness, an interpretation of consciousness as projected in the structure of language. In the later Heidegger, poetry will become the purest mode of interpretation of poetry because as the primal form of discourse or talk it is a disclosure of the "structural item that it necessarily possesses." The destruction of metaphysics, then, clears the way for the later meditations on the "way to language," by a discourse that reveals the structure hidden within "idle talk" or received historical understanding. As a method, the "destruction" can only be the reverse form of the later interpretation of poetry or "authentic" language, since as an interpretation of the "inauthentic" it is an interpretation of the world as "text," as fallenness, the "world" as already interpreted. The destruction makes way for "thinking," and for a kind of interpretative commentary which is reciprocal with the "saying" of poetry, with poetry as originary naming.

It is the status of the "language of Being," or language which situates the "nearness" of man and Being, that has been the object of Derrida's most severe questioning. (As he puts it in "Les Fins de l'homme," this "proximity" does not mark the relation between two ontological beings but between the "sense" of being and the "sense" of man—a kind of security that today is being displaced by a thinking that announces the "end of man" to be implicit in the language of Being.)[13] And ironically, as Heidegger has moved more and more toward the prophetic and oracular celebration of a "poetic" language as the "house of Being," and man as the "shepherd of Being," *Dasein* has tended to be displaced, and with "him" the structural model of discourse as "communication." Heidegger's later method, fully embracing poetic language as originary speech, has become increasingly less useful for literary criticism. Paul de Man, for example, has been one of the subtlest interpreters of Heideggerean hermeneutics for American criticism, arguing for the privilege, the "authenticity," of "poetic language."[14] But he stops short of embracing the "prophetic poeticism" of the later Heidegger.[15] Instead, he begins with Heidegger's interpretation of the "positive possibility for the most primordial kind of knowledge," which is hidden within language and derives from it a view of the irreducible doubleness of "literary language," which he can accommodate to even the most severe poststructuralist critiques of Heidegger.

De Man's interpretation of "literary language" as that which forever names the void lying between sign and meaning derives from Heidegger's nonexpressive view of a discourse that names the "existential possibilities of one's state of mind," in the sense that it always names the difference of understanding, of mediation. Thus literature, for de Man, always names itself as "fiction." It is the fore-knowledge of our understanding of the special nature of language. For de Man as for Heidegger, literary language is never self-deceived about the problematic that opens between the word and the thing; though unlike Heidegger, de Man will not prefigure what literary language does name, the void, as the site of an emerging "truth." De Man is a negative Heideggerean, like Maurice Blanchot. The privileging of literary language for de Man is not derived from its power of unconcealing but lies in its resistance to self-mystification, its refusal to name presence and its repeated naming of distance that is "nothing." (Perhaps de Man's use of "literary" language rather than "poetic" language is one evidence of this difference; he comes close to identifying literature with Derrida's rhetoric or grammatology rather than with Heidegger's presencing speech.)[16] For de Man there is the "void" rather than "proximity" or the "site." The "authenticity" of literary language lies in its persistent naming of itself as "fiction," and thus of its unique double function as the origin of the "self" and the naming of the self's nothingness, the naming of the "subject" as a necessary function.

III

De Man, then, begins as a "critic of consciousness" intent on putting that criticism within definite parentheses, marking the limits which govern the strengths (the blindness and insight) of the phenomenological critique. For de Man there can be an authentic criticism as well as an authentic literature, so long as that criticism is oriented toward the literary text as a kind of foreknowledge, as a totalized understanding of the absolute fissure between language and what it is presumed to name or to disclose. Inauthentic criticism, on the other hand, idealizes or mystifies poetry. And Heidegger's late "prophetic poeticism" is for him a form of this self-mystification.

De Man's reappropriation of Heidegger is not offered here simply as one form of American mistranslation, but because it points up some of the possible directions criticism takes from Heidegger's overthrowing of metaphysics. But de Man's interpretation of "literary" language as authentic does not derive solely from *Being and Time*; it comes as much by way of some intermediary texts. Both Blanchot's hermeneutics and de Man's move by way of the insertion of the "nothing" into the Heideggerean critique, the "nothing" of "What Is Metaphysics?" which is conceived as the "pure 'Other'" and as the "veil of Being." Heidegger's own philosophical "turn" (*Kehre*) from language as the structure of *Dasein* to language as the "house of Being" depends on his thinking of the abyss and thus on the thinking of "nothing" as a productive principle.

The consequences of this for his thinking of the nature of language is revealed in another early lecture, "The Origin of the Work of Art" (first read in 1935),[17] a deconstruction of the concept aesthetics as it is implicated in classical ontology. Though a bridge to the later thinking of poetry as the presencing of presence, the essay has not yet adopted the full-throated kerygmatic tones of the later meditations, perhaps because the essay's concern is as much with the "work" as "thing" as with the problem of origins. Still, Heidegger's ultimate concern is with art as truth (*aletheia*). Therefore, the opening of Being through language, while set against the metaphysical concept of the "subject" as origin and so against all theories of art as expression or representation, is presented as a metaphorical "rift." This is not the basic dualism of a subject become exterior, or an idea fallen into form, but the double nature of unconcealedness. Metaphorically, Heidegger presents this rift as between "earth" and "world," between the closed and the open, opposites always in conflict, reciprocal differences: "Truth is un-truth, insofar as there belongs to it the reservoir of the not-yet-uncovered, the un-covered, in the sense of concealment. In unconcealedness, as truth, there occurs also the other 'un-' of a double restraint or refusal. Truth occurs as such in the opposition of clearing and double concealing" (*PLT*, 60). One recalls the figural "place" of the poet in the Hölderin essays, situated in the "time" of the "double-Not" (need) of the old gods who have disappeared and the new ones who have "not yet" come.

The "rift" is a "between" that is a "measure." The conflictual situation of "earth" and "world," which seems to anticipate the later redefinitions of *physis* and *logos* in *An Introduction to Metaphysics* and elsewhere, is a "figural" place—the place as figure, the figure as place. "Createdness of the work means: truth's being fixed in place of the figure. Figure is the structure in whose shape the rift composes and submits itself" (*PLT*, 64). In the later essays, this place of poetry's opening will be presented figurally (as the "house of Being" or "bourne of Being," etc.), but a figure that is already doubly effaced and rendered as the Being of language (beyond metaphor). In this essay, the figure is double-faced, a Gestalt, a form of writing. Thus Heidegger opens up the possibility of a "figural" analysis of the kind proposed by de Man, in which the "rift" of the figure is the nothing it names, the distance between sign and meaning. But in Heidegger the figure is the "appearance," as opposed to the "expression," of truth. Language now appears as something other than the vehicle of communication: "language is not only and not primarily an audible and written expression of what is to be communicated. It not only puts forth in words and statements what is overtly or covertly intended to be communicated; language alone brings what is, as something that is, into the Open for the first time" (*PLT*, 73). Thus the reification of poetry as "inaugural naming."

In the same gesture, language for Heidegger is turned into a figure for some primal signification: "Language is not poetry because it is primal poesy"(*PLT*, 74); that is, poetry is the secondary sign, words, in which a primary language, poesy, takes its place. The primal is not the primitive but the originating. Art is historical for Heidegger in the sense that it reinvents the beginning of history as an opening. It is an appropriation and an overthrowing of the historical, and thus an original beginning (origin as *Ursprung* or "primal leap"). Poetic language overthrows "actual language," of which it is the origin; yet in its appearance it doubly effaces itself. Poetic language cannot be analyzed and criticized as a system of signs, but only prompted to bespeak itself. Veiled in a figural shape that has already disrupted the metaphoricity of actual language, it speaks of Being as at once inside and outside of metaphor. It introduces us to a "history" that holds out the hope for some full recovery of presence, as Derrida indicates in "La Différance," pointing to the evocation of "the first word of Being" in "Der Spruch des Anaximander." To "find a single word, the unique word," is the possibility harbored in "every language."[18]

Poetic language, then, portends a text that overthrows its own temporality. (Poetic) language is a metaphor of that which is the "author" of all metaphor, the nonmetaphoric Being. It is the "first word" without which the origin of language, Being, could not have its Being. Thus Being must also be metaphoric, already inscribed in the system as the name of the origin of the system—a system in Heidegger's case which fully declares itself as "language." (See Derrida's discussion of philosophical metaphorics in "La Mythologie blanche.")[19] Heidegger admits to the "mystery of language" which "admits to two things": "One, that it be reduced to a mere system of signs, uniformly available to everybody . . . ; and two, that language at one great moment says one unique thing, for one time only, which remains inexhaustible because it is ordinary" (*WICT*, 191–92).[20] The first recalls the "idle talk" of *Being and Time*, or "actual language," but even these "signs" do not submit to the materiality of linguistic description. Both written language and acoustical sounds are for him "abstractions." "Words" are "well-springs" (*WICT*, 130), and they can be named only metaphorically. They must be repeatedly "dug up." Thus poetic language is the excavation of language by language.

This operation, the gift of Being, can only be accomplished metaphorically: one can only dig in a "place." Things only bloom in a "field": "the saying [of poetic utterance or authentic thinking] *speaks* where there are no words, in the field between words" (*WICT*, 186). The remark comes in regard to a commentary on a text of Parmenides and emphasizes the "paratactic" grammar of this pre-Socratic style of thinking, including the significance of the graphic sign of punctuation, the colon. But contrary to the reading of such signs in modern linguistics or grammatology, Heidegger reads them as figural measures of a saying which speaks in silence. Thinking and saying *speak* in a "place" marked figuratively by the sign, but they speak a "proper word" to which "words" are related as Being is related (or articulated) to beings. Writing, or "script," on the other hand, is for Heidegger a near total repression of the "saying" of speech. Writing of Nietzsche, and of the sometime need to resort to writing, Heidegger remarks on the Nietzschean style as a generative violence directed against philosophical writing. If originary saying is related to speech, a response to some "call" or "appeal," there are occasions, says Heidegger, when only a "scream" will answer the "call." But the "scream" is difficult to achieve in writing:

Script easily smothers the scream, especially if the script exhausts itself in description, and aims to keep men's imaginations busy by supplying it constantly with new matter. The burden of thought is swallowed up in the written script, unless the writing is capable of remaining, even in the script itself, a progress of thinking, a way. (*WICT*, 49)

The privileging of speech over writing (speech as presenting-saying and not speech as acoustic sign, another form of writing) is, as Derrida points out, persistent and massive in Heidegger and is consistent with the valorization of presence which entangles him in the very metaphysical network he has so methodically overthrown and announced as ended. (Derrida thus marks the difference between the "closure" of metaphysics and the "end" of philosophy, as Heidegger announces it in his book on Nietzsche.) More of this later. But at this point it is necessary to consider the consequences for literary criticism of the suppression of the "text" explicit in Heidegger's view of (poetic) language. Quite obviously

---

the idea of a "text" has always included not only the idea of totalization but also the economy of the signifier—the "text" not only as scripted writing, as Derrida says, but as a "re-mark," a re-inscription of a previous discourse and its conceptualization. "Text" is therefore itself a metaphor for a totalization of elements which reveals itself as a metaphor of this totality.[21] For Heidegger, poetry or even "literature" cannot be this kind of re-marking, since it is original, the original speech of the (not-yet-disclosed) "proper word."

"Script," which smothers the "scream," is for Heidegger a kind of second-order language, representational, unless the style can overcome itself. Heidegger's example of Nietzschean writing which overcomes the "script" is an "aphorism," the writing of a poetic utterance which overthrows sense or ordinary understanding. The writing-speech of aphorism is therefore the utterance of the "one thought" that every true thinker repeatedly thinks, or the "one unique thing" that authentic language says "at one great moment" (WICT, 191). It is not rhetoric. Like the "single poetic statement" which at once rises from and remains concealed in the "site" (as "source") of every poet's saying, and "always remains in the realm of the unspoken" (OWTL, 160),[22] (poetic) language is a silence which speaks Being but has no being. The "source" of metaphor, the "site" of figure, it is nonfigural. And its origin is "natural," in the sense of *physis*. The poetic text, then, is only a kind of veil, or the rhythm of a passage, a trace of Being, a metaphoric detour which at the same time turns the "thinker" of the text toward the "site" and prevents his looking directly into its full light. (Poetic) language cannot be destroyed, or appropriated, in the sense of overthrowing the metaphysical concept; any interrogation of it must take the form of a "dialogue," a "poetic dialogue," that emerges in the "reciprocity between discussion and clarification" (OWTL, 160).

There is an "authentic" criticism, then, or an ideal commentary as de Man says, already posited in Heidegger's early writing, that emerges as a proximal possibility in his later work. If poets think the "holy," the true dialogue would be like a "conversation" between poets. On the other hand, there is the "dialogue" between "thinking" and poetry (as "saying"), or between two different kinds of discourse which share a "proper" "relation to language." But even in the conflictual reciprocity of this dialogue, Heidegger returns to the caution of the Hölderlin essays, that the critical statement must open a way to the pure utterance of the poem and in that act annihilate itself or become the silence of the "unique word": "in order that what has been purely written of in the poem may stand forth a little clearer, the explanatory speech must break up each time both itself and what it has attempted. The final, but at the same time the most difficult, step of every exposition consists in vanishing away together with its explanation in the face of the pure existence of the poem," allowing the poem to "throw light directly on the other poems" (*EB*, 234–35).[23]

Taken as a description of the critical discourse, this kind of statement might point toward a criticism which begins with individual poems but evolves into a study of the unitary metaphorics of the poetic canon, a criticism of consciousness as the exploration of the one poet's site. But this figural site is the site of all authentic poets, the site of "poetry" itself. Commentary, Heidegger writes, should ultimately sound like the "fall of snow on the bell" (*EB*, 234), the figure itself derived from Hölderlin, from authentic language. In the poetic fragment from which it is drawn, the metaphor of snow falling on a bell is a figure of dissonance, of that which smothers the "tune" of the bell which calls one to meals, to sustenance. (We might as well vulgarize Heidegger here and say that he considers most explanation a snow job.) Heidegger's deployment of this figure appears in a "Prefatory Remark to a Repetition of the Address," itself an explanation of his own repeated "smothering" of the pure self-interpretation of poetic language, and is thus a fore-structuring of his own "lecture" as that which will vanish in his utterance, re-membering the "poet" in the silence of its own end. Heidegger's essays on poets and poetry regularly "end" in the poet's words, with the poem which is the first and last word. Heidegger's dialogue with Hölderlin turns out to be an effort in self-annihilating "thinking," an apology for the reappropriation of pure "saying" in the explanation which transcribes, translates, and transgresses poetic language, turning it into its other. Thus Heidegger's "Preface" turns his after-word into a fore-word that fore-warns of its own dulling of the pure tones of the "holy." It marks off the critical text as a by-path to the poetry which has already explored the by-path of poetic homecoming.

The "Preface," then, repeats the essay's own theme of incompleteness, of the poetic deferral of the naming of the "holy." It repeats for us the poet's theme of poetic foreknowledge: "his knowledge of the mystery of the reserving proximity" (*EB*, 269). This site of "proximity" or place of mystery is the place of the "double-Not" (*EB*, 289). The "mystery" is not revealed by the poet, but is only protected. This "mystery" as "reserving proximity" is the mystery of language, its generative power or Being, that must be protected from writing. The poet, whose "singing" still lacks the proper word or "naming word," offers a "song without words," a song which holds open, by deferring, the "end" in which the "others" (the non-poets) may also have their "homecoming," the ultimate "understanding" of the proper word. As Heidegger interprets Hölderlin, the poet protects the "reserving proximity" so that the "others," those "of writing *and* of thinking," may always be directed toward the true source of language and not be sidetracked by its historical mis-adventures. The poet protects the "mystery" by calling to the others, by calling their thinking to his saying, thus re-membering the "community" of man.

IV

Derrida's critique of Heidegger's "metaphorics" takes not only the form of systematic questioning, but consists in itself of a methodological doubling of the "destruction," a strategy, as he warns, which must go beyond the fundamental "inversion" of basic concepts and mark a "divergence" which will prevent the conceptual reappropriation of those same concepts. Derrida finds the Heideggerean error to lie in this "destruction" which inverts and reappropriates, thus overthrowing metaphysics and reinscribing it fully within the thinking of presence. The question of the "resemblance" between their two methods—the "destruction" and the "deconstruction"—has compelled Derrida toward a statement on the nature of "écart" and "renversement."[24] Heidegger presents a problem for Derrida at every turn. He has been the subject of two essays in particular, but the "name" reverberates everywhere in the Derridean canon, as an example of the problematics involved in any metaphysical reappropriation or in any overthrow of metaphysics, not the least being the "inflation" of language and the relating of "literature" and truth in Heideggerean thinking.[25]

Derrida never underplays the difficulty of reading Heidegger, nor ignores the implications of turning a methodology against itself, of deconstructing the deconstructor. One might say, then, that Derrida *underwrites* Heidegger, in the various and contradictory senses of that word: to place the thinking of presence in italics, to become a signatory to the difference, to re-mark the metaphysical implications of writing an "end" to metaphysics, to submit Heidegger's valorization of speech to the mark of a *proto-écriture* which it tries to conceal, etc. Derrida's relentless questioning of the metaphysical hierarchy which places speech in a privileged relation to presence, and reduces writing to a secondary function, is literally an *underwriting* of the idea of a "poetic language," of language that claims to escape the double sense of the metaphoric.

In "La Différance," Derrida submits the Heideggerean text, "Der Spruch des Anaximander," to an extensive deconstruction, concentrating on the Heideggerean language of presence and the difference "between *presence* and *present*" (*SP*, 155–60).[26] The thrust of the Derridean critique inserts a double mark into Heidegger's attack on metaphysics which has, as Heidegger notes, "forgotten" the difference between Being and beings, Derrida submits the Heideggerean figure of the "trace" of the difference, which must be effaced in the appearance of being-present, to an irruptive discourse. What Heidegger calls the "matinal trace" (*Spur*) of the difference which effaces itself in the moment of Being's appearance, in order that Being might maintain its essence or its difference from beings, is also a figure analogous to what he calls the "mystery" of poetic language: the "difference between Being and beings" can be forgotten only if it is already "sealed in a trace that remains preserved in the language which Being appropriates" (quoted in *SP*, 156–57). Derrida's questioning of this "trace" traces it to its source in another language. In repeating the Heideggerean step, he disrupts the Heideggerean "way." The "trace" as "sustaining use" is a simulacrum of the name of Being, and not the appearance of the difference itself.

In this classic of deconstruction, Derrida interrupts the Heideggerean text in order to reveal that Heidegger's deployment of the concept "difference" reappropriates the metaphysical text it seems to disrupt; and in the same gesture, Derrida disrupts the thinking of hierarchical difference. "There is no essence of difference," he writes, and thus no "trace" or name for it that is not already a metaphysical inscription or another trace, the trace of a trace. Thus Derrida, who has already coined the name of "différance" as a trace of the concept difference which turns out to be a trace, a trace which has already effaced itself, provides a model of a critique which resists the reappropriation of the concept through inversion; he re-marks the divergence of a name that is not a word, not a concept, though it may simulate the concept (which is already a trace). (Derrida's neologism is *coined* in a manner to reveal the hidden functioning of priority in ontological concepts, wherein the phonetism of the letter "e" marks no "différence" from the letter "a," a *différance* marked only in writing.) Rather than examining a "text" for its concealed sense, or for its thematic differences which trace a hidden unity or promise a recovered word, Derrida inserts another language into the text, in order to reveal that the "text" is composed of different orders of signs and not signs which trace a single sense. The language of *différance* under*writes* the concept difference and renders it a "simulacrum" or "undecidable." It names the *name* of the difference, the word which is the name for all the possible substitutions for any of the commanding or privileged concepts which might govern the differences of the text—whereas Heidegger sees the metaphysical "forgetting" of the difference to be the determining movement of Being, and can thus promise in his own text what is always deferred in his interrogations of language, the ultimate overcoming of the difference of Being and being in the "proper name." But as Derrida concludes, the writing of *différance* reveals that there never was a "proper name" but only the "unnamable" play that produces "nominal effects," just as "the false beginning or end of a game is still part of the game" (*SP*, 159).

Now, it is not so much this interrogation of Heidegger which should instruct us here, as it is the Derridean thinking of textuality itself—though in this particular case, Derrida's critique of the Heideggerean "language of Being" is also a critique of the authenticity of poetic "speech." If poets are, as Heidegger wrote in "The Origin of the Work of Art," those who "sense the trace of the fugitive gods" and thus trace the realm of the "holy," they provide only traces of traces, and thus protect the "mystery" of the source (*PLT*, 94). "Language," which is "not poetry because it is primal poesy," is itself only a trace, a figural play of irreducible differences. Thus the expanding network of Heideggerean figures for present and presencing—site, house, bridge, etc.—might be analyzed as metaphorical traces of a word that is always already metaphorical, the name of the origin, the name that is already inscribed in every system as the "center." Language, for Heidegger, is the "name" of Being as presence, the name of naming. "Language" not only "gathers" the twofold, it is an already doubled metaphor. Heidegger features the double function of the *present* participal, at once noun and verb, as the temporal naming of Being—gathering, thinging, thinking, saying, bridging, dwelling, building, showing, relating, blooming, etc.

In *The Question of Being*, Heidegger speaks of authentic language as a "meaning-fullness." Its plenitude of sense is not an historical accumulation, but a "play" of unfolding, a "play which, the more richly it unfolds, the more strictly it is bound by the hidden rules" (*QB*, 105). The "play" of meaning is always commanded by an origin it can never fully name; the "meaning-fullness" of the word is determined by a rule that is fuller than meaning, by Being which appropriates that which in every appearance leaves it behind in bringing it to light. This is a "play" easily comprehended within the "tradition" in which we measure the depth of the work of art, a fathomless, resource-ful text which interpretation can never exhaust. Derrida, on the other hand, inserts into the thinking of the "text" and interpretation a more playful figure of "play," in which the production of meanings turns upon a meaninglessness, an absence of the commanding, originating word, and the play of the *supplément* which stands for that word (that center) in the text. In doing so, Derrida deprives us of literature in its relation to truth, only to give us back "literature" already in quotation marks, a text whose meaningfulness resides in its play of differences, including the insertion within it always of disruptive re-marks, other texts, signs that are not filled with meaning but are always already doubled and mark the double play of the text. Criticism begins with an insertion of a question into the opening provided by the text, into the double sense of the operative signifier; an operation which often consists of raising the illusory governing concept or "proper word" from the text in order to re-mark it, to mark its double sense and doubling function, and to trace its itinerary as a simulacrum. Thus Derrida's own (non-) concepts: *trace, différance, supplément, pharmakon, dissémination, écart, hymen, gramme*, etc., which he calls "undecidables" or "simulacra," words and concepts that are only the semantic mirage of real words and concepts, as if there were "real" words and concepts.

As example, we might point to the two complementary essays, "La Mythologie blanche"[27] and "La Double séance,"[28] which are both implicitly and explicitly deconstructions of the Heidegerrean principle of "thinking" and "saying." "La Mythologie blanche" is a rigorous interrogation of metaphor in philosophy; "La Double séance" is a systematic disruption of the "idea" of literature as truth, either as representation or as *aletheia*, at once a disruptive reading of an imaginative text (Mallarmé's *Mimique*) and of idealized or totalized readings of that text. Characteristically, Derrida's strategy is to approach one text through another, whether the second text is a reading of the first or not. The indirection or detour is consistent within the "nature" of all textuality— that is, a text is never self-sufficient or self-present, never in itself a totalization of meaning or a concealment/unconcealment of a unitary sense. "La Mythologie blanche" introduces the problematics of philosophical language through the imaginary dialogue of a "literary" or fictional text (by Anatole France), itself already a kind of parody of the philosophical dialogue. "La Double séance" opens in the "field" between a philosophical (Platonic) and an imaginative (Mallarmean) text, texts which in their way mark the opening and closing of metaphysics and in which is posed the question of the absolute reciprocal "difference" between two modes of "truth." This involves Derrida in an examination of various rhetorical strategies—including the placement and function of operational elements, both verbal and nonverbal, in the text, the deployment of the title, the use of epigraph, the function of grammatological marks. (The essay is the middle one in a "book," *La Dissémination*, which is introduced by a "Preface" about the function of prefaces, a preface with its own doubled title, "Hors Livre.")

The "central" text of "La Double séance" is Mallarmé's, the title of which already provides a *capital* instance of the question of representation and "what is represented?" But Derrida does not submit the work of "literature" to criticism. His "reading" is a re-marking of the text within other "readings" of it, in particular the impressive book of J.-P. Richard which incorporates the coherent thematic play of this one Mallarmé work into a totalized reading of the Mallarmé canon as an imaginary "world": a "world" or unity evident in the intricate play of thematic differences which dialectically unfold and enfold the unity of "consciousness" or "imagination." For Derrida, such readings of the thematic or semantic richness of work only reveal that the depth of the text is a semantic mirage generated by the play of heterogeneous signifiers which refuse to be commanded by any single element within (meaning) or without (author) the text. Thus Derrida deconstructs Richard's and other critical readings of Mallarmé by raising the textual undecidable, the "hymen," from its thematic role in order to show how it works as a grammatological function to disrupt the concept of mimesis named in the title and already displaced as an initiatory key to the text. It functions as a mark, a slash (/), and as a title with two faces; it functions always to disrupt the positioning of any representation that is not itself a representation of a representation. Thus it functions to upset the illusion that in literature there can be truth, or the "appearance" of an unrepresented in the represented, the concealed which is unconcealed yet hidden, a unity of consciousness or the "reality" of an imaginary "world."

There is nothing represented that is not already a representation, just as in "La Mythologie blanche" there is no pure or natural origin of metaphor which stands behind or beneath the play of traces, but only metaphorical play itself. Derrida's strategic re-marking of concepts, by a forceful inversion followed, as he says, by a divergence, is necessary to keep his own undecidables in play and to resist the overpowering tendency of the "names" to be reconceptualized. Thus Derrida's artful footwork of renaming his "positions" so as to avoid any one of his "names" falling into a position of initiatory concept: most obviously, the undecidable *écriture* which many critics of Derrida have tried to locate as his privileged position. (He has even been called a nominalist, even though nominalism is a classical form of representation, the privileging of the word-concept.) All of his undecidables recall, like a distant echo or a veiled shape, some etymological legacy which they at the same time *underwrite*, trace, and efface. Thus, the conflictual nature of the Derridean text inverts the Heideggerean conflict and diverges from it; Derrida's gap or break or hymen redoubles Heidegger's rift; his dissemination disrupts Heideggerean flowering.

Écriture is not the name for the physical mark of writing, but the doubleness of which the physical mark is always a sign—a sign that has no signified except another sign. Thus the productive function of *écriture* which, like *différance*, initiates by an instant re-play. The limitlessness of "literature" is not the concealed fullness of language, but its disruptive and temporalizing function. "Literature" is neither a full text nor an empty text, neither a presence nor an absence. There is no "literary language," not even in de Man's sense, for there can be no privileged language. Derrida's critique disrupts the classical play of difference which always begins or ends with one of the two terms in a "position" of "authority." "Literature" can be privileged, then, only because it is the purest function of the self-dissimulating movement of writing. "Literature" is writing—the "figure" of a productive function for which the produced text is only a simulacrum, a facsimile, a fac-simile, a "factor." The literary text is a play of textuality, not simply in the obvious sense that a "work" of art always originates in the historical field of predecessors. Its own play of differences mirrors its displacement and reappropriation of other texts, and anticipates the necessary critical text which must "supplement" it, insert into it the undecidable or raise the undecidable which is dissimulated in it as a unique word. The Derridean rhetoric names the double-play of chance as the (non-) law of "literature." Thus Derrida threatens to disrupt the whole cultural order which has given literature a "place" at the center because it could assume that literature was the *arche* and *eidos* of order. But then, he gives us back "literature" as the double-name of man, who makes metaphor, who interprets.

Derrida is a kind of Dupin, whose literary function he explores in a recently published essay, "Le Facteur de la vérité"[29]—a de-cipherer in pursuit of a letter which is always moving, always displaced, always doubled, always at hand and underhanded, an "author" who is already only the sign of another (pre-) text.

Dupin who:

observed them [the edges of the exterior of the letter] to be more *chafed* than seemed necessary. They presented the *broken* appearance which is manifested when a stiff paper, having once been folded and pressed with a folder, is refolded in a reversed direction, in the same creases or edges which had formed the original fold. This discovery was sufficient. It was clear to me that the letter had been turned, as a glove, inside out, re-directed, and re-sealed.

Dupin who: through the distracting ruse of some "pretended lunatic" reappropriates the letter and replaces it with a *"fac-simile* (so far as regards externals)," but with an inside which is a sign reappropriated from literature and marking its transgressions.

Dupin who: is the double of the narrator, shares the sign ("D——") of the thief, and is the double-name of author-interpreter-seducer, who cannot *write* either a beginning or end to literature, who cannot escape the circuit of the sign as the "factoring" (bearing, like a mailman) of a "truth" that never gets outside "literature," and is never fully delivered.

Notes

1. "Les Fins de l'homme," *Marges, de la philosophie* (Paris: Éditions de Minuit, 1972), pp. 135–36, 161. Translated as "The Ends of Man," *Philosophy and Phenomenological Research*, 30 (Sept. 1969): 31–57.

2. See, for example, "La Parole soufflée," *L'Écriture et la différence* (Paris: Éditions du Seuil, 1967), pp. 253–92; and "La Double séance," *La Dissémination* (Paris: Éditions du Seuil, 1972), pp. 199–317.

3. *The Fate of Reading, and Other Essays* (Chicago: University of Chicago Press, 1975), p. 107.

4. See "Criticism and Crisis," *Blindness and Insight: Essays in the Rhetoric of Contemporary Criticism* (New York: Oxford University Press, 1971), pp. 3–19. First published in 1967, this essay situates the present "crisis" in criticism, the challenge of structuralism to a criticism of consciousness or to a criticism which privileges the subject, within Mallarmé's pronouncement almost a century earlier of a "crisis" in poetry, and concludes that creative periods are always critical, marked by pronouncements of rupture, displacements, violent changes, discontinuities, etc., enacted upon and within received conventions. So, in any such pronouncement, the crisis lies in the criticism.

5. *The Question of Being*, trans. William Kluback and Jean T. Wilde (New Haven, Conn.: College and University Press, 1958), p. 105. Hereinafter noted in text as: *QB*.

6. *Being and Time (Sein und Zeit)*, trans. John Macquarrie and Edward Robinson (New York: Harper & Row, 1962). Hereinafter noted in text as: *BT*.

7. See *An Introduction to Metaphysics*, trans. Ralph Mannheim (New York: Anchor Books, 1961), p. 47.

8. "Ousia et Grammé," *Marges*, pp. 73–74. Trans. Edward S. Casey, in *Phenomenology in Perspective*, ed. F. J. Smith (The Hague: Martinus Nijhoff, 1970), pp. 54–93; see esp. p. 89.

9. "La Différance," *Marges*, p. 29. Trans. by David B. Allison as "Differance" in *Speech and Phenomena, and Other Essays on Husserl's Theory of Signs* (Evanston, Ill.: Northwestern University Press, 1973), pp. 129–60; see esp. pp. 159–60.

10. *Blindness and Insight*, pp. 30–31.

11. Ibid., pp. 30–31.

12. See Derrida, "Les Fins de l'homme," *Marges*, pp. 160–61 ("The Ends of Man," pp. 54–55), on this restoration of "humanism" as the determination of the "end" of man in the thinking of Being. The major thrust of the essay is a deconstruction of Heidegger's thinking of proximity. In his conclusion, Derrida offers a project of two

kinds of deconstructive thinking, and thus marks the difference between Heidegger's and his own. I will discuss this in the last section of the essay.

13. *Marges*, pp. 160–61 ("The Ends of Man," pp. 54–55).

14. *Blindness and Insight*, pp. 29–32, 76, and *passim*.

15. Ibid., p. 100.

16. See also Paul de Man, "The Rhetoric of Temporality," *Interpretation: Theory and Practice*, ed. Charles Singleton (Baltimore: Johns Hopkins University Press, 1969), pp. 173–209; and "Semiology and Rhetoric," *Diacritics* 3 (Fall 1973): 27–33.

17. In *Poetry, Language, Thought*, trans. Albert Hofstadter (New York: Harper & Row, 1971), pp. 17–87. Hereinafter noted in text as: *PLT*.

18. *Marges*, p. 29; *Speech*, p. 160.

19. *Marges*, pp. 247–324. Translated as "White Mythology," in *New Literary History* 6 (Autumn 1974): 5–74.

20. *What Is Called Thinking*, trans. Fred D. Wieck and J. Glenn Gray (New York: Harper Torchbooks, 1968). Cited in text as: *WICT*.

21. See Jacques Derrida, *Positions* (Paris: Éditions de Minuit, 1972), pp. 81–82, and *passim*. Parts of this text are translated in *Diacritics* 2 (Winter 1972): 35–43; and *Diacritics* 3 (Spring 1973): 33–46.

22. *On the Way to Language*, trans. Peter D. Hertz (New York: Harper & Row, 1971). Cited in text as *OWTL*.

23. *Existence and Being*, trans. Werner Brock (Chicago: Gateway ed., 1949). Cited in text as: *EB*.

24. *Positions*, pp. 73, 81; see *Diacritics* 2 (Winter 1972): 40–43. See also *Marges*, pp. 162–64 ("The Ends of Man," pp. 56–57).

25. See *De la grammatologie* (Paris: Éditions de Minuit, 1967), pp. 33 ff.; and references in footnote 2.

26. *Marges*, pp. 24–29.

27. Ibid., pp. 247–324. (See footnote 19.)

28. *La Dissémination*, pp. 199–317.

29. "Le Facteur de la vérité," *Poetique* 21 (1975): 96–147. This essay, translated in *Yale French Studies*, is a "reading" of the Lacanian "Seminar" on "The Purloined Letter," and thus a reading of the psychoanalytic appropriation of literature as truth. Derrida reads "The Purloined Letter" in and through the interpretations of Marie Bonapart and Jacques Lacan and in the context of Freud's reading of a "literary" text.

Gerald Gillespie

Scientific Discourse and Postmodernity
Francis Bacon and the Empirical Birth of "Revision"

Good faith demands that broad speculations about culture be so labeled. Admittedly, this paper speculates about matters which may seem at best tenuously related: on the one hand, the emergence of scientific discourse, its influence, and its originally antitraditionalist program in the Anglo-American world; on the other hand, the revaluative, transformational, and apocalyptic thought of postmodernism. My purpose is not to erect a grandiose thesis, such as that repeated lapses of cultural memory enable us "unconsciously" to imitate an earlier key set of ideas and strategies vis-à-vis our own tradition. Yet, since "reformation" and "renaissance" were long ago elevated as guiding concepts of Anglo-American culture, the process of change may well have required eventually that we forget we are repeating a pattern, in order to forestall a genuine rebellion against the sustaining "myth" of transformation itself. For example, resistance to further questioning of the epochal transformation of culture soon appeared in Protestantism, which from the start developed its own conservative strains. Moreover, if to some extent today we merely imagine we are rejecting and superseding a heritage (which, paradoxically enough, is characterized by "progress"), then it follows that when the logic of our denial of tenacious paradigms does indeed conduct to antinomian or nihilistic obliteration of imposed imperatives and inherited traits, such incidents of extremism, too, may fit the overall historical pattern.

William Spanos cogently expresses a ruling postmodern bias when he endorses a sweeping deconstruction of culture in his paper on "Breaking the Circle: Hermeneutics as Dis-closure":

despite the alternations between its idealistic and realistic manifestations—and the significant exceptions to its binary structure—the Western literary tradition from the classical Greeks to Proust, Joyce, Yeats, and Eliot has been by and large, and increasingly, a metaphysical or logocentric tradition motivated by the Will to Power over existence.[1]

"Willful objectification of the 'mystery' " and "spatialization of the temporality of being" threaten suffocation and petrification, whereas

destruction or deconstruction of the Western literary heritage . . . promises the paradoxically liberating double retrieval (*Widerholen*). I mean the dis-covering not only of texts "buried" in and by the hardened tradition (i.e., the "meaning" for us in the present), but also of a stance before the Western literary tradition, especially as it has been formulated by the ontotheological New Critics and Structuralists, that opens up the possibility of a perpetually new—a postModern or an authentically modern—literary history, a history that, in focusing on disclosure, both validates the inexhaustibility of literary texts (i.e., literary history as mis-reading) and commits literature to the difficult larger task of "overcoming metaphysics"—a history, in other words, that puts literature at the service of being rather than being at the service of literature.[2]

That is certainly an admirable program in its aim, but it raises momentous issues about the way in which our discovery of the "mystery" may or may not, as experience, flow and rechannel itself in myriad courses through the contingencies of language, memory, culture, history.[3]

Therefore, if I concentrate on only one set of symptomatic terms in the above passage, it is to address the general bias (and not necessarily to dispute specific points, such as the well-taken critique of most structuralist and semiotic approaches). "Liberating double retrieval," "a perpetually new . . . literary history," and " 'overcoming metaphysics' " strike me as reformulations of several sacrosanct tenets of "our" culture supposedly under scrutiny and attack. While it is true that Spanos, drawing nourishment from thinkers such as Heidegger, avoids (pseudo-)scientific, and prefers philosophic, expressions, this momentarily distracts attention from what is fundamentally the restatement of a persistent binary relationship to existence. M. H. Abrams and others have shown that the progressive secularization of Western thought since the Renaissance has involved not just the reformulation of religious ideas "within the prevailing two-term system of subject and object" but also the assimilative poetization of the triumphant natural sciences in the eighteenth and nineteenth centuries.[4] The romantics, too, had high hopes for a "perpetu-ally new" poetry, which would simultaneously "overcome" and thereby redeem or "retrieve" the moribund past, as well as "liberate" existence as "becoming." Hence postmodern propositions haunt me like ghostly echoes which cannot be disentangled from other ancestral contexts, those spectral families hardly banished into the recesses of memory—as into the dictionary and history book. Must I join them (ahead of wish) and drag with me into oblivion the corpse of the language and culture I did *not* invent, in order to help unclutter and unfetter Being? Yes; if I accept the most extreme conclusion deriving from Lord Bacon's veiled declaration that, as of the Renaissance, being in possession of a vocabulary—man's inherited burden—constitutes the gravity of Origi-nal Sin. Speech, even speech concerning the inauthenticity of speech, prevaricates meanwhile.

Perhaps my recalcitrant admission that I believe I have already re-jected *earlier* versions of redemption by or as some radical break in con-sciousness only brands me as a hardened reifier and spatializer, an unbe-liever lacking the amazing grace to be reborn in the spirit. Others may call this predicament a paradox. I merely report that even my alienation from my own culture strikes me as "typical"; it has resulted from my as-siduous deconstruction of its myths and pretenses. I learned this ability from preceding European anatomizers; it isn't very difficult any more. So when I deconstruct postmodern habits of mind, I sense I am co-imitating the postmodernists' imitation of the very ancestors to whom—quite rightly—they impute the elaboration of the crucial ideas which underlie modernity. In this respect, postmodernism constitutes another gyre in the *circulus vitiosus* within which Western "identity" twists and turns to avoid ceasing to be what it is. Since postmodernism strikes me as paradigmatic of recapitulation, thus subtly conservative, a release from the reality of the contemporary world, I am not surprised that a con-siderable segment of the postmodern camp waits with millenarian ex-citement in the penumbra of an oncoming (requisite) Apocalypse. Rather than question the thematics of decadence inherited from fin-de-siècle literature, postmodern theoreticians merely repeat a favorite negative version of the cliché of a purgatorial revaluation of values—including their own. That proposition is mildly reflected in the title of Ihab Has-san's essay "Beyond a Theory of Literature: Intimations of Apocalypse?"

Yet, like most theoreticians, Hassan can only set up lists of authors now "in," the approach to whose works is not facilitated or understood by older theoreticians. We are offered a few symptomatic terms, such as "non-telic," but Hassan soon has recourse to tired nineteenth-century notions of disappearance and silence when he hierophantically invokes the postmodern prophets of apocalpyse and rebirth (Kierkegaard, Heidegger, Norman O. Brown, D. H. Lawrence).[5] Postmodernists now busily deconstruct modernity, their immediate Babel and Babylon, with their own epochal jargon, zealous to break out of the intractable morass which encumbers existence.

The mainstay of modernity *and* postmodernity *is* imitation of scientific discourse, the mature habit of demystification, of deconstruction and reconstruction. The intrusion of science into art already seemed oppressively evident in positivism a century ago, and half a century ago some observers saw further baleful omens in the reconstructive approach to culture and myth practiced by important modernists. For example, reviewing *Ulysses* in the *Freeman* (July 19, 1922), Mary G. Colum noted:

The alarming thing about "Ulysses" is very different [from the charge of obscenity]; it is that it shows the amazing inroads that science is making on literature. Mr. Joyce's book is of as much interest as science as it is as literature; in some parts it is of purely scientific and non-artistic interest. It seems to me a real and not a fantastic fear that science will oust literature altogether as a part of human expression; and from that point of view "Ulysses" is a dangerous indication.[6]

Contrary to expectations, perhaps, American criticism did not abandon the all-embracing pretenses of modernist literature when theoreticians started turning away from the representative microcosm of the "verbal icon"; rather, by supposed or prophesied acts of total revaluation, the theoreticians arrogated to themselves the aura of "wholeness." René Wellek has astutely sensed that, in rejecting the "art" of literature, "recent criticism—and not only criticism in America—looks constantly elsewhere, wants to become sociology, politics, philosophy, theology and even mystical illumination."[7] Allan Rodway has detected an analogous expansionism in the British turning from New Criticism, but in my view he misjudges the metacritical mimicry of scientific discourse by equating it in some cases with actual science: "Moreover this sort of work seems scientific. Indeed it often is scientific, and that is why, as theorists in rival categories were to point out, it is not strictly literary criticism but metacriticism: a specialised form of sociology or psychology, history, biography or anthropology."[8] Nonetheless, the metacritical drive of postmodern criticism reveals itself in forms as virulent as the romantic climax.

When postmodern theoreticians turn against spatialization of consciousness and extol a liberated art of time, two things tend to occur in critical practice. By deconstruction adherent critics alter slightly the literary and critical canon, shifting our attention to the latest qualifications for inner right(eous)ness. By reconstruction they also circle back to the primary "rebirth" experience of romanticism and, before that, of the Renaissance and Reformation, when the dynamics of time were discovered[9] and time relationships, which shape entire bodies of discourse, were made into the chief subject of the emergent superdiscourse after 1600. Now joyfully (Rabelais), now perplexedly (Donne), European intellect—having taken apart the Medieval system—considered culture in its totality, under the rubric of stages of history, as an educational happening, a redemptive becoming. Henceforth, each new extremely difficult passage, progressively adjusting to the traumatic recognition of the unmanageable products of prolific Western thought, could eventually be interpreted as postfiguration of the initial break: "just" another dissociation of sensibility.[10]

Before discriminating major post-Renaissance directions of Western rationalism (Descartes' radical doubting, Leibniz' ontological optimism, etc.), most cultural historians can more or less agree that all modes have focused initially on these propositions:

(A) the existence of a plethora of cultural data, often seemingly contradictory, at times ludicrous, nonsensical;
(B) the need for a critical assessment and arrangement of such data;
(C) the advisability of devising a "method"
    (1) to increase exponentially the capacity of the mind to sort and store,
    (2) to avoid the past pitfalls and errors of the mind, which are deplorably evidenced in the cultural record,
    (3) to create and expand certain knowledge.

The above amounts essentially to the empiricist program.

Spanos, too, indicts in particular the Cartesian quest for "certainty";

with the advent of the romantic and modern period, Hegelian dialectics, symbolist-imagist iconicity, and Nietzschean Will to Power provide not so much responses to the metaphysical aggression which has elaborated the positivistic "world picture," as omens of its end. Spanos prophesies that the ontotheological relay team of Plato, Aquinas, Descartes, Leibniz, and Hegel will not be able to hand on the baton (or as Bacon would say, the "torch").[11] It is curious how insistent the apocalyptic tone is in postmodern pronouncements; the only other comparisons—aside from the immediately antecedent Schopenhauerian and Spenglerian pessimism underlying Modernism—are the expectations and dejections of the romantics at the time of the French Revolution, or of the liberal and radical Protestants in the earlier seventeenth century.[12] In startling contrast, with the prospect of a triumph of rationalism on the threshold of the Enlightenment, when Leibniz looked at the multiplicity of forms of being as a flowing dynamics of energies, he saw their composite vector as a meaningful happening in time. His time-consciousness tended to make him delight in "accidents," surface phenomena, because his craving was to understand the invisible "rules" shaping the phenomena. For Leibniz, the intervening use of "artificial memory" and instrumental systems of abstractions (combinatory art, calculus) implied nothing "wrong" with earthly givens; rather, it portended a qualitative surge in spiritual evolution through the discovery of "method." The Leibnizian ecstasy is to believe confidently that the middle state of muddle and confusion is being overcome; man spirals onto a new plane and can reinstate his Adamic hopes, because he can render a critique of the mind's contents and even of the mind's operations. Thus with "control" over itself, the mind is promised a new start, virtually unlimited potential— a glorious prospect.[13]

Though Bacon and Descartes, in contrast, earlier approached the "results" of past mental life (human history) with grave suspicion about the operations as well as products of the mind, their critiques, too, had as their constructive aim a radical, qualitative break in consciousness and the eventual attainment of a comparable "certainty." And since American education has been so extensively colored by the empiricist bias, I shall concentrate on the Baconian complex to illustrate the longer-range implications of scientific discourse for all discourse. The most fundamental point is that scientific discourse set out programmatically to subordinate and even to swallow poetic discourse. Bacon converts the pattern of the Fall and Apocalypse into a historical vision of the contest between entrapment in degenerative cycles and breaking out of the "circle" (*Works* IV, 52, 383) into "continuation and further progression" (IV, 449) of a linear temporal pathway.[14] With the Puritan millenarians he shared his specific belief that a major cycle had turned and that in the midst of epochal disorder a providential momentum was building for a redemptive alteration of the mind. The evidence consisted, among other things, in the regeneration of Reformation hopes, the irreversible impact of printing and its attendant intellectual renascence, the actual new achievements in the pure sciences, and the literal expansion of civilizatory scope through exploration and colonization of the globe. The promise existed that men could permanently cease "wandering round and round as in a labyrinth" (IV, 81) by engaging in an ostensible act of cultural humiliation, abjuring the fantastic constructs and vagaries of their philosophic and religious heritages. Beyond revising the Renaissance principle of *docta ignorantia* whereby scholasticism and medieval discourse generally had been undermined, Bacon now espouses an aggressive deconstruction which must include even his own mental life. By the radical new start from a zero position, the inductive method will permit the mind to "arrive at a knowledge of causes in which it can rest" (IV, 32), that is, to regain on a higher plane the lost Adamic state of the final "sabbath" (IV, 33; VII, 221). Guibbory notes:

Paradoxically, however, the forward advance of knowledge is really a return to the original state of wisdom before the Fall. The linear path of progress which Bacon substitutes for the cycles of the past will actually complete the circle of mankind's history by leading man to the end of redemption which touches the prelapsarian state of bliss where the circle began.[15]

Milton grandiloquently translated the Baconian anthropological approach into poetic terms in *Paradise Lost* and *Regained,* as well as in his treatises on education and freedom of expression. But the most persistent post-Baconian tendency was the pseudo-scientific curbing of language out of suspicion about its insidious powers and, since natural language was seemingly unmanageable, the search for a substitute for language. Both compulsions are symptomatic of the rationalist attempt to escape from the intractable web of contingency. The Renaissance and Reformation rejection of scholastic values as tottering edifices of words intensifies into a concerted drive for a new discourse when Bacon suspects the schoolmen's books reveal that, if the mind works only "upon itself, as the spider worketh his web, then it is endless, and brings forth indeed cobwebs of learning, admirable for the fineness of thread and work, but of no substance or profit" (III, 285–86). The story is well known: Locke extends Bacon's distrust of "idols of the human mind" (IV, 51) into an unrelenting epistemological *Essay Concerning Human Understanding*, and taking the hint jocoseriously, Sterne eventually exhibits the mysterious dilemma of identity as circumscription in a hermeneutic circle. In my view, when Bacon says "Circular motion is interminable, and for its own sake" (V, 478), he expresses the fundamental ill ease which surfaces again so powerfully in existentialism and in postmodern literary theorizing.

James Stephens has traced the stages in which Bacon attempted to unfold his program for science and was forced to make adjustments based on the hard realities of communicating his elitist goals.[16] Though accepting the need for "one method for the cultivation, another for the invention, of knowledge" (IV, 42), Bacon was concerned that the newly reconstituted tradition—Renaissance learning—was oriented to rhetoric for its own sake rather than for delivery of pertinent modern knowledge. Stephens seconds Karl R. Wallace in deeming Bacon's contribution to reside in the application of Renaissance psychology to the communication process on behalf of a new progressive learning. In the long run, rhetoric had to be pressed into service appropriately, since an effective style was required to recommend reason and understanding to the imagination. In Bacon's attack on that refractory faculty, "which may at pleasure make unlawful matches and divorces of things" (*De augmentis scientiarum*, 11, 13), we can detect the inroads of the late Renaissance dissociation of sensibility. Though art must play a role in skillful management of the various components of an audience, words remain suspect through their association with inherited errors and as sources of potential erring. Among ways to offset the danger posed by language, Bacon uses the aphoristic approach, representing fragments of knowledge and stimulating the intelligent reader to contribute extensions and conclusions, hence to discover. Similarly, the acroamatic approach seeks "by obscurity of delivery to exclude the vulgar from the secrets of knowledge."

Both approaches give scope to Bacon's emblematic proclivity. Since words are but "symbols of notions," yet embroil humankind in intractable muddles, he is fascinated by hieroglyphs, ideograms, characters, and gestures, because these suggest the possibility of an alternative universal language of pictures or signs:

Moreover it is now well known that in China and the provinces of the furthest East there are in use at this day certain *real characters,* not nominal; characters, I mean, which represent neither letters nor words, but things and notions; insomuch that a number of nations whose languages are altogether different, but who agree in the use of such characters . . . communicate with each other in writing; to such an extent indeed that any book written in characters of this kind can be read off by each nation in their own language.

The Notes of Things then which carry a signification without the help or intervention of words, are of two kinds: one *ex congruo,* where the note has some congruity with the notion, the other *ad placitum,* where it is adopted and agreed upon at pleasure. Of the former kind are Hieroglyphics and Gestures; of the latter the Real Characters . . . Gestures are as transitory as Hieroglyphics. For as uttered words fly away, but written words stand, so Hieroglyphics expressed in gestures pass, but expressed in pictures remain. (*De augmentis scientiarum,* IV, 1)

When Bacon resorts to mythmaking in the *New Atlantis* to lend moral authority to science as successor to man's earlier religious heritage, hieroglyphic reduction of "intellectual conceptions to sensible images" (*De augmentis,* V, 5) obviates any affront or exposure to vulgar (mis-)-understanding; and at the same time, the elitist code does not compromise the revolutionary role of science as true religion. For the scientist as intellectual hero is compelled "to sweep away all theories and common notions" (*Aphorisms,* XCVII), sows "for future ages the seeds of a purer truth" (*Aphorisms,* CXVI), and would "let the human race recover that right over human nature which belongs to it by divine bequest" (*Aphorisms,* CXXIX).

The postmodern bias against the older "image," against closed self-referential expression, seems to me to be one of the many latter-day step-children of Baconian empiricism. Hence, for example, since the imagist Ezra Pound was ever striving after an authentic "objective correlative" or the equivalent of Chinese ideograms in poetry, it amounts to sibling rivalry to attack Pound's "hieroglyphs" as unwittingly captive of their own terms, rather than as a deliberate means to restore language to a proper role. Postmodern "deconstruction" and "reconstruction" does, nonetheless, pursue another branch of the iconoclastic Baconian impulse to overcome "tainted and corrupted" learning enshrined in language, to topple "idols of the mind," dogmas which work an "enchantment from progress." Bacon's antibook orientation is based on the supposition that words maintain false images cast by the human mind as a distorting "enchanted glass"—the theme which his contemporary Cervantes vigorously pursued in the *Quixote*. Though Bacon "rescues" the revered ancient philosophy with its colorful symbols and myths, he does so only to exploit it as a resource to recruit the special elite. Bacon's rationalist mythmaking serves in the final analysis (like Cervantes' indirect rescue of romance?) as a means to replace tenacious old structures and convert the finest minds to science, the difficult "second Scripture." Bacon judges that even such carefully cultivated "literate experience" will remain inferior to the direct interpretation of nature, but he recognizes that it is a necessary channel and that only by passage through it can men be led to an awareness and overcoming of its limits. We can speak of the superiority complex of Western intellectuals who, since Bacon, take pride in their capacity to play with terms which—in varying degrees of openness or aggression—they are debunking and dismantling. It is a game from which the vast slave population (i.e., ordinary users of language as a repertory of commonplaces) are excluded.

The difficulty with this attitude becomes apparent as soon as we consider the divergence which indeed set in between science, promoting the search for new codes liberated from the past, and art, beholden to the contingent media of expression whether it will or not. With the invention of the calculus at the end of the seventeenth century, a threshold was crossed in the drive to elaborate a notational system which could engender virtually unlimited growth for mathematical language. It became not only possible but highly attractive to shift from qualitative (language-oriented) to a quantifiable (sign-oriented) examination of things, once mathematics had attained to its own complex, satisfying symbolism. The desire for the order, power, and purity epitomized in the liberated hard sciences gradually penetrated other realms, and in my view it has continued to fire the redemptive and apocalyptic aspirations of many sectors of the literary world down to the present. Poetic experiments to push language in the direction of a calculus and to release its potential as a primal code through the *ars combinatoria* and other "logics" were already being undertaken in the seventeenth century. In certain respects, Joyce continued to experiment with ways to reconcile rhetoric and logic in a polyphonic code and tested the limits for a natural language. But such reconcilements with or exaggerated hopes for natural language have been matched by an almost unbroken post-Renaissance tradition of suspicion and even hatred of language. Since language is doomed to remain incommensurate (except for a few anti-Baconians), the need to use it can be regarded as demeaning servitude or spiritual martyrdom, as Rimbaud, Hofmannsthal, and others have discovered in a less humorous vein than Sterne.[17]

Richard F. Jones has demonstrated how the Baconian prejudice against language was widely endorsed by the scientific community, who eventually helped bring about a stylistic reformation of English in the seventeenth century.[18] Their "aversion and contempt for the empty study of words" (Boyle) often goes hand in hand with antipathy for the older humanist cultivation of languages for the sake of the heritages transmitted in them. The leading educational philosophers for the Puritans, notably Comenius and Dury, opposed the study of the classics as a pursuit lacking intrinsic value. Instead, the time-robbing acquisition of languages should be subordinate "unto Arts and Sciences," because in themselves languages "are worth nothing towards the advancement of our Happiness." The extent to which contemporary American rejection of language training still mimics the thought of our Puritan forebears bears witness to the spellbinding appeal of the new superdiscourse of science. Not satisfied with deconstructing the human past and scrapping it almost wholly as outmoded, the scientific coteries of the Puritans and Royal Society wanted to deconstruct language itself as an unreliable instrument and to reconstruct a linguistic counterpart for the natural philosophy of the age, on the grounds that the consideration of the truth of ideas could not proceed without strictly controlled definitions.[19] The scientists' call for a plain language, stripped of superfluous adornments, purged of ambiguity, eventually found its counterpart in the attack on rhetoric in the pulpit as betokening corrupt habits or fanaticism.[20] By the close of the century, theological seriousness of purpose, too, came to be closely associated with ascendant neoclassical traits, and rehabilitations of figurative language increasingly rested on the virtues of less vulnerable primary sources such as the Bible, "true" eloquence close to the primal experience of the race.

The even more radical attempt to replace natural language with a "real character" gained impetus when Comenius in *The Way of Light* (1641) reconsidered Bacon's speculation in *The Advancement of Learning* (1605) about Chinese ideograms as one model for a symbolic code —though with unfortunate defects.[21] To help restore harmony to the "commonwealth of humanity" and mobilize the "innate Principles" of "knowing, willing, and achieving" rooted in "Human General Intelligence," Comenius proposed it was first paramount to overcome the powerful obstacle "which consists in the multitude, the variety, the confusion of language." This means finally the establishment of "a language absolutely new, absolutely easy, absolutely rational, in brief a pansophic language, the universal carrier of light." The ecumenical ambition and linguistic correlates of Comenius and Hartlib appear to underlie directly the elaborate treatises on pure, rational discourse by Dalgarno and Wilkins. In the *Ars signorum vulgo character universalis et lingua philosophica* (1661), Dalgarno begins, like the Lullian-Ramian encyclopedist Alsted, the German Calvinist mentor of Comenius, by postulating seventeen—later twenty-three—classes of irreducible ideas and by beginning every word in a primary class with the same letter as an unmistakable sign. Further modifications and subdivisions are marked by second, third, and subsequent letters, so that an adequately large vocabulary of artificial objective words can be generated by further application of this *ars combinatoria*. In a similar vein, Wilkins' *Essay towards a Real Character and a Philosophical Language* (1668) presented to the Royal Society an incredibly detailed, encyclopedic analysis of all categories of things, processes, and relations for conceptualizing matters mundane or divine. Next he offered a rationalistic anatomy of "natural grammar" and assigned to every structural function in the grammar a written mark or character; by combination and modification, every nuance of an objective discourse could be represented ideogrammatically. People of various nations would thus be able to "communicate by a *Real Character*, which shall be legible in all [natural] Languages," because it can be "made *effable*," that is, read as phonemes "in a distinct Language."[22] In addition, Wilkins constructed a tentative example of an international "Philosophical Language" which could be uttered as composed sounds, even though the words were generated artificially, as in the case of the exclusively ideogrammatic parallel, "Real Character."

Soon after entering Oxford in 1661, the young Newton, in the wake of

Dalgarno and others, was sketching his own project for a universal language based on an alphabetic shorthand.[23] The evidence is abundant that the British scientific mind was intrigued by the possibility of bringing the use of language and the formulation of metaphysical and theological insights into conformity with mathematically rigorous empiricism. The urge to "reify" thought is disguised since the trend of such reductionism is to create manipulable abstractions, a cipher of neutral, pure signs; in the beginning, the crusade against older, language-bound "metaphor," "emblems," "conceits," etc., lends the appearance of an escape from the trammels of a confused "pictorial" imagination, the residual habits of archaic fallen man. As already mentioned, the phase of quantifying all phenomena set in not just with Newton's theory of universal gravitation but also with his invention of the calculus, whose notational system liberated mathematical signs as a self-generative, self-correcting code. Yet, as is well known, Newton still clung fervently to his belief in divine revelation and redemption.[24]

The example of Newton cautions us against assuming that fundamental Protestant (hence late Christian) aspirations were simply displaced relentlessly by science. Rather, it strengthens the suspicion that Anglo-American empiricism absorbed and furthered the deeper drives of the millenarian Baconians. The Puritan stress on reform; their cult of education; doctrine of hard work; desire to rebuild lost Eden through scientific, technological control over nature; and their ecumenical program for the eventual restoration of fallen humankind became elements of a generally accepted mission for Western science *and* civilization. As Webster has argued, it was the Puritan eschatological vision which spurred them to the cultivation of science. Furthermore, the radical Protestant speculation about the creation of an elitist confraternity—Bacon's House of Solomon, Comenius' and Boyle's "invisible college," etc.—began to be realized on a practical level by the establishment of the Royal Society. On the Continent, the early parallel, especially among German Calvinists, was the Rosicrucian notion of an "Invisible College."[25] We tend to forget the importance of the interconnected webbing of *illuminati* movements in Western nations during the surge of pre-Revolutionary science, industrialization, and capitalism because so many features seem too bizarre to pertain to the formation of modern elitist sentiments. But the history of "secret" societies shows the relatively greater early success of Masonism in Protestant, and notably Calvinist, areas and its appeal especially to liberal (and often nominal) Catholics as a channel for associating with Enlightenment forces; and the theosophical and pansophical contribution to Masonic and Rosicrucian lore has been thoroughly documented.[26] If our memory of these links needs refreshing, we can engage in an intensive review with Hans Castorp under the tutelage of Settembrini in *The Magic Mountain*.

My point here is that the modern surface world dominated by the "pure" signs of scientific discourse rests on the elitist "secret" discourse which once was being actively pursued against the perceived monstrously deforming forces of human nature, against the voices of unauthentic authorities and institutions. The conviction in the efficacy of scientific discourse flourished when the fusion of Protestant craving for a radical transformation and of humanist gnostic yearnings occurred. The latter drives, expressed through magic-mystical, hermetic-occult pursuits, provided a rich soil in which conviction in the efficacy of "purified" scientific discourse flourished.

I have recollected how, in the Hesperidean branch, the new discourse was accompanied by an ever-intensifying skepticism about natural language and the operation of the mind, reflected in the culture's patchwork "vocabulary." Rationalist epistemological theory remained adamant in its zeal to debunk the mind, to grasp its archaic procedures, to dispel its obscurities, to control its waywardness. Perhaps the supreme monument to this attack on mendacious (i.e., natural) discourse by a contemporary of Newton was Locke's celebrated *Essay on Human Understanding*. In the Eastern branch, however, the new discourse took an altogether different approach to the vexatious evidence of some identity between structures of language and operations of mind.

The "linguistic model," which underlies a variety of approaches to literature, other arts, and culture generally, has acquired particular refinements by many hands. But, simplifying the larger history of this model, we can say the notion that methodological linkages between several subjects can be established because they can all be treated as *languages*, that is, codes, results in large measure from the line of thinking traceable from Leibniz over Humboldt to today's structural linguists (Chomsky et al.) and anthropologists (Lévi-Strauss et al.) and the literary formalists related to them. (Certain extreme formalists will probably dismiss the foregoing statement as an irrelevant "genetic" explanation for what now "is" diacritical knowledge has small worth to those more interested in schematizing coordinates in a synchronic slice of life to detect the "grammar" imbedded in their specimen.) Leibniz was among the first to see that innatist views of natural languages—as having had a common (Adamic) origin, but having evolved over time in territorial and ethnic environments, subject to sometimes complex conditions, and working out their own grammars and vocabularies in a series of "accidents"— promised more than convenient compatibility with the religious tradition of the dispersion of tongues after Babel. He recognized that the "accidents" displayed an actual organic continuum and that through and in human languages nature expressed possibilities, the manifold collective devising, acquiring, conflating, altering of codes which anthropologists can study as "cultures," "myths," "interchange," and so forth. Whereas a medieval realist theory threatened to convert humanity into a frightening collection of speakers of ideolects in loosely overlapping groups because it failed to explain the actual enormous diversity of tongues and peoples which the Renaissance savants, explorers, colonizers, and missionaries had (re-)discovered, nominalism *and* innatism in combination provided a more satisfactory key.

Leibniz grasped the proposition that the fundamental capacity which characterized a "human" being was the inborn ability to acquire and use "a"—that is, any—language. He conceived of the rules of languages as a deep structure in the mind resulting from earlier stages of evolution which eventually led to the point where, with this common genetic heritage established, "humanness" appeared biologically as an inherent attribute of each human monad. The activity of receiving, using, imperceptibly altering one—or with education or cultural experience more than one—code as utterance (in thoughts, spoken words, or recorded speech) was from that juncture the most significant kind of participation with other monads in shaping complicated levels of human symbiosis known as society, culture, religion, etc. Leibniz' thinking evidences the advanced Protestant consciousness of language and culture but it bears symptomatic resemblance to advanced Catholic theorizing such as that by Athanasius Kircher. Crucial for both as a point of convergence of ideas is their early obsession with the possibility of a "combinatory art." The dream of an *ars combinatoria* continued the Renaissance drive for control over all the profuse data with which the renewed civilization had to cope; and largely from it, as I have noted above, sprang the key Enlightenment concepts of a philosophic *methodus* and mathematical *calculus*. Thus, looking backwards from Kircher and Leibniz, we can discern among their superseded common ancestors Ramus and other sixteenth-century speculators about a "method" which would permit mechanistic manipulation of fundamental categories of definition and eventually of entire "codes." The first efforts, then, involved a fusion of the laws of rhetorical analysis and synthesis with the laws of logic.

The Lullian-Ramian project was to identify the universal fundamentals in a hierarchy of concepts, to arrange these in tables as signs, and to work toward solutions of difficult problems through permutations and combinations of alphabetic algorithms. Kircher believed, moreover, that ultimately it would be possible to *invent* totally new concepts by generating them from the initially established ones, so that the valid underlying structure would yield further "sentences" or complicated combinations which conformed to the abstract code. The earlier Renaissance search had been for "artificial memory," some means of mnemonic control of the recoverable repertory of knowledge, which had already proven to be enormous and still growing; in fact, the decline of the Dark and Middle Ages could be and was described largely as actual loss of vast treasures, a slowdown and shutdown of considerable extents of the human mind. Beyond mnemonic control by means of hierarchically organized encyclopedias, the later Renaissance search turned more aggressively to the expansion of the conceivable repertory literally through creation of ideas, to self-sustaining scientific "invention" (and not mere rhetorical *inventio*) as a new form of discourse. Kircher proposed, but never carried out, the construction of a *cista* ("box") in which all the perfected extant *tabellae* would be coordinated so as to permit combinatory crossing on various axes from framework to framework of values: a forerunner of the modern computer with memory storage. Kircher not only believed that such a device would produce new propositions but vaunted that by means of it eventually even "children and idiots" could operatively manipulate the various "languages"—natural tongues, musical composition, mathematical procedures, painting, etc. Several decades later, toward the end of his life, Leibniz advanced the similar view that, in effect, various bodies of theory and practice—arts and sciences—are semiotic systems living out of their own evolved rules and that these systems are analogous to the natural spoken languages.

Indeed, Leibniz was groping for the profoundest level of deep structure, the irreducible logic of the mind that would explain the universal grammar which is capable of generating particular sentences in any natural language, mathematical thought, musical expression, etc. He hoped to abstract from all these operations a "general" or "universal" language, a supercode reducible to notation in terms of which other codes could be scrutinized. Like Comenius, he also yearned to anticipate the ecumenical confraternity of expanding enlightenment by furthering the creation of an artificial, rational language for international communication. This language he understood variously in relation to sound, mathematical thought, and signs. According to his ideal, it could be expressed in numbers, spoken in phonemes, composed as abstract music, or written as ideograms (once more, as Bacon mused, after the supposed model of Chinese)—alternately or simultaneously. Leibniz suggested that there was a European family of languages which had evolved from some archaic unity—in a rough outline genially corresponding to today's picture of the several branches as reconstructed by etymological philologists and comparative grammarians. In Rome, Kircher sought to schematize the mythological complexes of several great cultures, including the Egyptian and the Greco-Roman, and coordinated their features in patterns to which Biblical and Christian lore could be compared as supposed governing form; however, his abstraction of common underlying structure amounted to a beginning of a new branch of scientific discourse: the anthropological study of comparative religion. In the case of both "Protestant" Leibniz and "Catholic" Kircher, we note the powerful fascination for representation by visual signifiers, a search to discover the pictorial base in primal layers of known languages as well as in more complicated formulations from later layers. The theory that the alphabets of the Mediterranean basin had evolved from pictorial signs, the perception of nominal roots as being the metaphoric heart of conceptual terms, the interest in Egyptian hieroglyphs and Chinese ideograms as a possible emblematic code—these and similar notions shared by such savants belong to a complex which deeply marked the poetry, drama, and fiction of their age and its successors. The practices of "spatialization" are rooted in their investigation and application of pictorialism.

By the foregoing I do not mean to imply that imitation of scientific discourse could or should be avoided in contemporary writing or criticism. Quite to the contrary, my skepticism is two-edged. I share

the view which Donald Davie advances that a lack of historical awareness of the vast assimilation of scientific terms, which had subsequently
lost their metaphoric vividness, prompted the standard charge that the
atmosphere of the mechanistic, quantifying Newtonian age was inimical to poetry, even though, contradictorily, critics deemed the influence
of the Royal Academy beneficial to English prose.[27] After the romantics, literary history largely failed to distinguish between creative scientists themselves, with whom poets shared much vocabulary, and philosophers commenting on what scientists appeared to be doing. Yet the
philological evidence tends to show that, simultaneously, eighteenth-
century literary use of terms from the natural sciences helped support
Lockean assumptions in ethics and psychology and in turn was stimu-
lated by the philosophers acting as middlemen. The new vocabulary
also appeared in the language of satirical and comic writers—such as
Berkeley, Pope, and Swift—who opposed the whole materialist trend.
One general result of the adoption of new scientific terms into common
usage was the initial awareness that many elevated words used for centuries had been formed earlier in the same way; thus both these older
and also the newer terms (e.g., "gravitation," "profound") could be and
were deflated by humorists. As in the time of Rabelais, at a moment
when language seemed to be changing too rapidly, writers had to consider the relative value of stabilizing the process versus benefiting from
its fluidity, since in fact the scientists were one of their most fruitful
sources of new words or new senses for old words. Davie is convinced
that thorough investigations by historical semanticists into terms like
"spirit" will reveal the extent to which the earlier eighteenth century
clung to metaphors bridging disparate realms; "the distinction which we
make between the scientific and the moral was unnecessary, positively
unwanted."[28] Once chemistry had freed itself from physics as a separate
discipline, the romantics turned to it as a natural science which could be
an ally against the mechanistic view of things and source of revisionary
metaphors—whence yet another wave of vocabulary. So we ought not to
be surprised that actual or psuedo-sciences today (compare alchemy and
chemistry in the Renaissance) still affect literary discourse as deeply as
they do.

But there are curious contradictions—*not* paradoxes—in the pervasive postmodern attempt to stake a moral claim for the deconstructive
labors of those who battle the power of the "image," take apart and ex-

pose in all nakedness extant metaphoric systems, etc. In contrast to the Elizabethans, Davie argues, the Augustans had become more eclectic in deriving metaphors from virtually any source; Augustan metaphors, because they are just figures of speech, can thus refer to several incompatible world pictures: "Here is certainly a contraction, not in the field of metaphor, but in man's notion of its validity"—probably furthered more by philosophers of science than by scientists themselves.[29] Strangely, some postmodern critics nonetheless act as if the most extreme romantic wishdream of a magical key or a modernist iconic poem represents the normative conditioning delusion embodied in (somehow not yet debunked) poetic language and constructs today; rather than acknowledging the extreme nominalistic pluralism of our own age. The same critics can demand a radical rebeginning, a new holistic vision which mysteriously follows what amounts to purgation, even though it is evident the new vision may not last long, of course, if another deconstructor arrives on the scene with his iconoclast's hammer in hand and quickly once more reduces all to fragments of *dead* (already predeconstructed) vocabulary out of which his predecessor has temporarily constructed a poetic utterance. The zeal to smash another's idol and to heap up piles of rubble as one's own transitory monument indeed seems to be the trademark of many a critic today. These traits might be termed the postmodern panic.

A less deprecatory view of today's fashionable mutual deconstructing can be gained from Meyer's discussion "Concerning the Sciences, the Arts—AND the Humanities" in the inaugural issue of *Critical Inquiry*.[30] According to Meyer, artists tried to devise propositional programs in the early twentieth century out of the mistaken belief that science meant novelty and that it was sufficient to achieve the limited duration of scientific propositions. Meyer, reverting cautiously to the New Critical stance that a work of art is a "fabricated microcosm," argues that the truer analogy is between the single work of art and the collective body of practices and theories characterizing science.[31] Although ideas in a work of art lose their strangeness with time, as does a new scientific theory, its unique pattern never wholly does; for there is no supersession in works of art, neither confirmation nor disconfirmation of "truth." The credibility of works of art is corroborated by general human experience, and their content can thus have some active impact on our concept of human behavior, no matter how unlikely the generic or epochal features may appear to the overly rationalistic observer of a later era; hence the survival of "classics" over centuries and millenia. Like Davie, Meyer recognizes that scientific theories can furnish matter for aesthetic delight once they are registered phenomena in the cultural world. But the model of natural language is more applicable to art because men use and understand the medium without explanation, and each enjoys the personally variant possibility of a gradualistic increase and refinement of appreciation. Acquired rules and vocabulary of a language are first presumed to be in the minds of others on a tacit intersubjective basis, rather than discovered as conceptual knowledge. Beyond the finding that art like language is broadly characterized by "synthesis" and science by "analysis," Meyer expatiates on the impediments to any general psychological explanation of audience experience and reception. I must pass over his interesting comments on the methodological challenge of qualifying our approach to fit the nature of each distinct medium (fiction, painting, music, etc.), as well as on the practical nullity of discovering the behavioral neurobiological explanation for particular instances of artistic creation and reception. The important point is that, meanwhile, criticism, too, remains a kind of art. Inductive taxonomies comparing features of style do not lead to successively better hypotheses for the reason that the principles of organization of works of art alter from age to age and culture to culture (even on the same hierarchical level of structure, as well as in the articulation of variables). Only by adducing *ad hoc* propositions can the critic deal with actual cases. Despite all our attempts to identify generic modes and structures, the categories run up against limits imposed by the intrusion of unexpected associations (conflation), reversal or adaptation of function, etc., in actual works; and rhetorical systems persist mainly on the grammatical, not the semantic, level.

Returning an instant to Bacon, it is instructive to note that for him

the art of Memory is built upon two intentions: Prenotion and Emblem. . . . By prenotion I mean a kind of cutting off of infinity of search. For when a man desires to recall anything into his memory, if he have no prenotion or perception of what he seeks, he seeks and strives and beats about hither and thither as if in infinite space. But if he have some certain prenotion, this infinity is at once cut off, and the memory ranges in a narrower compass. (*De augmentis,* V, 5)

When facing the hermeneutic problem of initiating direction, though he suspects the human mind of inveterate habits of self-deception, Bacon momentarily concedes human dependence on an intuitive step. But he does not devote himself to investigating, for their possible positive implications, the internal operations of the mind which permit us to possess a prior basis of knowledge or the creative will.[32] Stephens points out that Bacon simply admits that "no man can give a just account of how he came to that knowledge which he hath received" (*Valerius terminus*, cap. 18); Bacon assumes that a hermeneutic directedness permits the search for valid axioms and counsels intermediate rests for stocktaking so that the written form of the new philosophy will not contradictorily defeat its own goal.[33] Today we can cite Wittgenstein among extreme exponents of confidence in language as the valid, determining matrix of thought; the attribution of crucial ontological dimensions to language has flourished, as mentioned, in the line from Leibniz over Humboldt to the innatists in contemporary linguistics. Of course, Bacon propounds his psychology of discovery without the benefit of later romantic perceptions of the fragment as a jagged nexus, a puzzle piece suggesting the total context; when Bacon uses the fragment to stimulate a sense of the total context within which a scientist works, he does not embark on questions which offer strong clues for alternatives to a sensationalist theory of the mind. Sensationalism followed comfortably the British materialist penchant. In essence, then, postmodern antipathy to symbolism, imagism, etc., because these supposedly give readers a false sense of unity and completion, is a shadowy descendant of Baconian dislike of rhetorical system such as represented by Ciceronian elegance. The traditional Anglo-American habit is to drift into loathing the familiar furniture of the mind and to feel great satisfaction in clearing out the clutter—and refurnishing in a newer chic fashion. The mould of fashion is what philosophers say about science, directly or indirectly.

Meyer proposes, as a corrective to our misunderstanding of the role of science, that "Nature, Human Behavior, and Works of Art are antecedent to the theories explaining them."[34] Not only are theories in the humanities still necessarily "plural" and "discrete," but further works of art can be affected by theories (e.g., Freudian notions in surrealism), whereas in the realm of science there is no feedback from successive theories to phenomena of nature. The physical laws have always been operative in nature; however, the "composition" of church architecture, for example, has varied in startling ways over the centuries. Furthermore, Meyer holds that only the humanist-theorist can aspire to emulate the scientist, while the critic resembles, on the one hand, the historian, and on the other, various performers. The critic deals with a plethora of "texts" (events, documents), usually in relation to a larger body of "context" (traditions, codes); he interprets the "text" to some extent as a musician does a musical score. The contrast between "political science" and the "art of politics," between "medical science" and the "practice" or "art of medicine," etc., applies to the relationship between theorist and critic. The latter deals not just with general principles and typological analysis but with the nonrecurring interaction of variables and idiosyncratic details which mark the work of art as a unique entity. The physician treats an actual person at an actual moment, just as the politician considers the given body politic and the critic speaks about the actual work of art. Applying Meyer's idea to the seeming paradox of postmodern deconstruction-reconstruction, I see in this drive to remake our vision the supreme value traditionally attributed to *new* synthesis in the West. However, today the value often is asserted through (at times fanatical) denial of older syntheses, which are mistakenly regarded not simply as cultural givens, available vocabulary, but as wicked determinants and inhibitors.

That would be all well and good if, as Davie points out, it reflected merely the age-old eagerness of poets to embrace new vocabulary and renew their idiom—which is their primary objective, after all. Toughminded historians might dismiss the postmodern yearning for an apocalyptic cleansing as another amusing spectacle of absurd objectives. But some could take it more seriously as another symptom of deep malaise in the intellectual community of the so-called "developed" world. If the very culture is widely resented by disaffected intellectuals as repressive and muddled, this condition sometimes seems to resemble the grim rejecting mood of many factions, in the Reformation era. The moral spleen, the thirst for justification, the iconoclastic itch may well derive from a profound religious need the satisfaction of which our scientific age has, to some extent, stifled. But, ironically, the righteous fervor in much postmodern commentary strikes me as negatively imitative of scientific discourse in its early Baconian moment; for when empiricism took over the iconoclastic function of radical Protestantism, our world of "progress" and "revision" was born.

The most accelerated rejection of humanistic revision of Christian values, bringing the savage denunciation of Enlightenment norms and Kantian objective categories, appears with startling clarity in the postromantic work of Max Stirner, often regarded as the spiritual forerunner of the most extreme atheistic existentialism. For Stirner, Western humanism and rationalism were a fraud, as was Hegelianism and all attempts to rescue German idealism. This anarchic nihilist declared Man as well as God to be dead and (to the chagrin of Karl Marx) already denounced socialism-communism as a resuscitation of the unholy church which always assumes power on the pretext of knowing the good, but then through power programmatically oppresses actual—that is, transitory, mortal, creative—existence. In *The Ego and Its Own*, Stirner "posited [himself] on nothing," engaged in a radical devaluation of all values, and hurled a revolutionary challenge at the structure of the world as otherness.[35] Though his quest for a complete revaluation starting from the irreducible Cartesian datum of his own existence may strike many modern readers as "paradoxically" tainted by gnostic passion, Stirner in fact typifies a broad class of Western thinkers who experience the worst repercussions of the late Renaissance "dissociation of sensibility," a trauma which was already indelibly marked by gnostic sentiments at the start of the Renaissance. From Pascal to Sartre, we can trace the features of a modernized Western gnosticism, which in its latest guise today goes under the name of existentialism.

Hans Jonas has identified the symptomatic resemblances of our latterday cosmic terror as that of aliens who are compelled, by their recognition of estrangement, to live in a ceaseless dynamics of realization. Supposedly, rest in the joy and certainty of a perceived reality no longer is conceivable.[36] Whereas earlier gnostic dualism at least pictured man heroically reclaiming his birthright against an antagonistic, antidivine nature, existentialism reflects the total depreciation of nature, which (as a negative result of continuing scientific discourse) has become, or been unmasked as, indifferent toward man. The Pascalian thinking reed—crushed by a blind universe, no longer feeling kinship with a cosmic order but rather regarding himself as cast into prison—is still unable, now as post-Christian "unhoused" man, to repair the ruins of ancient cosmic piety and repossess the therewith linked ethics of classical civilization. Nietzsche saw that nihilism could spring from the devaluation of the interim highest values, if this process were finally interpreted as the collapse of the possibility of obligatory values. In the citadel of reason, Sartre reinstated the antinomian argument of the gnostics that, since there is no sign of a transcendent, man must regard himself as abandoned and reclaim his freedom, making himself his own project. Pneumatic man is beyond good and evil and creates in the intensely temporal mode of the Heideggerian "moment," with no real rest or place in the present since acceptance may merely be a masked relapse or brings the danger of entrapment in degeneracy (*Verfallenheit*).

The Platonic contemplation of immutable divine order (*theoria*), the beholding of eternal objects in relation to which human experience in time can be placed (as Dante still understood this), has, since antiquity, lost its status virtually in parallel with the deanthropomorphization of nature. According to postmodern thought, the Renaissance program of epochal renewal, the Reformation recharting of course toward the goal of universal salvation, and in turn even the Enlightenment secular doctrine of perfectibility and the romantic revisions thereof have been replaced by the permanent eschatological tension of crisis: the commitment to constant futurity. One of the main charges postmodern thinkers have leveled against modernism is that (because of or despite its apocalyptic awareness) it tried to gather, codify, exhibit, and thereby rescue, in some necessarily transmuted consciousness, the complete Western heritage. But now, the modernist tendency to iconize and reify all relationships has been denounced as often as the word Liberty was printed in the era of the American and French revolutions. In my view, however, major exponents of postmodern literary theorizing, once more exhibiting a resurgence of gnostic forces in Western civilization, again conceive of life under the classically gnostic metaphoric notions of forlornness and dread. Though the tenacious concept of "homesickness" is no longer stressed in an environment of atheism, the existential notion of authenticity reinstates the gnostic concept of the "noise of the world," the confusing discourse of blinded captives and of unworthy laws, to which the spirit responds by "awakening." The ancient gnostics regarded man's spirit (*pneuma*) as caught in a falling or sinking which resulted from his "being-cast-into-the-world" (Heidegger's *Geworfenheit*, Pascal's "Cast into the infinite immensity of spaces of which I am ignorant, and which know me not, I am frightened"). The feeling of an absolute rift "between man and that in which he finds himself lodged—the world" was and again is primary (compare Heidegger's *Riss*). Against the mindlessness of a creation based on ignorance and passion, the gnostic rebel projects himself by a radical revaluation of otherness—which in today's terms ostensibly includes the entire Western heritage as inhibitory "noise." (Of course, existentialism is just more such "noise" to antignostics.)

An even more negative assessment of postmodern literary concepts results if we regard them as one bundle of many gnostic symptoms in the larger context of contemporary cultural and political thought and apply a critique based on Volume IV of Erich Voegelin's monumental study *Order and History*.[37] Voegelin renders a qualitative judgment of the two principal modes of understanding fashioned by Near Eastern, Mediterranean, and European civilization in antiquity: the *noetic* illumination (whose highest standard was achieved by Plato) and the *pneumatic* (whose epitome was St. Paul in the train of the prophets). In the several centuries leading to the formation and then collapse of the Roman Empire, ancient philosophy had to cope with a series of imposed traumatic redirectings of the impulse to create an ecumenic totality, the justification for which was the purported need to subsume diverse cultures under a mediating order. The great transition in antiquity was from culturally self-contained older empires with their complete cosmological system (Egypt) to universalistic empires which gradually rationalized "concupiscential" drives through an expansion of the mythological horizon in order to accommodate imperialist ambitions (Alexander to Augustus). In the Judeo-Christian line of religious development, the disappointment over the lack of congruence—between spiritual aspirations for an ecumene on the plane of real time in history and the use and acquisition of power ostensibly to bring order—was another confirmation of "disorder." Given the special Jewish sense of the "chosen" people displaced in history, Paul definitively transferred expectations of eventual fulfillment of order to a transcendental plane. Achievement of a universal plan would proceed in a different realm than that of time, since the elect suffered and were manifestly impotent on earth; the Judeo-Christian kingdom of God replaced the Greco-Roman pagan vision of ecumenical empire. Thus the tension between imperfect time and perfect eternity was intensely experienced, and generations of late pagan and early Christian thinkers began to elaborate that sense of another in-between kind of time which partakes of eternity and lends order to temporality—a kind of time which has a structure marked by cardinal points or turnings (*kairoi*) and directedness toward an ending (*apokalypsis*). This shaped the Western view of time processes and made the laws of time into the significant factor, the medium of experience underlying Western realist mimesis—the subject Erich Auerbach has examined. As Frank Kermode has shown, it deeply informed the Western idea of the special realm of "fiction."

The craving for a superconstruct which would overcome real disorder in human affairs has never died. It was central in the thinking of liberal and radical Protestants in the late Renaissance when, after the disappointment in the failure of the Reformation and out of the trauma of bitter civil war, they reconstituted their faith in a radical break in consciousness. It was apparent in the ecumenical vision of romantics such as Novalis who were reacting to the disappointments and trauma attendant upon the French Revolution (e.g., in *Christianity or Europe*). It thrives in the ecumenic-imperialist dogmas of a communist world revolution in the twentieth century. Voegelin characterizes the latter as a virulent focus of gnostic forces because, after several millenia, the main thrust of gnostic "rebellion" remains the destructive hatred of "what is," and the method of self-validation for adherents is largely through a disguised nihilistic attack on life and nature, though it also often enough occurs openly. Real humaneness is postponed puritanically on behalf of an hypostatized future. Like Jonas, Voegelin views the problem of the twentieth century as analogous to (*not* identical with) that of antiquity. Vast masses of disturbed peoples, to a great extent consisting of hordes of uprooted barbarians imploding into or from lower layers within the "developed" world, seeth with resentment. Gnostic attitudes encourage rage by the displaced against a supposed "system" which denies real satisfaction yet fails to achieve order in compensation. Modern gnostics foster readiness to follow a variety of ecumenical crusades. Since Napoleon's refurbishing of the hallowed imperial symbols, tailored into an explicit costume for the French Revolution as a unifying complex, we have had our fill of fascistic and totalitarian appeals by modernizers who wish to shortcut their imitation or overwhelming of the developed countries.

In Voegelin's analysis, the confusion of the twentieth century reflects, then, the attempt at evasion of our ineluctable involvement in reality. He points to the age-old awareness of man's being grounded in the cosmos, yet of man's necessary moving from this ground toward "God"; consciousness of this motion (which entails the "separation" of individuation) has from the beginning constituted and still constitutes the inner basis of the human psyche. Seeking to become regrounded, man senses himself to be in a distressful in-between state (Plato's *metaxy*), even though his condition is the natural cause of his particular identity as a creature. The danger to man arises not from being "in-between," but from falsifications of his situation which exacerbate it without leading to any further peak moments of "illumination." Gnosticism is perverse insofar as it encourages the hypostatizing of constructs which seem to offer redemption, and thus induces human beings to pursue concupiscential goals—crimes and aggression—against all the *evidence* of history respecting the true nature of imperialist motives and imperialist exploitation of religious cravings and symbolism.

I, too, sense in much of postmodern discussion the undertow of re-channeled religious hysteria which extensively pervaded romantic metaphysical and social speculation and radical humanist and Protestant ideas before that. Nietzsche's suspicions against the religious mentality as the fountainhead of nihilism seem not so farfetched, even if—as René Girard believes—Nietzschean fulminations, too, are tainted as an act of mimetic struggle with Europe's "shadow" and are provoked out of envy toward genuinely creative personality.[38] Postmodern existentialist criticism assails modernism for having in effect hypostatized the organizing scheme of modern consciousness and the whole repertory of cultural possessions; this drive to control everything in an iconic construct supposedly subverts authentic being, which should be a constant "becoming." Even though modernism pretends to bring everything pertaining to time process into copresence, most extremely in the symbolist "perfection" of a work of art, the literary habit of "spatialization" falsifies the temporal dimensions of life. But from my perspective, postmodernism in turn indulges in another variation of the gnostic escapism described by Voegelin, because in its zealous reversal of values postmodernism hypostatizes the basis of self-experience of the psyche, declares the process of discovering motion out of the ground to be the effective producer of values and creator of the future, and elevates "becoming" (confuses it) as equivalent to *real* temporal process in its vast wholeness.

The rebellion against discovered groundedness takes its most immediate expression in the aggressive desire to dismantle "history," to deconstruct the encumbering paradigms and traditions and understandings and evolved relationships of the extant, complex, real, and contingent world. The gnostic analogue is battling the inimical "archons." On the pretext of an absolute "reconstruction" from *zero*, the postmodern mind as *pancrator* thus arrogates to itself the stature of a transmundane godhead. With few distinguished exceptions, postmodernism bypasses the tedious pathway of considering the minutiae of science, that unpleasant involvement in contingency. (A deeper artistic involvement with scientific lore and the mysteriously heavy plethora of details can, however, be illustrated by writers such as Pynchon.)

But postmodernity will not and perhaps cannot dispense with the formal trappings of scientific discourse; thus this ruling discourse pervades even our critical efforts to grasp "authenticity" and participate in a fruitful art. Someday—doubtless in the lifetime of many present readers—mention of postmodern ideas will evoke nostalgia, because they will be part of memory of what has passed in a series of events closely related to modernism.[39]

Notes

1. William V. Spanos, "Breaking the Circle: Hermeneutics as Dis-closure," *boundary 2*, 5 (Winter 1977): 435.

2. Ibid., p. 446.

3. In an excellent overview of contemporary theories of "The Hermeneutic Circle and the Art of Interpretation," *Comparative Literature* 24 (Spring 1972): 97–117, Wallace Martin points out that the intense late twentieth-century discussion of hermeneutics was rekindled from German romantic pronouncements, notably Schleiermacher's. Wallace eventually undermines the notion of a "hermeneutic circle" and favors a rational, objective, but antipositivistic structuralism like Barthes's (pp. 110–17), which acknowledges that literary interpretation is "historically contingent" because it is profoundly conditioned by "a critic's world view" (whether adequate or inadequate) and that "literature exists only in temporal movement" (uses of language by various others and ourselves). Literature can "shatter the individual languages we impose on other features of our world," and a work of art guides us toward a point of view, as we encounter it, much as does "ordinary" living speech.

4. Meyer Howard Abrams, *Natural Supernaturalism: Tradition and Revolution in Romantic Literature* (New York: W. W. Norton, 1971), p. 13.

5. Ihab Hassan, "Beyond a Theory of Literature: Intimations of Apocalypse?" in *Comparative Literature: Matter and Method*, ed. A. Owen Aldridge (Urbana: University of Illinois Press, 1969), pp. 25–35. Norman O. Brown's influence as a latter-day prophet surged following his Phi Beta Kappa address at Columbia University (May 31, 1960), published, with introductory commentary by Benjamin Nelson, under the title "Apocalypse: The Place of Mystery in the Life of the Mind," *Harper's*, May 1961, pp. 46–49. This address—which invokes Emerson's—exhibits many key motifs symptomatic of a traditional Anglo-American malaise: "mystic academies" and "disclosure" versus mechanistic, democratized learning; "ideogram" versus "alphabet" (routinized language); liberating "imagination" versus the tyranny of "books"; Dionysus (or an apocalyptic Christianity) versus normalized Christ. Like the modernists, Brown finds the roots of dilemma in the late Renaissance crisis of dissociation: "Read again the controversies of the seventeenth century and discover our choice: we are either in an age of miracles, says Hobbes, miracles with authenticate fresh revelations; or else we are in an age of reasoning from already received Scripture" (p. 49b). In my view, Brown typifies the (often historically blind) love-hate relationship toward the givens of culture and human nature when he echoes the programmatic call of early British science to overturn the deadening weight of Scripture; and thus his opposition to "scientific method" as the "attempt to democratize knowledge" is a standard confusion, because he mimics the elitism of the first radical Protestant empiricists.

6. Cited by Herbert Gorman, *James Joyce*, 2d ed. (New York: Rinehart & Co., 1948), p. 299.

7. René Wellek, "Philosophy and Postwar American Criticism," in *Comparative Literature: Matter and Method*, p. 23. Wellek recognizes that the "new motif of American criticism in recent years is Existentialism" (p. 21) but finds that critics today tend to use literature "only as a vehicle for ideas"—in the words of Karl Shapiro, for "'culture criticism or theology, ill concealed'" (p. 23).

8. Allan Rodway, "Crosscurrents in Contemporary English Criticism," in *Comparative Literature: Matter and Method*, p. 54. Rodway lists the ruling fallacies in nonstylistic modes of British criticism as the "historicist, personalist, romantic, biographical, or intentionalist and effective" (p. 57) and notes the rise of a "linguistic fallacy" (p. 58), that is, structuralism.

9. Among works demonstrating the significance of this development, special mention should be made of Herschel Baker, *The Race of Time: Three Lectures on Renaissance Historiography* (Toronto: University of Toronto Press, 1967), and Ricardo J. Quinones, *The Renaissance Discovery of Time* (Cambridge: Harvard University Press, 1972).

10. On the epochal interrelation of new metaphysics and science with literary revaluation and trauma in the late Renaissance, consult Hiram Haydn, *The Counter-Renaissance* (New York: Harcourt, Brace & World, 1950).

11. "Breaking the Circle," p. 437.

12. The importance of millenarian excitation for the breakthrough of scientific discourse and empiricism in Britain is convincingly and thoroughly documented by Charles Webster in *The Intellectual Revolution of the Seventeenth Century* (London and Boston: Routledge and Kegan Paul, 1974), and *The Great Instauration: Science, Medicine and Reform 1626–1660* (London: Duckworth, 1975). Illustrative of links to radical Protestants on the continent, who desired a sure "method" and encyclopedic

control, is the German Calvinist John Henry Alsted, treated in ch. 3 of *Puritans, the Millennium and the Future of Israel: Puritan Eschatology 1600–1660*, ed. Peter Toon (Cambridge and London: James Clarke & Co., 1970).

13. For bibliography on Leibniz's contribution to psychology (concept of the unconscious, evolution of mind), linguistics (deep structure), and cultural anthropology (ontological basis of systems of signs), consult my forthcoming article "Primal Utterance: Observations on Kuhlmann's Correspondence with Kircher, in View of Leibniz' Theories," in *Wege der Worte: Festschrift für Wolfgang Fleischhauer* (Köln: Böhlau Verlag, 1978). On the search for a universal medium of discourse, consult D. P. Walker, "Leibniz and Language," *Journal of the Warburg and Courtauld Institutes*, 35 (1972): 294–307.

14. The statements by Bacon interpolated in this paragraph are cited from Achsah Guibbory's excellent treatment of "Francis Bacon's View of History: The Cycles of Error and the Progress of Truth," *Journal of English and Germanic Philology* 74 (July 1975): 336–50. Like Guibbory, I will continue to cite from *The Works of Francis Bacon*, 14 vols., ed. James Spedding, Robert L. Ellis, and Douglas D. Heath (London 1857–74; fascimile rpt. Stuttgart: Friedrich Frommann Verlag Günther Holzbood, 1963), but will refer by title to chief works already conveniently subdivided by Bacon.

15. "Francis Bacon's View of History," p. 348. Brian Vickers's study of *Francis Bacon and Renaissance Prose* (Cambridge: Cambridge Univ. Press, 1968) is still indispensable for a primarily *literary* understanding of Bacon's "style" and its rhetorical structures. Since Bacon's impact clearly was not that of a scientific theorist or experimentalist, but that of an exponent of "method" who caught the imagination of his age, Vickers scrutinizes his habits of organizing a diverse range of writings and speeches for characteristic features; when one bridges the supposedly separate categories of Bacon's political, legal, literary, and "scientific" works, one discovers that rhetorical structurings, such as *partitio*, are central to the latter, too, and may well explain why they were received with respect. Contrary to Stephens, Vickers (ch. 3) does not assume that Bacon's main reason for using the aphorism is to conduct a psychological strategy. Rather, in the Renaissance, the aphorism already enjoyed special status, being associated with authoritative statement of laws and principles; and Bacon, essentially a creative writer, regarded it as one of several means at his disposal, though he recognized it was especially suited for the initial stages of guiding superior minds, as well as for avoiding the snares of faulty systems.

16. James Stephens, *Francis Bacon and the Style of Science* (Chicago: University of Chicago Press, 1975).

17. The German modernist confrontation with the "imperative" or problem of silence—and notably Hugo von Hofmannsthal's "Letter" of Lord Chandos to Francis Bacon ("Ein Brief" [1902])—is explored in Oskar Seidlin's essay "The Shroud of Silence," in *Essays in German and Comparative Literature* (Chapel Hill: University of North Carolina Press, 1961).

18. Jones examines the epochal shift, mightily furthered by the natural alliance of the Puritan and scientific elites, in "Science and Language in England of the Mid-Seventeenth Century," *Journal of English and Germanic Philology* 31 (1932): 315–31, and "Science and English Prose Style in the Third Quarter of the Seventeenth Century," *PMLA* 45 (December 1930): 977–1009.

19. The educational program of the Puritan intellectual leaders and their ties with

advanced Protestant thought on the continent are examined by G. H. Turnbull in his study of *Hartlib, Dury and Comenius* (Liverpool: University Press of Liverpool, 1947). These same connections are also treated in chs. 6 and 7 of Paoli Rossi, *Clavis universalis: arti mnemoniche e logica combinatoria da Lullo a Leibniz* (Milan: Riccardo Ricciardi, 1960), within the fuller European context of a reconstituted global vision of the "drama" of history, modern rationalist encyclopedism and illuministic pansophism, and the search for a reliable "method," as well as for a universal language and real character.

20. The impact of science and rationalist philosophy is convincingly demonstrated in Richard F. Jones's study of "The Attack on Pulpit Eloquence in the Restoration: An Episode in the Development of the Neo-Classical Standard for Prose," *Journal of English and Germanic Philology* 30 (1931): 188–217.

21. See Benjamin DeMott, "Comenius and the Real Character in England," *PMLA* 70 (December 1955): 1068–81; the interpolated wordings in translation from Comenius' *Via Lucis* are cited by DeMott.

22. John Wilkins, *An Essay towards a Real Character and a Philosophical Language*, fascimile ed. (Menston, England: Scolar Press Ltd., 1968), p. 385.

23. See Ralph W. V. Elliott, "Isaac Newton's 'Of an Universal Language,'" *Modern Language Review* 52 (January 1957): 1–17.

24. On Newton's theological views and the essential correspondence between divine and scientific truth for him, consult especially Frank E. Manuel, *The Religion of Isaac Newton* (Oxford: Oxford University Press, 1974). Newton's cultural anthropological speculations on the evolution and corruption of religious and metaphysical knowledge since remote antiquity can be more fully appreciated against the background presented in D. P. Walker's study, *The Ancient Theology: Studies in Christian Platonism from the Fifteenth to the Eighteenth Century* (London: Duckworth, 1972).

25. In *The Rosicrucian Enlightenment* (London and Boston: Routledge and Kegan Paul, 1972), Frances Yates examines seventeenth-century British-German cultural relations and affinities, and relevant French and Italian sentiment, which help explain the favorable climate for Protestant acceptance of a scientific elite and furtherance of the Royal Society. A condensed version of her findings is given in her review essay on Webster's study *The Great Instauration: Science, Medicine, and Reform 1626–1660*, appearing under the title "Science, Salvation, and the Cabala," *New York Review of Books*, May 27, 1976, pp. 27–29.

26. On British-German-Italian connections in particular, as well as the neomythic theme of a Salomonic "temple" and heritage among European *illuminati*, consult Karl R. H. Frick, *Licht und Finsternis: Gnostisch-theosophische und freimauerisch-okkulte Geheimgesellschaften bis an die Wende zum 20. Jahrhundert, Teil 1: Ursprünge und Anfänge* (Graz: Akademische Druck- und Verlagsanstalt, 1975).

27. Donald Davie, *The Language of Science and the Language of Literature, 1700–1740* (London and New York: Sheed and Ward, 1963).

28. Ibid., p. 59.

29. Ibid., p. 85.

30. Leonard B. Meyer, "Concerning the Sciences, the Arts—AND the Humanities," *Critical Inquiry* 1 (September 1974); 163–217.

31. Ibid., p. 182.

32. Bacon's two "intentions" bear a rough resemblance to Descartes' two "acts" of

---

the mind, "intuition" and "deduction," as described under Rule III of *Rules for the Direction of the Mind* (*Philosophical Essays*, trans. Laurence J. Lafleur [Indianapolis: Bobbs-Merrill, 1964]). For example:

We can therefore distinguish an intuition of the mind from certain deduction by the fact that in the latter we perceive a movement or a certain succession of thought, while we do not in the former; and furthermore, because present evidence is not necessary to the latter, as it is to intuition, but rather, in a certain measure, it derives its certainty from memory. From this it follows that certain propositions which are immediately derived from first principles can be said to be known in different ways, now by intuition, now by deduction. But the first principles themselves are known only by intuition, while, on the other hand, ultimate conclusions are known only by deduction. (p. 155)

Though beginning confidently from the irreducible primal intuition of existence as a mind, Descartes—like Bacon—encounters language as a peril: "Now I am truly astonished when I consider [how weak my mind is and] how apt I am to fall into error. For even though I consider all this in my mind without speaking, still words impede me, and I am nearly deceived by the terms of ordinary language" (*Second Meditation*, p. 89).

33. Stephens recognizes (pp. 69 ff.) that a rational art of "memory" necessarily is useful to the reformer Bacon because this faculty is associated with history, whose unrealized resources must be mobilized for a radical change of course; but he emphasizes that, for Bacon, "rhetoric" plays no significant role in the process of discovery. This crucial question is also explored by Frances Yates in *The Art of Memory* (Chicago: University of Chicago Press, 1966), pp. 370–73, and by Paolo Rossi in *Francis Bacon: From Magic to Science*, trans. Sacha Rabinovitch (Chicago: University of Chicago Press, 1968), pp. 207–14. Perhaps because Bacon emphasizes such a grand leap or breaking out of cultural captivity, he largely satisfies his own libertarian-redemptive impulse and so does not become obsessed with hermeneutic circularity as a repetitive problem on a lesser scale. Once underway, the pilgrim mind (as represented by the scientific elite) makes its gradualistic progress out of and beyond the labyrinth, over waystations of concretized findings (emblematic formulations of discovery). See also Wallace Martin's "The Hermeneutic Circle and the Art of Interpretation."

34. "Concerning the Sciences," p. 203.

35. Stirner (1806–1856), who has had a significant impact on the Anglo-American anarchist and nihilist streams, is the subject of an excellent recent monograph by R. W. K. Paterson, *The Nihilistic Egoist Max Stirner* (London and New York: Oxford University Press, 1971). A more accurate translation of Stirner's *Der Einzige und sein Eigentum* would be *The Solitary* (or *Singular*) and *His Property* (or *Ownness*); actually, Stirner proposed that identity is absolute as an "open (or manifest) phrase," whereas concept or name is "a contentless word" ("offenbare—Phrase," "das inhaltsleere Wort"; *Kleinere Schriften*, ed. John Henry Mackay [Berlin: Schuster & Loeffler, 1898], p. 115). Stirner accepts the void he becomes in order actually to be:

Im *Einzigen* kehrt selbst der Eigner in sein schöpferisches Nichts zurück, aus welchem er geboren wird. . . . Stell. Ich auf Mich, den Einzigen, meine Sache, dann steht sie auf dem Vergänglichen, dem sterblichen Schöpfer seiner, der sich selbst verzehrt, und ich darf sagen: Ich hab' mein Sach' auf Nichts gestellt. (*Der Einzige und sein Eigentum*, ed. Ahlrich Meyer [Stuttgart: Reclam, 1972], p. 199.)

In the singular (sole one), the owner himself returns into his creative nothingness, out of which he is born. . . . If I posit Myself, the singular, my thing, then it rests on the transitory, the mortal creator of himself, who consumes himself, and I may say: I've posited my thing (affair) on nothing.

36. See Jonas's brilliant "Epilogue: Gnosticism, Existentialism, and Nihilism" in his book *The Gnostic Religion: The Message of the Alien God and the Beginnings of Christianity*, 2nd. rev. ed. (Boston: Beacon, 1963).

37. Erich Voegelin, *The Ecumenic Age*, vol. 4 of *Order and History* (Baton Rouge: Louisiana State University Press, 1974).

38. Girard demotes Nietzsche in spiritual contrast to Wagner and Dostoevsky in "Superman in the Underground: Strategies of Madness—Nietzsche, Wagner, and Dostoevsky," *MLN* 91 (December 1976): 1161–85. Despite Nietzsche's boast to kill the dead law, supposedly he slips into a competitive love-hate relationship characteristic of Western intellectuals; his "vision is turned into one of the countless inverted ethical Manicheanisms that the contemporary world produces in such abundance" (p. 1170).

39. I would exclude the apparently "different" thinker Heidegger from my assessment of the closeness of modern and postmodern ideas were it not for the fact he continuously transcribes paradigms worked out by Hölderlin—thus furthering the ontological developmental myth which Hölderlin, as well as Hegel and Schelling, imbibed from the same secularized theosophical-pansophical fountains of radical Protestantism. Heidegger describes the Renaissance shift beyond the medieval *argumentum ex verbo* and *argumentum ex re* (words from the correlative Book of Nature) to empirical gradualistic revision in his essay "The Age of the World View" (trans. Marjorie Grene, *boundary 2*, 4 [Winter 1976]: 341–55). He observes astutely how, once permeated by the spirit of science, even "history as research projects and objectifies the past" (p. 346), and how having and elaborating a worldview characterizes the imitative humanistic disciplines. As man becomes increasingly subject and world concomitantly object (representational product, conquered picture, etc.), "the modern age races to the fulfillment of its nature with a velocity unknown to its participants" (p. 353); however, deeper reflection on the uniqueness of the historical moment "sets the man of the future in that in-between area, in which he belongs to being and yet remains a stranger to the existent" (p. 354). To me this sounds like merely another gyre of the revisionary Western mind, too in love with the pattern "in-betweenness" and "transformation" to overcome the mythic spell. If Voegelin is right, the most depressing "sameness" of our condition is the age-old inability to resist the misdirected craving for justification and meaning which springs from the tension so poignantly addressed by Heidegger.

Nietzsche's Prefiguration of Postmodern American Philosophy

You ask me about the idiosyncracies of philosophers? . . . There is their lack of historical sense, their hatred of even the idea of becoming, their Egyptianism. They think they are doing a thing *honour* when they dehistoricize it, *sub specie aeterni*—when they make a mummy of it. All the philosophers have handled for millennia has been conceptual mummies; nothing actual has escaped from their hands alive. They kill, they stuff, when they worship, these conceptual idolaters—they become a mortal danger to everything when they worship. Death, change, age, as well as procreation and growth, are for them objections—refutations even. What is, does not *become*; what becomes, *is* not.
Nietzsche, *Twilight of the Idols*

What I relate is the history of the next two centuries. I describe what is coming, what can no longer come differently: *the advent of nihilism*. This history can be related even now; for necessity itself is at work here. This future speaks even now in a hundred signs, this destiny announces itself everywhere; for this music of the future all ears are cocked even now. For some time now, our whole European culture has been moving as toward a catastrophe, with a tortured tension that is growing from decade to decade: restlessly, violently, headlong, like a river that wants to reach the end, that no longer reflects, that is afraid to reflect.
Nietzsche, *The Will to Power*

Nietzsche is the central figure in postmodern thought in the West. His aphoristic style—the epigram as style—governs the elusive texts of postmodern philosophers such as Ludwig Wittgentstein and E. M. Cioran. His antihermeneutical perspectivism underlies the deconstructive stance of postmodern critics such as Jacques Derrida and Paul de Man. His genealogical approach, especially regarding the link between knowledge and power, regulates the neo-Marxist textual practice of postmodern critic-historians such as Michel Foucault and Edward Said. And his gallant attempt to overcome traditional metaphysics is a major preoccupation of postmodern thinkers such as Martin Heidegger, Hans-Georg Gadamer, and Jean-Paul Sartre.

In this paper, I will try to show the ways in which Nietzsche prefigures the crucial moves made recently in postmodern American philosophy. I will confine my remarks to two of Nietzsche's texts: *Twilight of the Idols* and *The Will to Power*.[1] The postmodern American philosophers I will examine are W. V. Quine, Nelson Goodman, Wilfred Sellars, Thomas Kuhn, and Richard Rorty. The three moves I shall portray are: the move toward antirealism or conventionalism in ontology; the move toward the demythologization of the Myth of the Given or antifoundationalism in epistemology; and the move toward the detranscendentalization of the subject or the dismissal of the mind as a sphere of inquiry. I then shall claim that Nietzsche believed such moves lead to a paralyzing nihilism and ironic skepticism unless they are supplemented with a new worldview, a new "countermovement" to overcome such nihilism and skepticism. Lastly, I will suggest that postmodern American philosophy has not provided such a "countermovement," settling instead for either updated versions of scientism (Quine and Sellars), an aristocratic resurrection of pluralistic stylism (Goodman), a glib ideology of professionalism (Kuhn), or a nostalgic appeal to enlightened conversation (Rorty). Such weak candidates for a "countermovement" seem to indicate the extent to which postmodern American philosophy—similar to much of postmodern thought in the West—constitutes a dead, impotent rhetoric of a declining and decaying civilization.

Antirealism

The originary figures of modern analytic philosophy—Gottlob Frege, Alexius Meinong, Bertrand Russell, and G. E. Moore—are the acknowledged ancestors of postmodern American philosophers. These figures constituted a formidable realist revolt against psychologism, conventionalism, and idealism.[2] Frege revolted against J. S. Mill's psychologism and J. Venn's conventionalism in logic; Meinong, against Franz

Brentano's psychologism in object theory; Russell and Moore, against F. H. Bradley's Hegelian idealism in metaphysics and epistemology. Each separate attack shares a common theme: an attempt to resurrect realism.

There are many forms of realism in modern analytic philosophy, including naive realism, Platonic realism, critical realism, and internal realism.[3] The basic claims of any form of realism are that objects, things, states of affairs, or the world exist externally to us and independently of our sense experience; and that these objects, things, states of affairs, or this world, in some fundamental way, determine what is true, objective, and real.

This two-prong definition of realism suggests two important elements of any realist position. First, it links any realist position to some notion of correspondence (or re-presenting) between either ideas and objects, words and things, sentences and states of affairs, or theories and the world. Second, this definition proposes something other than human social practice to serve as the final court of appeal which determines what is and what we ought to believe. To put it crudely, realism is preoccupied with assuring us that there is an external world and with obtaining the true (accurate, objective, valid) copy of this world.

Postmodern American philosophers affirm the first prong of the definition of realism—thus bypassing idealism—but see no need to build the notion of correspondence into the way the claim is stated. In short, they are highly critical of the subject-object problematic embodied in the first prong of the definition such that grasping reality consists of crossing the subject-object hiatus, leaving one's inner world in order to get in contact with the external world, and of one's ideas copying or corresponding to the world.

Postmodern American philosophers reject the second prong of the definition of realism—thus promoting conventionalism in ontology. They refuse to accept the view that the world determines truth or that the world is the final court of appeal which compels us to accept what is or believe as we ought.

This rejection is based on two major insights of postmodern American philosophers: the conventional character of constructing (reductionist or nonreductionist) logical systems of the world and the theory-laden character of observations. The first insight crystallized after Rudolf Carnap's highly acclaimed yet unsuccessful attempt in his *Logical Con-*

struction of the World (1928) (and better known as his *Aufbau*) to rationally reconstruct the process of acquiring knowledge by reducing (or translating) statements about the world to those of immediate experience. The second insight was gained from A. J. Ayer's popular yet no less unsuccessful attempt in his *Language, Truth and Logic* (1936) to defend the verificationist theory of meaning (or roughly promoting the primacy of observational evidence for determining the meaningfulness of a sentence).

Almost a decade after his painstaking study of Carnap's *Aufbau* in his masterful work, *The Structure of Appearance* (1951), Goodman concluded in his renowned essay, "The Way the World Is,"

What we must face is the fact that even the truest description comes nowhere near faithfully reproducing the way the world is . . . for it has explicit primitives, routes of construction, etc., none of them features of the world described. Some philosophers contend, therefore, that if systematic descriptions introduce an arbitrary artificial order, then we should make our descriptions unsystematic to bring them more into accord with the world. Now the tacit assumption here is that the respects in which a description is unsatisfactory are *just those respects in which it falls short of being a faithful picture;* and the tacit *goal* is to achieve a description that as nearly as possible gives a living likeness. But the goal is a delusive one. For we have seen that even the most realistic way of picturing amounts merely to one kind of conventionalization. In painting, the selection, the emphasis, the conventions are different from but no less peculiar to the vehicle, and no less variable, than those of language. The idea of making verbal descriptions approximate pictorial depiction loses its point when we understand that to turn a description into the most faithful possible picture would amount to nothing more than exchanging some conventions for others.[4]

After his search for a criterion of adequacy for constructional systems, such as Carnap's phenomenalistic one, or for scientific theories, such as Einstein's special theory of relativity, Goodman held that the choice is not based primarily on mere agreement with the facts, that is, observational data, but rather on, among other things, structural simplicity. In his influential essay, "The Test of Simplicity," he writes,

Thus selection of a theory must always be made in advance of the determination of some of the facts it covers; and, accordingly, some criterion other than conformity with such facts must be applied in making the selection. After as many points as we like have been plotted by experiment concerning the correlation of two factors (for example, of time and deterioration of radioactivity), we predict the remaining points by choosing one among all the infinitely many curves that cover the plotted points. Obviously, simplicity of some sort is a cardinal factor in making this choice (we pick the "smoothest" curve). The very validity of the choice depends upon whether the choice is properly made according to such criteria. Thus simplicity here is not a consideration applicable after truth is determined but is one of the standards of validity that are applied in the effort to discover truth.[5]

In a later essay, "Art and Inquiry" and in his most recent work, *Ways of Worldmaking* (1978), Goodman advances the notion of fitness as appropriate to (and as replacement for) talk about truth.

Truth of a hypothesis after all is a matter of fit—fit with a body of theory, and fit of hypothesis and theory to the data at hand and the facts to be encountered.[6]

Briefly, then, truth of statements and rightness of descriptions, representations, exemplifications, expressions—of design, drawing, diction, rhythm—is primarily a matter of fit: fit to what is referred to in one way or another, or to other renderings, or to modes and manners of organization. The differences between fitting a version to a world, a world to a version, and a version together or to other versions fade when the role of versions in making the worlds they fit is recognized. And knowing or understanding is seen as ranging beyond the acquiring of true beliefs to the discovering and devising of fit of all sorts.[7]

In his famous essay, "Two Dogmas of Empiricism," Quine observed that in Ayer's attempt to correlate each meaningful sentence with observational evidence, that is, empirical confirmation, Ayer remained tied to Carnap's reductionist project by trying to reduce the meaningfulness of a sentence to its empirical import.

But the dogma of reductionism has, in a subtler and more tenuous form, continued to influence the thought of empiricists. The notion lingers that to each statement, or each synthetic statement, there is associated a unique range of possible sensory events such that the occurrence of any of them would add to the likelihood of truth of the statement, and that there is associated also another unique range of possible sensory events whose occurrence would detract from that likelihood. This notion is of course implicit in the verification theory of meaning.

The dogma of reductionism survives in the supposition that each statement, taken in isolation from its fellows, can admit of confirmation or infirmation at all. My countersuggestion, issuing essentially from Carnap's doctrine of the physical world in the *Aufbau*, is that our statements about the external world face the tribunal of sense experience not individually but only as a corporate body.[8]

Quine extended his critique of updated empiricism to the most cherished notion of modern analytic philosophers—the notion of analyticity, the idea that a statement is true by virtue of meanings and independently of fact. Given his Duhemian holism, the idea of an isolated statement being true without empirical confirmation is as unacceptable as the idea of an isolated statement being true with empirical confirmation. His main point is that the basic "unit of empirical significance is the whole of science,"[9] namely, competing theories (versions or descriptions) of the world, not isolated statements, since the truth-value of such statements can change relative to one's theory of the world.

If this view is right, it is misleading to speak of the empirical content of an individual statement—especially if it is a statement at all remote from the experiential periphery of the field. Furthermore it becomes folly to seek a boundary between synthetic statements, which hold contingently on experience, and analytic statements, which hold come what may. Any statement can be held true come what may, if we make drastic enough adjustments elsewhere in the system. Even a statement very close to the periphery can be held true in the face of recalcitrant experience by pleading hallucination or by amending certain statements of the kind called logical laws. Conversely, by the same token, no statement is immune to revision.[10]

Goodman and Quine are the (retired, Harvard) patriarchs of postmodern American philosophy. Their respective holistic critiques of Carnap and, to a lesser degree, Ayer, constitute the emergence of postmodernity in American philosophy and mark the Americanization of analytic philosophy.[11] If Goodman and Quine are the patriarchs, then Richard Rorty and Thomas Kuhn are the renegade stepchildren. Rorty and Kuhn have followed through most thoroughly on the antirealist, historicist and conventionalist implications of the views of Goodman and the early Quine.

In his celebrated article, "The World Well Lost," Rorty concludes that the theory-laden character of observations relativizes talk about the world such that appeals to "the world" as a final court of appeal to determine what is true or what we should believe is viciously circular. We cannot isolate "the world" from theories of the world, then compare these theories of the world with a theory-free world. We cannot compare theories with anything that is not a product of another theory. So any talk about "the world" is relative to the alternative theories available. In response to the second prong of the definition of realism—to the notion that the world determines truth—Rorty states,

Now, to put my cards on the table, I think that the realistic true believer's notion of the world is an obsession rather than an intuition. I also think that Dewey was right in thinking that the only intuition we have of the world as determining truth is just the intuition that we must make our new beliefs conform with a vast body of platitudes, unquestioned perceptual reports, and the like.[12]

Kuhn, the other stepchild of Goodman and Quine, has received more attention than any postmodern American philosopher of science primarily because he has provided a new descriptive vocabulary which gives a new perspective on a sacrosanct institution, that is, natural science, in our culture in light of the early Quine's pragmatism and Goodman's conventionalism. His controversial yet highly acclaimed book, *The Structure of Scientific Revolutions* (1962) serves as a rallying point for antirealists owing to statements such as the following:

A scientific theory is usually felt to be better than its predecessors not only in the sense that it is a better instrument for discovering and solving puzzles but also because it is somehow a better representation of what nature is really like. One often hears that successive theories grow ever closer to, or approximate more and more closely to, the truth. Apparently generalizations like that refer not to the puzzle-solutions and the concrete predictions derived from a theory but rather to its ontology, to the match, that is, between the entities with which the theory populates nature and what is "really there."

Perhaps there is some other way of salvaging the notion of 'truth' for application to whole theories, but this one will not do. There is, I think, no theory-independent way to reconstruct phrases like 'really there'; the notion of a match between the ontology of a theory and its "real" counterpart in nature now seems to me illusive in principle.[13]

If I am right, then 'truth' may, like 'proof', be a term with only intra-theoretic applications.[14]

There surely have been antirealists (such as Hegel), conventionalist philosophers of science (such as Pierre Duhem) and pragmatists (such as John Dewey) prior to the rise of postmodern American philosophy. But I claim that it is Nietzsche who most openly and unequivocally prefigures the antirealist, conventionalist move made by postmodern American philosophers.

For example, in the section entitled, "How the 'Real World' at Last Became a Myth" in *Twilight of the Idols*, Nietzsche comically mocks the notion of a theory-free world, a "world" that can be appealed to in adjudicating between competing theories of the world.

4. The real world—unattainable? Unattained, at any rate. And if unattained also *unknown*. Consequently also no consolation, no redemption, no duty: how could we have a duty towards something unknown?

(The grey of dawn. First yawning of reason.
Cockcrow of positivism.)
5. The 'real world'—an idea no longer of any use, not even a duty any longer—an idea grown useless, superfluous, *consequently* a refuted idea: let us abolish it!
(Broad daylight; breakfast; return of cheerful-
ness and *bon sens*; Plato blushes for shame; all
free spirits run riot.)
6. We have abolished the real world: what world is left? the apparent world per-haps? . . . But no! *with the real world we have also abolished the apparent world!*
(Mid-day; moment of the shortest shadow; end
of the longest error; zenith of mankind;
INCIPIT ZARATHUSTRA.) (*T1*, pp. 40–41)

Nietzsche clearly subscribes to the insight of postmodern American philosophers which holds that facts are theory-laden. He writes in *The Will to Power*,

Against positivism, which halts at phenomena—"There are only *facts*"—I would say: No, facts are precisely what there is not, only interpretations. We cannot establish any fact "in itself": perhaps it is folly to want to do such a thing. (*WP*, p. 267)

There are no facts, everything is in flux, incomprehensible, elusive; what is rela-tively most enduring is—our opinions. (*WP*, p. 327)

Goodman's pleas for a pluralism of versions of the world as manifest in the following passages:

The movement is from unique truth and a world fixed and found to a diversity of right and even conflicting versions or worlds in the making.[15]

There are very many different equally true descriptions of the world, and their truth is the only standard of their faithfulness. And when we say of them that they all involve conventionalizations, we are saying that no one of these different descriptions is *exclusively* true, since the others are also true. None of them tells us *the* way the world is, but each of them tells us *a* way the world is.[16]

echoes Nietzsche's quip,

No limit to the ways in which the world can be interpreted; every interpretation a symptom of growth or of decline.
    Inertia needs unity (monism); plurality of interpretations a sign of strength. Not to desire to deprive the world of its disturbing and enigmatic character! (*WP*, p. 326)

As we saw earlier, for Goodman, this pluralism suggests multiple criteria for accepting versions of the world—in science and art.

Truth is not enough; it is at most a necessary condition. But even this concedes too much; the noblest scientific laws are seldom quite true. Minor discrepancies are overridden in the interest of breadth or power or simplicity. Science denies its data as the statesman denies his constituents—within the limits of prudence. . . . Truth and its aesthetic counterpart amount to appropriateness under different names. If we speak of hypotheses but not works of art as true, that is because we reserve the terms "true" and "false" for symbols in sentential form. I do not say this difference is negligible, but it is specific rather than generic, a difference in field of application rather than in formula, and marks no schism between the scientific and the aesthetic.[17]

Similarly for Nietzsche, seeking after 'truth' is essentially a matter of positing a goal and achieving that goal.

The ascertaining of "truth" and "untruth," the ascertaining of facts in general, is fundamentally different from creative positing, from forming, shaping, overcoming, willing, such as is of the essence of philosophy. To introduce a meaning—this task still remains to be done, assuming there is no meaning yet. Thus it is with sounds, but also with the fate of peoples: they are capable of the most different interpretations and direction toward different goals.

On a yet higher level is to *posit a goal* and mold facts according to it; that is, active interpretation and not merely conceptual translation. (*WP*, p. 327)

Note the way in which Nietzsche's perspectivism, most clearly stated in the following passage,

That the value of the world lies in our interpretation (—that other interpretations than merely human ones are perhaps somewhere possible—); that previous interpretations have been perspective valuations by virtue of which we can survive in life, i.e., in the will to power, for the growth of power; that every elevation of man brings with it the overcoming of narrower interpretations; that every strengthening and increase of power opens up new perspectives and means believing in new horizons—this idea permeates my writings. The world with which we are concerned is false, i.e., is not a fact but a fable and approximation on the basis of a meager sum of observations; it is "in flux," as something in a state of becoming, as a falsehood always changing but never getting near the truth: for—there is no "truth." (*WP*, p. 330)

anticipates the early Quine's pragmatism, best articulated in this famous paragraph,

As an empiricist I continue to think of the conceptual scheme of science as a tool, ultimately, for predicting future experience in the light of past experience. Physical objects are conceptually imported into the situation as convenient intermediaries—not by definition in terms of experience, but simply as irreducible posits comparable, epistemologically, to the gods of Homer. For my part I do, qua lay physicist, believe in physical objects and not in Homer's Gods; and I consider it a scientific error to believe otherwise. But in point of epistemological footing the physical objects and the gods differ only in degree and not in kind. Both sorts of entities enter our conception only as cultural posits. The myth of physical objects is epistemologically superior to most in that it has proved more efficacious than other myths as a device for working a manageable structure into the flux of experience.[18]

Note also the crucial role of utility and human interests in the early Quine's pragmatism and Nietzsche's perspectivism.

The quality of myth, however, is relative; relative, in this case, to the epistemological point of view. This point of view is one among various, corresponding to one among our various interests and purposes.[19]

The apparent world, i.e., a world viewed according to values; ordered, selected according to values, i.e., in this case according to the viewpoint of utility in regard to the preservation and enhancement of the power of a certain species of animal.

The perspective therefore decides the character of the "appearance"! (WP, p. 305)

Postmodern American philosophers, unconsciously prefigured by Nietzsche, are aptly described by Rorty, when in the process of delineating what he calls 'edifying' philosophers such as Dewey, Kierkegaard, and the later Heidegger, he writes,

These writers have kept alive the suggestion that, even when we have justified true belief about everything we want to know, we may have no more than conformity to the norms of the day. They have kept alive the historicist sense that this century's "superstition" was the last century's triumph of reason, as well as the relativist sense that the latest vocabulary, borrowed from the latest scientific achievement, may not express privileged representations of essences, but be just another of the potential infinity of vocabularies in which the world can be described.[20]

Nietzsche catches the flavor of this passage when he writes, "That the destruction of an illusion does not produce truth but only one more piece of ignorance, an extension of our 'empty space,' an increase of our 'desert'" (WP, p. 327).

Demythologizing the Myth of the Given

The Myth of the Given is an attempt to secure solid foundations for knowledge-claims; it is a quest for certainty in epistemology.[21] The Myth of the Given roughly holds that there is a given element—a self-justifying, intrinsically credible, theory-neutral, noninferential element —in experience which provides the foundations for other knowledge-claims and serves as the final terminating points for chains of epistemic justification. Therefore the attempt of postmodern American philosophers to demythologize the Myth of the Given is a move toward antifoundationalism in epistemology. It is not surprising that such antifoundationalism is akin to the antirealism, holism, and conventionalism we examined earlier.

The two major proponents of the Myth of the Given in modern analytic philosophy are C. I. Lewis, a beloved teacher of Quine and Goodman, and H. H. Price, an appreciative student of Russell.[22] For both philosophers, the given element and its interpretation constitute the basic characteristics of knowledge and experience. As Lewis states: "There are in our cognitive experience, two elements, the immediate data such as those of sense, which are presented or given to the mind, and a form, construction, or interpretation, which represents the activity of thought."[23] Price also notes after acknowledging the data of the historian, general, and detective,

But it is obvious that these are only data relatively and for the purpose of answering a certain question. They are really themselves the results of inference, often of a very complicated kind. We may call them data *secundum quid*. But eventually we must get back to something which is a datum *simpliciter*, which is not the result of any previous intellectual process.[24]

As we said earlier, for Lewis and Price, the very foundations of knowledge are at stake in this distinction. Lewis is quite candid about this,

If there be no datum given to the mind, then knowledge must be altogether contentless and arbitrary; there would be nothing which it must be true to. And if there be no interpretation which the mind imposes, then thought is rendered superfluous, the possibility of error becomes inexplicable, and the distinction of true and false is in danger of becoming meaningless.[25]

Similarly for Price, the phenomenological investigation of the particular modes of perception (which lies outside of science) provides the foundations for science. "Empirical Science can never be more trustworthy than perception, upon which it is based."[26]

We are fortunate to have Goodman's direct response to Lewis's two-component view of knowledge owing to a symposium in which they both (along with Hans Reichenbach) took part at an American Philosophical Association meeting at Byrn Mawr in 1951. Needless to say, Goodman is critical of Lewis's view. He replies not by denying the notion of the given but by severing any links of a given element with notions of the true, false or certain.

But this all seems to me to point to, or at least to be compatible with, the conclusion that while something is given, nothing given is true; that while some things may be indubitable, nothing is certain. What we have been urged to grant amounts at most to this: materials for or particles of experience are given, sensory qualities or events or other elements are not created at will but presented, experience has some content even though our description of it may be artificial or wrong and even though the precise differentiation between what is given and what is not given may be virtually impossible. But to such content or materials or particles or elements, the terms "true", or "false", and "certain" are quite inapplicable. These elements are simply there or not there. To grant that some are there is not to grant that anything is certain. Such elements may be indubitable in the vacuous sense that doubt is irrelevant to them, as it is to a desk; but they, like the desk, are equally devoid of certainty. They may be before us, but they are neither true nor false. For truth and falsity and certainty pertain to statements or judgments and not to mere particles or materials or elements. Thus, to deny that there are empirical certainties does not imply that experience is a pure fiction, that it is without content, or even that there is no given element.[27]

Five years later in his essay on Carnap, "The Revision of Philosophy," Goodman picks up the given-interpretation issue again and this time he rejects the distinction outright.

Any such view rests on the premise that the question "What are the original elements in knowledge?" is a clear and answerable one. And the assumption remains uncontested so long as we are dominated by the tradition that there is a sharp dichotomy between the given and the interpretation put upon it—so long as we picture the knower as a machine that is fed experience in certain lumps and proceeds to grind these up and reunite them in various ways. But I do not think this view of the matter will stand very close scrutiny.[28]

And in his latest book, the very notion of epistemological foundations and the given element in experience are dismissed and dispensed with.

"With false hope of a firm foundation gone, with the world displaced by worlds that are but versions, with substance dissolved into function, and with the given acknowledged as taken, we face the questions how worlds are made, tested, and known."[29]

The most explicit attempts in postmodern American philosophy to demythologize the Myth of the Given are those of Wilfred Sellars and Richard Rorty. For Sellars, the Myth of the Given results from a confusion between the acquisition of knowledge and the justification of knowledge, between empirical causal accounts of how one comes to have a belief and philosophical investigations into how one justifies a belief one has. This confusion dissolves when one realizes that knowledge begins with the ability to justify, the capacity to use words. Everything else, he holds, is a noncognitive causal antecedent. Sellars's psychological nominalism claims that there is no such thing as prelinguistic awareness; or, to put it positively, that all awareness—of abstract and particular entities—is a linguistic affair. According to his view, "not even the awareness of such sorts, resemblances, and facts as pertain to so-called immediate experience is presupposed by the process of acquiring the use of a language."[30]

Sellars's view precludes the possibility of any form of the Myth of the Given because it rules out any self-justifying, intrinsically credible, theory-neutral, noninferential epistemic element in experience. This is so because if knowledge begins with the ability to justify, then its beginnings (or "foundations") are public and intersubjective, matters of social practice.

For example, one of the forms of the Myth of the Given subscribed to by traditional empiricist philosophers,

is the idea that there is, indeed must be, a structure of particular matter of fact such that (a) each fact can not only be noninferentially known to be the case, but presupposes no other knowledge either of particular matter of fact, or of general truths; and (b) such that the noninferential knowledge of facts belonging to this structure constitutes the ultimate court of appeals for all factual claims—particular and general—about the world.[31]

This privileged stratum of fact is justified by appeals to prelinguistic awareness of self-authenticating, 'phenomenal' qualities. Price tries to defend this view by characterizing a normal perceptual situation—of a tomato under regular circumstances of light—in which he arrives at certain indubitable beliefs.

One thing however I cannot doubt: that there exists a red patch of a round and somewhat bulgy shape, standing out from a background of other colour-patches, and having a certain visual depth, and that this whole field of colour is directly present to my consciousness. . . . This peculiar manner of being present to consciousness is called *being given* and that which is thus present is called a *datum*. The corresponding mental attitude is called *acquaintance, intuitive apprehension*, or sometimes *having*.[32]

Sellars then replies,

that one couldn't have observational knowledge of any fact unless one knew many other things as well. . . . For the point is specifically that observational knowledge of any particular fact, e.g., that this is green, presupposes that one knows general facts of the form X is a *reliable symptom* of Y. . . . The essential point is that in characterizing an episode or a state as that of *knowing*, we are not giving an empirical description of that episode or state; we are placing it in the logical space of reasons, of justifying and being able to justify what one says.[33]

Sellars concludes that the conception of knowledge based on the Myth of the Given, along with its concomitant picture of epistemology,

is misleading because of its static character. One seems forced to choose between the picture of an elephant which rests on a tortoise (What supports the tortoise?) and the picture of a great Hegelian serpent of knowledge with its tail in its mouth (Where does it begin?). Neither will do. For empirical knowledge, like its sophisticated extension, science, is rational, not because it has a *foundation* but because it is a self-correcting enterprise which can put any claim in jeopardy, though not *all* at once.[34]

Rorty's epistemological behaviorism extends Sellars's psychological nominalism, accenting even more the intersubjective, that is, social character, of the "foundations" of knowledge.

Explaining rationality and epistemic authority by reference to what society lets us say, rather than the latter by the former, is the essence of what I shall call "epistemological behaviorism," an attitude common to Dewey and Wittgenstein. This sort of behaviorism can best be seen as a species of holism—but one which requires no idealist metaphysical underpinnings.[35]

Following Sellars's attack on the Myth of the Given and linking this attack to Quine's holism, Rorty claims,

A holistic approach to knowledge is not a matter of antifoundationalist polemic, but a distrust of the whole epistemological enterprise. A behavioristic approach to episodes of "direct awareness" is not a matter of antimentalistic polemic, but a distrust of the Platonic quest for that special sort of certainty associated with visual perception.[36]

By combining the insights of Sellars and Quine, Rorty arrives at his own radical conclusion.

When Sellars's and Quine's doctrines are purified, they appear as complementary expressions of a single claim: that no "account of the nature of knowledge" can rely on a theory of representations which stand in privileged relations to reality. The work of these two philosophers enables us . . . to make clear why an "account of the nature of knowledge" can be, at most, a description of human behavior.[37]

In *Twilight of the Idols*, Nietzsche acknowledges that fundamental quest in Western philosophy for self-authenticating, self-justifying, intrinsically credible beliefs and concepts must rest, to use Stanley Cavell's Wittgensteinian phrase, "outside language games."[38] For Nietzsche, as for Sellars, such beliefs and concepts must presuppose some other kind of knowledge rather than serve as the foundation of our knowledge; they are grounded on what we already know rather than serve as the grounds for all that we know. He writes in section 4 of his chapter entitled " 'Reason' in Philosophy,"

The *other* idiosyncrasy of philosophers is no less perilous: it consists in mistaking the last for the first. They put that which comes at the end—unfortunately! for it ought not to come at all!—the 'highest concepts', that is to say the most general, the emptiest concepts, the last fumes of evaporating reality, at the beginning *as* the beginning. It is again only the expression f their way of doing reverence: the higher must not be *allowed* to grow out of the lower, must not be *allowed* to have grown at all. . . . Moral: everything of the first rank must be *causa sui*. Origin in something else counts as an objection, as casting doubt on value. (*TI*, p. 37)

Nietzsche considers the quest for certainty and the search for foundations in epistemology—any forms of the Myth of the Given—unattainable and ultimately self-deceptive. Any such quest and search must be subordinate to an inquiry as to why the will to power takes the form of such a quest and search.

It might seem as though I had evaded the question of "certainty." The opposite is true; but by inquiring after the criterion of certainty I tested the scales upon which men have weighed in general hitherto—and that the question of certainty itself is a dependent question, a question of second rank. (*WP*, p. 322)

Any attempt to ground knowledge-claims must be demystified such that the practical aims and goals concealed by such an attempt are disclosed.

Theory and practice.—*Fateful distinction, as if there were an actual* drive for knowledge that, without regard to questions of usefulness and harm, went blindly for the truth; and then, separate from this, the whole world of *practical* interests—

I tried to show, on the other hand, what instincts have been active behind all these *pure* theoreticians—how they have all, under the spell of their instincts, gone fatalistically for something that was "truth" *for them*—for them and only for them. The conflict between different systems, including that between epistemological scruples, is a conflict between quite definite instincts (forms of vitality, decline, classes, races, etc.).

The so-called drive for knowledge can be traced back to a drive to appropriate and conquer. (*WP*, p. 227)

Nietzsche's rejection of foundationalism in epistemology results from his acceptance of the Heraclitean flux, of the world of becoming which forever slips out of the arbitrary conceptual schemas through which humans come to "know" the self and world.

The character of the world in a state of becoming as incapable of formulation, as "false", as "self-contradictory." Knowledge and becoming exclude one another. Consequently, "knowledge" must be something else: there must first of all be a will to make knowable, a kind of becoming must itself create the deception of beings. (*WP*, p. 280)

A world in a state of becoming could not, in a strict sense, be "comprehended" or "known"; only to the extent that the "comprehending" and "knowing" intellect encounters a coarse, already-created world, fabricated out of mere appearances but become firm to the extent that this kind of appearance has preserved life— only to this extent is there anything like "knowledge"; i.e., a measuring of earlier and later errors by one another. (*WP*, p. 281)

For Nietzsche, as for Quine, Goodman, Sellars and Rorty (and against Plato, Aristotle, Descartes, Kant, Kripke, and Lévi-Strauss), knowledge is not a matter of grasping fixed forms, static essences or permanent substances and structures. Rather knowledge is a matter of perceiving phenomena under a description, within a theory or in light of a version in order to, to use a Wittgensteinian phrase, "help us get about." On this point, the early Quine's pragmatism and Nietzsche's perspectivism again converge.

Each man is given a scientific heritage plus a continuing barrage of sensory stimulation; and the considerations which guide him in warping his scientific heritage to fit his continuing sensory promptings are, where rational, pragmatic.[39]

Not "to know" but to schematize—to impose upon chaos as much regularity and form as our practical needs require.

In the formation of reason, logic, the categories, it was *need* that was authoritative: the need, not to "know", but to subsume, to schematize, for the purpose of intelligibility and calculation. (*WP*, p. 278)

Nietzsche's conception of knowledge as elastic in character and creative in content is echoed in Goodman.

Furthermore, if worlds are as much made as found, so also knowing is as much remaking as reporting. All the processes of worldmaking I have discussed enter into knowing. Perceiving motion, we have seen, often consists in producing it. Discovering laws involves drafting them. Recognizing patterns is very much a matter of inventing and imposing them. Comprehension and creation go on together.[40]

Coming to know means "to place oneself in a conditional relation to something"; to feel oneself conditioned by something and oneself to condition it—it is therefore under all circumstances establishing, denoting, and making-conscious of conditions. (*WP*, p. 301)

Nietzsche debunks the Myth of the Given because, for him, knowledge is not a set of beliefs to be "grounded," but rather a series of linguistic signs which designate and describe the world in light of our evolving needs, interests, and purposes. "It is an illusion that something is *known* when we possess a mathematical formula for an event: it is only designated, described; nothing more!" (*WP*, p. 335). He surely would agree with Rorty that demythologizing the Myth of the Given—and promoting antifoundationalism in epistemology—results in, "preventing man from deluding himself with the notion that he knows himself, or anything else, except under optimal descriptions."[41]

The last crucial move of postmodern American philosophy I will examine is the detranscendentalizing of the subject—the dismissing of
the mind as a self-contained sphere of inquiry. This move is a natural
consequence of the antirealism, holism, conventionalism, and antifoundationalism we examined earlier.

It is important to note that notions such as the subject, self-
consciousness, ego, and "I" were under attack by modern analytic philosophers. Therefore this last move of postmodern American philosophers is part of the general trend of modern analytic philosophy.

For example, Quine's treatment of this matter follows, in many ways,
the logical behaviorist position put forward in Gilbert Ryle's classic
work, *The Concept of Mind* (1949). This position, largely intended to
debunk the Cartesian myth of the "ghosts in machines," roughly holds
that talk about mental states, that is, an intentional idiom, is but a
clumsy and confusing way of talking about dispositions to behave in certain ways under specific circumstances, that is, a behavioristic idiom.
Quine's well-known passage in his *Word and Object* (1960) summarizes
his own behavioristic position,

One may accept the Brentano thesis either as showing the indispensability of intentional idioms and the importance of an autonomous science of intention, or
as showing the baselessness of intentional idioms and the emptiness of a science
of intention. My attitude, unlike Brentano's, is the second. To accept intentional
usage at face value is, we saw, to postulate translation relations as somehow
objectively valid though indeterminate in principle relative to the totality of
speech dispositions. Such postulation promises little gain in scientific insight if
there is no better ground for it than that the supposed translation relations are
presupposed by the vernacular of semantics and intention.[42]

Underlying this viewpoint is Quine's eliminative materialist position,
namely, the view that there simply are no mental states, but rather neural events. In this way, Quine detranscendentalizes any notion of the
subject.

Rorty deepens this version of detranscendentalizing the subject by
abandoning the very notion of mind-body identity. On his view, the
social practice of speaking in neural events (by those who know neurology) and the social practice of speaking in mental states (by those who
do not know neurology) "are just two ways of talking about the same

thing."[43] And the "thing" being talked about in each case is that which is posited within one's theory. As Sellars points out, such thing-talk, be it neurological or commonsensical, occurs in,

a framework of "unobserved," "nonempirical" "inner" episodes. For we can point out immediately that in these respects they are no worse off than the particles and episodes in physical theory. For these episodes are "in" language-using animals as molecular impacts are "in" gases, not as "ghosts" are in "machines." They are "nonempirical" in the simple sense that they are *theoretical*—not definable in observational terms. . . . Their "purity" is not a *metaphysical* purity, but, so to speak, a *methodological* purity . . . [and] the fact that they are not introduced as physiological entities does not preclude the possibility that at a later methodological stage, they may, so to speak, "turn out" to be such.[44]

Sellars's methodological behaviorism—his way of detranscendentalizing the subject—permits him to be a behaviorist (like Quine) without thinking that all one's theoretical concepts in relation to "mental events" will turn out to refer to neurological phenomena (unlike Quine)—though, of course, they may. "The behavioristic requirement that all concepts should be introduced in terms of a basic vocabulary pertaining to overt behavior is compatible with the idea that some behavioristic concepts are to be introduced as theoretical concepts."[45]

Nietzsche's dismissal of the mind as a self-contained sphere of inquiry is illustrated in section 3 of his chapter entitled, "The Four Great Errors" in *Twilight of The Idols*.

the conception of a consciousness ('mind') as cause and later still that of the ego (the 'subject') as cause are merely after-products after causality had, on the basis of will, been firmly established as a given fact, as *empiricism*. Meanwhile we have thought better. Today we do not believe a word of it. The 'inner world' is full of phantoms and false lights: the will is one of them. The will no longer moves anything, consequently no longer explains anything—it merely accompanies events, it can also be absent. The so-called 'motive': another error. Merely a surface phenomenon of consciousness, an accompaniment to an act, which conceals rather than exposes the *antecedentia* of the act. And as for the ego! It has become a fable, a fiction, a play on words: it has totally ceased to think, to feel and to will! . . . What follows from this? There are no spiritual causes at all! The whole of the alleged empiricism which affirmed them has gone to the devil! (*TI*, p. 49)

Like Ryle, Nietzsche's detranscendentalizing of the subject begins with a critique of Descartes.

"There is thinking: therefore there is something that thinks": this is the upshot of all Descartes' argumentation. But that means positing as "true a priori" our belief in the concept of substance—that when there is thought there has to be something "that thinks" is simply a formulation of our grammatical custom that adds a doer to every deed. In short, this is not merely the substantiation of a fact but a logical-metaphysical postulate. (*WP*, p. 268)

Similar to Rorty and Sellars, Nietzsche views subject-talk as mere convention, a matter of social practice rooted in our needs, interests, and purposes.

"Everything is subjective," you say; but even this is interpretation. The "subject" is not something given, it is something, added and invented and projected behind what there is. (*WP*, p. 267)

However habitual and indispensable this fiction may have become by now—that in itself proves nothing against its imaginary origin: a belief can be a condition of life and nonetheless be false. (*WP*, p. 268)

He concludes that subject-talk is a linguistic social practice derived from our grammar, namely, the subject-predicate structure of our judgments.

In every judgment there resides the entire, full, profound belief in subject and attribute, or in cause and effect (that is, as the assertion that every effect is an activity and that every activity presupposes an agent); and this latter belief is only a special case of the former, so there remains as the fundamental belief that there are subjects, that everything that happens is related attributively to some subject. (*WP*, p. 294)

Nihilism

If Nietzsche prefigures certain important developments in postmodern American philosophy, then it is appropriate to note briefly that he believed such developments ultimately lead to nihilism unless they are supplemented with a new worldview. He makes this point clearly in his Preface to *The Will to Power*.

For one should make no mistake about the meaning of the title that this gospel of the future wants to bear. "*The Will to Power:* Attempt at a Revaluation of All Values"—in this formulation a countermovement finds expression, regarding both principle and task; a movement that in some future will take the place of this perfect nihilism—but presupposes it, logically and psychologically, and certainly can come only after and out of it. For why has the advent of nihilism become *necessary?* Because the values we have had hitherto thus draw their final consequence; because nihilism represents the ultimate logical conclusion of our great values and ideals—because we must experience nihilism before we can find out what value these "values" really had.—We require, sometime, *new values.* (*WP*, pp. 3–4)

For Nietzsche, this nihilism results from certain ideals of modern Europe, especially those ideals which presuppose belief in the categories of "aim," "unity," and "truth." Nihilism is a natural consequence of a culture (or civilization) ruled and regulated by categories which mask manipulation, mastery, and domination of peoples and nature.

Suppose we realize how the world may no longer be interpreted in terms of these three categories, and that the world begins to become valueless for us after this insight: then we have to ask about the sources of our faith in these three categories. . . .

Conclusion: The faith in the categories of reason is the cause of nihilism. We have measured the value of the world according to categories *that refer to a fictitious world.*

Final conclusion: All the values by means of which we have tried so far to render the world estimable for ourselves and which then proved inapplicable and therefore devaluated the world—all these values are, psychologically considered, the results of certain perspectives of utility, designed to maintain and increase human constructs of domination—and they have been falsely *projected* into the essence of things. (*WP*, pp. 13–14)

Nihilism ushers in an era in which science—the great pride of modern Europe—provides greater and greater instrumentalities for world domination. As Maurice Blanchot observes,

The moment Nihilism outlines the world for us, its counterpart, science, creates the tools to dominate it. The era of universal mastery is opened. But there are some consequences: first, science can only be nihilistic; it is the meaning of a world deprived of meaning, a knowledge that ultimately has ignorance as its foundation. To which the response will be that this reservation is only theoretical; but we must not hasten to disregard this objection, for science is essentially productive. Knowing it need not interpret the world, science transforms it, and by this transformation science conveys its own nihilistic demands—the negative power that science has made into the most useful of tools, but with which it dangerously plays. Knowledge is fundamentally dangerous . . . for a universe cannot be constructed without having the possibility of its being destroyed . . . [and] by making science possible, Nihilism becomes the possibility of science—which means that the human world can be destroyed by it.[46]

Nietzsche considers nihilism to be "partly destructive, partly ironic" (WP, p. 14). It is marked by philosophical positions of antirealism, conventionalism, relativism, and antifoundationalism. We have seen that postmodern American philosophers support such positions. Quine describes himself as a "relativist,"[47] yet warns against associating him with the "epistemological nihilism"[48] of Kuhn. Goodman labels his position "as a radical relativism under rigorous restraints, that eventuates in something akin to irrealism."[49] Rorty calls himself an "historicist"[50] and Kuhn admits to subscribing to a form of relativism.[51]

The crucial moves made by postmodern American philosophers are highly significant in that these moves disclose the unwarranted philosophical assumptions and antiquated theoretical distinctions upon which rests much of modern analytic philosophy. Yet—and in this regard they resemble their counterparts in postmodern literary criticism—postmodern American philosophers have failed to project a new world view, a countermovement, "a new gospel of the future." Quine's and Sellars's updated versions of scientism not only reflect their positivist heritage, but, more importantly, reveal their homage to an outmoded cultural mode of thought. Goodman's attempt to infuse the idea of style with new life is intriguing yet ultimately resorts to an old aristocratic preoccupation. Kuhn's unequivocal promotion of the proliferation of learned societies (or groups) engaged in puzzle-solving under converging paradigms amounts to an unimaginative ideology of professionalism. And Rorty's ingenious conception of philosophy as cultured conversation rests upon a nostalgic appeal to the world of men (and women) of letters of decades past. These viewpoints do not constitute visions, worldviews, or, to use Gilles Deleuze's phrase, "discourses as counter-philosophies"[52] to the nihilism to which their positions seem to lead. Instead their viewpoints leave postmodern American philosophy hanging in limbo, as a philosophically critical yet culturally lifeless rhetoric mirroring a culture (or civilization) permeated by the scientific ethos, regulated by racist, patriarchal, capitalist norms, and pervaded by debris of decay.

Notes

1. The English translations I shall refer to throughout this essay are: *Twilight of the Idols*, trans. R. J. Hollingdale (Middlessex, U.K.: Penguin, 1968), and *The Will to Power*, trans. W. Kaufman and R. J. Hollingdale (New York: Vintage, 1968). References to these editions, designated *TI* and *WP*, respectively, will be incorporated in the text. The first work, written in 1888, was one of Nietzsche's last and best texts; the second is a selection from Nietzsche's notebooks, 1883–1888. Nietzsche's philosophical (and metaphilosophical) views have not been examined in relation to the latest developments in postmodern American philosophy primarily because of the distance between his work and Anglo-American philosophy. This distance exists owing to two basic reasons. First, Nietzsche and Anglo-American philosophers radically disagree on the appropriate mode of philosophizing, on how philosophy should be done, pursued, and codified. For Nietzsche, philosophy is a consuming passion, a gay vocation—hence more adequately pursued in a literary mode for a general intelligent audience; whereas, for most Anglo-American philosophers, philosophy is a pedagogical activity, a serious profession—hence more adequately pursued in a technical mode for a highly specialized audience. Second, Anglo-American philosophers are noted (and notorious) for "their lack of historical sense." Therefore, their interest in and attention to philosophical figures preoccupied with history, for example, Hegel, Kierkegaard, Marx, Nietzsche, is minimal. It is not surprising that of the five major books on Nietzsche in English—Walter Kaufman's *Nietzsche: Philosopher, Psychologist, Antichrist* (Princeton: Princeton University Press, 1975), R. J. Hollingdale's *Nietzsche* (London: Routledge & Kegan, 1973), Arthur Donto's *Nietzsche as Philosopher* (New York: Macmillan, 1965), Crane Brinton's *Nietzsche* (Cambridge: Harvard University Press, 1941), and J. P. Stern's *Friedrich Nietzsche* (New York: Penguin, 1979)—only one is written by an Anglo-American philosopher, namely, Arthur Danto. And Danto is an atypical Anglo-American (or analytic) philosopher, with diverse interests and publications ranging from Croce, philosophy of history, and Sartre to Nietzsche and Schopenhauer.

2. It comes as no surprise that analytic philosophy, with its "lack of historical sense," has produced little historical reflection and interpretation of itself. Besides Richard Rorty's early introductory essay in *The Linguistic Turn* (Chicago: University of Chicago Press, 1967) and his recent book, *Philosophy and the Mirror of Nature* (Princeton: Princeton University Press, 1979), there is only John Passmore's *A Hundred Years of Philosophy* (Middlesex, U.K.: Penguin, 1970) which is pedantic reportage and straightforward exposition—neither historical reflection nor interpretation—of late nineteenth and twentieth century developments in European philosophy. The pertinent works of Frege, Meinong, Russell, and Moore that I have in mind are Frege's classic "On Sense and Reference," in Peter Geach and Max Black, eds., *Translations from the Philosophical Writings of Gottlob Frege* (Oxford: Oxford University Press, 1952); Meinong's "The Theory of Objects," in Roderick Chisholm, ed., *Realism and the Background of Phenomenology* (California: Glencoe, 1960); Russell's "Meinong's Theory of Complexes and Assumptions," *Mind* 13 (1904): 204–19, 336–54, 509–24; and Moore's "The Refutation of Idealism," in *Philosophical Studies* (London, 1922).

3. For noteworthy examples of naive (or commonsensical) realism, see G. E. Moore's "A Defense of Common Sense" and "Proof of an External World," in his *Philo-*

sophical Papers (London, 1959); for Platonic realism, see Bertrand Russell's *Principles of Mathematics* (Cambridge, 1903) and to a lesser extent his *Problems of Philosophy* (New York, 1912); for critical realism, see Roy W. Sellars's *Critical Realism* (Chicago, 1916) and his "A Statement of Critical Realism," *Revue internationale de philosophie* 1 (1938–39): 472–98; and for internal realism, see Hilary Putnam's recent work, *Meaning and the Moral Sciences* (London: Routledge & Kegan Paul, 1978), Part 4 entitled "Realism and Reason."

4. Nelson Goodman, *Problems and Projects* (New York: Bobbs-Merrill, 1972), pp. 29–30.

5. Ibid., pp. 279–80.

6. Ibid., p. 118.

7. Nelson Goodman, *Ways of Worldmaking* (Indianapolis: Hackett, 1978), p. 138.

8. Willard Van Orman Quine, *From a Logical Point of View* (New York, 1963), pp. 40–41.

9. Ibid., p. 42.

10. Ibid., p. 43.

11. Wilfred Sellars, son of the aforementioned Roy Sellars, deserves a similar place, alongside Quine and Goodman. But his highly technical style of writing as well as his position at the University of Pittsburgh (slightly removed from the center of fashionable intellectual activity and notoriety) unfortunately has rendered his writings less accessible and influential.

12. Richard Rorty, "The World Well Lost," *Journal of Philosophy* 69, 19 (1972): 661.

13. Thomas S. Kuhn, *The Structure of Scientific Revolutions*, 2d ed. (Chicago: Univ. of Chicago Press, 1970), p. 206.

14. Thomas S. Kuhn, "Reflections on My Critics," *Criticism and the Growth of Knowledge*, ed. Imre Lakatos and Alan Musgrave (Cambridge: Cambridge University Press, 1970), p. 266.

15. *Ways of Worldmaking*, p. x.

16. *Problems and Projects*, pp. 30–31.

17. Ibid., pp. 117, 118.

18. *From A Logical Point of View*, p. 44.

19. Ibid., p. 19.

20. *Philosophy and the Mirror of Nature*, p. 367.

21. This phrase was popularized by Wilfred Sellars's influential University of London lectures originally entitled "The Myth of the Given: Three Lectures on Empiricism and the Philosophy of Mind" and now known simply as "Empiricism and the Philosophy of Mind," *Minnesota Studies in the Philosophy of Science* 1, Herbert Feigl and Michael Scriven, eds. (University of Minnesota Press, 1956). For a brief, cogent, and sympathetic elaboration on this myth, see Michael William's *Groundless Belief: An Essay on the Possibility of Epistemology* (New Haven: Yale University Press, 1977), chapter 2 and for the only treatment I know of how this myth functions in traditional philosophical hermeneutics, see my essay, "Schleiermacher's Hermeneutics and the Myth of the Given," Special Hermeneutics Issue, *Union Seminary Quarterly Review* 34, 2 (Winter 1979): 71–84.

22. For C. I. Lewis's pertinent work, see his *Mind and the World Order* (New York: Dover, 1956) and "The Given Element in Empirical Knowledge," *The Philosophical Review* 61, 2 (April 1952): 168–73. For H. H. Price's relevant work, see his classic

Perception (London: Methuen & Co., 1964). Lewis's book was first published in 1929, Price's in 1932. More recent defenders of the Myth of the Given include A. J. Ayer, *The Foundations of Empirical Knowledge* (London: Macmillan & Co.; New York: St. Martin's Press, 1958), R. M. Chisholm, *Theory of Knowledge*, 2d ed. (Englewood Cliffs, N.J.: Prentice Hall, 1977), Jonathan Bennett, *Locke, Berkeley, Hume: Central Themes* (Oxford: Oxford University Press, 1971), and John L. Pollack, *Knowledge and Justification* (Princeton: Princeton University Press, 1975). For a survey of the variety of versions of the Myth of the Given, see J. J. Ross, *The Appeal to the Given* (London: Macmillan, 1970). Lastly, for a fascinating and original attempt to reject the myth and Quine's holism (at the same time!), see Clark Glymour's *Theory and Evidence* (Princeton: Princeton University Press, 1980).

23. *Mind and the World Order*, p. 38.
24. *Perception*, p. 4.
25. *Mind and the World Order*, p. 39.
26. *Perception*, p. 1.
27. *Problems and Projects*, pp. 61–62.
28. Ibid., p. 9.
29. *Ways of Worldmaking*, p. 7.
30. "Empiricism and the Philosophy of Mind," p. 289.
31. Ibid., p. 293.
32. *Perception*, p. 3.
33. "Empiricism and the Philosophy of Mind," pp. 298–99.
34. Ibid., p. 300.
35. *Philosophy and the Mirror of Nature*, p. 174.
36. Ibid., p. 181.
37. Ibid., p. 182.
38. Stanley Cavell, *The Claim of Reason* (Oxford, 1979), p. 226.
39. *From A Logical Point of View*, p. 46.
40. *Ways of Worldmaking*, p. 22.
41. *Philosophy and the Mirror of Nature*, p. 379.
42. Willard Van Orman Quine, *Word and Object* (Cambridge, 1960), p. 221.
43. *Philosophy and the Mirror of Nature*, p. 122.
44. "Empiricism and the Philosophy of Mind," p. 319.
45. Ibid., p. 316.
46. Maurice Blanchot, "The Limits of Experience: Nihilism," *The New Nietzsche: Contemporary Styles of Interpretation*, ed. and intro. David B. Allison (New York, 1977), pp. 122–23.
47. W. V. Quine, *Ontological Relativity and Other Essays* (New York, 1969), pp. 50ff.
48. *Ontological Relativity*, p. 87.
49. *Ways of Worldmaking*, p. x.
50. *Philosophy and the Mirror of Nature*, pp. 9, 10.
51. "Reflections on my Critics," p. 264.
52. Gilles Deleuze, "Nomad Thought," *The New Nietzsche*, p. 149.

Index

Abrams, M. H., 233
Absurdists, postmodern, 23–24
Academy, literary, 6
Aeschylus, 83–85
Allen, Donald, 42
Ammons, A. R., 115, 173
Analyticity, 269–70
Antifoundationalism, 275
Anti-humanism, 109–10, 118
Antiliterature, 72–73
Antin, David, 188–206
Antin, Eleanor, 197–200
Antirealism, 266–74
Aphorism, 221, 261 n.15
Arcadians, 80
Arendt, Hannah, 112
Aristotle, 26
Arnold, Matthew, 108
Art, 40–41, 210–11, 217–19
Ascent, 158
Ashbery, John, 124, 173
Auden, W. H., 46–48
Autobiography: in poetry, 124–25, 197
Ayer, A. J., 268–70

Bacon, Francis, 237–44, 251–52, 261
    n.15
Barthes, Roland, 24
Baudelaire, Charles, 55–57, 61
Beat poets, 73–76
Behaviorism, 282–83
Being, 212–26. *See also* Heidegger

Belatedness, psychology of, 170–74
Bergson, Henri, 18
Bester, Alfred, 95–96
Biography: in poetry, 52
Black Mountain poets, 63, 68, 73–76
Blackmur, R. P., 13
Blake, William, 92
Blanchot, Maurice, 216, 217, 285
Bly, Robert, 108, 112–13, 116–17, 120
Body, the, 176
boundary 2, 4, 7, 8, 14 n.3, 15 n.5
Bronowski, J., 80–81
Brooks, Cleanth, 61–62
Brown, Norman O., 235, 260 n.5
Burroughs, William, 93–94

Cage, John, 91, 109, 191–92, 195–204
Calvinism, 244–45
Canon, literary, 15 n.5, 170–71
Capital, 1, 10
Carnap, Rudolf, 267–70
Cassirer, Ernst, 103
Catholicism, 245, 246
Cecil, David, 42
Cendrars, Blaise, 68–70
Certainty, 275–76, 279
City, 18–19, 26–28, 30–34, 56–57
Civil rights, 5–6, 11
Codes: as language, 241–48
Coleridge, Samuel Taylor, 102–3
Collage, 48–52, 57, 58, 63, 64, 161
Colum, Mary G., 235

Comenius, 242–43
Concrete universal, 104–8
Consciousness, 20–38, 79–88, 95, 208, 215. *See also* De Man; Heidegger; New Gnosticism
Contrast, semantic, 62–63
Correspondence, in realism, 267
Corso, Gregory, 74, 122
Cosmography, 154–59
Creeley, Robert, 120, 124, 127, 205
Criticism, 210; American, 235–36; as art, 251; and Heidegger, 207–31; postmodern, 258; schools of, 6
Critics, postmodern, 4–16, 250, 253
Curtius, Ernst Robert, 168–70

Dalgarno, Melvin, 243
Dasein, 20, 212–16. *See also* Heidegger
Davie, Donald, 249–50
De-composition, 26–27
Deconstruction, 209–10, 235–36, 240–42
Decreation, 108
Dehistoricization, 15 n.5
Deleuze, Gilles, 16 n.8, 286
Delgado, Dr. José, 90
De Man, Paul, 210, 214–18, 221, 230 n.4
Derrida, Jacques, 8, 167, 207–31
Descartes, 237, 262–63 n.32, 283–84
Descent, 157
Destruction, 209–15, 223
Detranscendentalization: of the subject, 282–84
Dickey, James, 107, 120, 129
Dickinson, Emily, 171–72
Dislocation, 30
Disorder, 256–57
Dostoevsky, Fyodor, 20, 22
Doyle, Sir Arthur Conan, 21, 25–26
Dread, 19–20, 26–27
Duncan, Robert, 68, 105–7, 115, 132, 161

Ego, 123–24, 160–62
Einstein, Albert, 80, 89
Eliade, Mircea, 87
Eliot, T. S., 44, 53, 60–61, 104, 131, 165–66; *Sweeney Agonistes*, 22, 28; *The Waste Land*, 48–49, 64
Ellul, Jacques, 88
Emerson, Ralph Waldo, 163, 165, 172
Empiricism, 236, 244, 269–70, 276, 277
Epistemology. *See* Knowledge
Essent, 117–19
Etymology, 127. *See also* Language
Existentialism, 18–23, 26, 32, 254

Falsity, 276
Fear, 19
Feinberg, Gerald, 84–85
Feminist criticism, 8, 11–12
Figure: in Heidegger, 218–22
Fitness, 269. *See also* Truth
Foucault, Michel, 8, 16 n.8
Frye, Northrop, 165–66
Fuller, Buckminster, 79, 89, 190–94, 198–99

Geneva school, 208
Geography, literary representations of, 15 n.6. *See also* City
Ginsberg, Allen, 59, 71
Girard, René, 258
Given: Myth of the, 275–81; notion of, 276–77
Gnosticism, 254–58
Goethe, 84
Goodell, Larry, 205–6
Goodman, Nelson, 268–73, 276–77, 281, 286
Guibbory, Achsah, 238

Hartman, Geoffrey, 210–11
Hassan, Ihab, 234–35
Hecht, Anthony, 109
Hegel, G. W. F., 92, 108
Heidegger, Martin, 19–20, 23, 27, 116–21, 207–31; *Being and Time*, 211–19
Heinlein, Robert, 95
Heller, Erich, 92
Heraclitus, 116, 129–30
Hermeneutics, 208–9
Hesiod, 84

Heterogeneity, 62
Historian, role of the, 148–50
History: of history, 209; importance of, 128–29; and poetry, 48–54; as process, 130–31; rejection of, 128
Hölderlin, Friedrich, 221–23
Homer, 168–69, 188, 192
Hulme, T. E., 117–18, 125
Husserl, Edmund, 114–15, 209–10

Image, 114–15
Imagination, creative, 102–8
Imagism, 102–4, 114
Immanentist thinking, 102, 123–25, 137 n.6
Improvisation: oral poetry, 193, 201–3
Incarnation, 104–6
Instruction, Scene of, 171–73
Interaction: art, 196
Interpretation, 212–15
Ionesco, Eugene, 25–27
Irony, 62

Jameson, Fredric, 1, 2, 4, 9–10, 15 n.5
Jarrell, Randall, 42, 46–48, 50–51
Jonas, Hans, 254
Jones, Richard F., 242
Joyce, James, 242; *Portrait of the Artist as a Young Man*, 29–31; *Ulysses*, 175–87, 235
Jung, Carl, 157

Kant, Immanuel, 117
Kelly, Robert, 115
Kenner, Hugh, 190, 191
Kerényi, C. K., 84–86
Kierkegaard, Søren, 19, 20, 27, 113–14
Kinesis, 29, 32
Kircher, Athanasius, 246–48
Knowledge, 275–81
Koch, Kenneth, 109
Kuhn, Thomas, 49, 270–71, 286

Laforgue, Jules, 70–71
Language, 125–27, 242; and Heidegger, 211–15, 218–19; natural, 242–47, 251; philosophical, 243; poetic, 215–

16, 218–21, 224; universal, 240, 244, 248. *See also* Codes; Scientific discourse
Leibniz, Gottfried Wilhelm Freiherr von, 237, 246–48
Levertov, Denise, 116–17, 126, 131–32, 135
Lewis, C. I., 275–76
Lichtenstein, Roy, 40
Lilly, John C., 91
Literature: classification of, 169; and the mind, 91–93; as metaphor for truth, meaning, 210
Locke, John, 239, 245
Lord, Albert, 188, 192, 194, 199
Lowell, Robert, 52–58, 63, 111–12, 171
Lynch, William F., 85

McLuhan, Marshall, 29, 90
Mailer, Norman, 97–98, 171
Mallarmé, Stéphane, 227, 230 n.4
Martin, Wallace, 259 n.3
Marx, Karl, 13, 47
Marxism, 48. *See also* Jameson
Masonism, 245
Meaning, 114, 121, 226. *See also* Language
Mediation, 124, 127, 128
Melville, Herman, 53
Merwin, W. S., 124
Metaphor, 219–22, 249–50
Metaphysics, end of, 208–10
Meter, 59–60, 63
Metonymy, 49
Meyer, Leonard B., 250–53
Miles, Josephine, 110
Miller, J. Hillis, 104
Milton, John: *Paradise Lost*, 171–74, 238
Mimesis, 18
Mind, the, 238–39, 245
Modern, the, 4, 40
Modernism, 6–9, 41, 110; as developed by Eliot, Tate, and Brooks, 60; establishing, 42; high, 4–5; late, 4; reaction against Western humanism, 17–18; and postmodernism, 40–76; symbolist, 18, 22–23, 28–29, 102–4

Modernist tradition, metaphysical, 63–64
Mumford, Lewis, 33
Murdoch, Iris, 37
Music: metaphor of, 64–66; interpretation, 75
Myth, 80–81, 131–33

Name, 225–26, 228
Nashville critics, 50
Neumann, Erich, 87
New Criticism, 10, 18, 22, 29, 104–7, 125
New England Myth, 53
New Gnosticism, 77–99
New Historicism, 12
Newton, Isaac, 81, 244
New York school, 75–76
Nietzsche, Friedrich Wilhelm, 15 n.5, 122, 209–10, 254–55, 258, 264–89
Nihilism, 284–86

Objectism, 160
Objectivism, 114
O'Hara, Frank, 73–74
Olson, Charles, 58–59, 63–68, 105–9, 114, 116, 122–24, 130–31, 140–62, 205
Oppen, George, 115

Pater, Walter, 30
Periodization, 15 n.5
Personae, 160
Perspectivism, 273
Phenomenology, 208–9. *See also* Heidegger
Philosophy, postmodern American, 266–89
Pictorialism, 248
Poetics, iconic, 31–33
Poetry: American, 41–42, 59, 70–71; anti-, 59, 71–72; and authentic language, 215; confessional, 112; image, 189; as literature, 70–71; metaphysical, 61; modernist, 49–50, 61, 73, 104; oral, 188–206; postmodern, 104, 114
Postmodern, the: and history, 129; thought, 255
Postmodernism, 1, 4, 7, 18; scien-

tific discourse, 232–64; theory and interpretation of, 11; values, 122
Poststructuralism, 209
Pound, Ezra, 48, 64–66, 68, 70–71, 73, 240
Price, H. H., 275–78
Prometheus, 82–85
Props, use of: oral poetry, 199
Protestantism, 110, 232, 244–46, 257
Psychoanalysis, 48–50, 52
Purism, 40
Puritanism, 242, 244
Pynchon, Thomas, 6, 166–67, 173

Quine, Willard Van Orman, 269–71, 273–74, 281–83, 286

Ransom, John Crowe, 59–60, 64
Rationalism, 236–37
Realism, 267
Reappropriation: of metaphysics, 211–13
Reconstruction, 235–36, 240–42
Reformation, 236, 238
Reification, 15 n.5
Renaissance, 21, 236–39, 247
Resistance, 11–13
Revisionism, 171
Rexroth, Kenneth, 116
Rhetoric, 239, 242
Richards, I. A., 61–62
Ritual, primitive: poetry of, 133
Robbe-Grillet, Alain, 109
Rodway, Allan, 235–36
Roethke, Theodore, 115
Romanticism, 170
Romantics, 101, 103, 234, 249
Rorty, Richard, 270–71, 274, 278–83, 286
Rosenberg, Harold, 79, 132
Rosicrucians, 244–45
Roszak, Theodore, 81
Rothenberg, Jerome, 189, 195
Royal Society, 242
Ryle, Gilbert, 282

Sacramentalism, 100, 106
Sartre, Jean-Paul, 5, 9, 10, 23–25, 27, 33, 255

Sauer, Carl, 129
Schneidau, Herbert, 128
Scholars, literary: in Alexandria, 169–70
Scholem, Gershom, 166–67
Schwartz, Barry, 88
Schwartz, Delmore, 43–49, 59, 71–72
Science, 88–91. *See also* Technology
Science fiction, 94–96
Scientific discourse, 232–64. *See also* Codes; Language
Scott, Nathan, 38, 106
Script, 220–21
Selby, Hubert, Jr., 195
Sellars, Wilfred, 277–80, 283, 286
Semiotics, 247
Sensationalism, 252
Shapiro, Karl, 46
Shelley, Mary, 84–85
Shelley, Percy, 84–85
Sign, 176, 219–20
Signifier, 176–82, 221, 226, 248
Simpson, Louis, 105
Snyder, Gary, 130
Sorrentino, Gilbert, 74
Spanos, William, 232–33, 236–37
Spatialization, 15 n.5, 236, 248
Spears, Monroe, 110
Speech, 119, 215, 220. *See also* Heidegger; Language
Stasis, 29–32
Stephens, James, 239, 252, 263 n.33
Sterne, Laurence, 239
Stevens, Wallace, 7, 104
Stirner, Max, 254, 263 n.35
Sturgeon, Theodore, 96
Sukenick, Ronald, 94
Symbolism, 102. *See also* Modernism
Symbolists, 18, 33, 38, 137 n.6

Tate, Allen, 42, 44, 46, 57–59, 64, 71, 104–6, 115

Teaching, 167, 173–74
Technology, 80–82, 88–91
Technophiles, 80
Teilhard de Chardin, Pierre, 79, 87
Text, 179, 214, 220–21
Thomas Aquinas, Saint, 31
Thompson, William Irwin, 81
Tillich, Paul, 19, 27–28
Time, 256–57
Tradition, literary, 163–74
Translation, 127
Trilling, Lionel, 5
Truth, 218, 269, 273, 276

Union: of subject and object, 120–21
University, the, 2–3
Utility, 274

Value: and postmodern poetry, 114; postmodern theory of, 108
Vickers, Brian, 261 n.15
Vietnam War, 5, 35–36
Voegelin, Erich, 256–58

Wallace, Karl R., 239
Wellek, René, 5, 235
Whitehead, Alfred North, 114, 120–22, 129, 138 n.15
Wiener, Norbert, 89
Wilbur, Richard, 110–11
Wilkins, John, 243
Williams, William Carlos, 64–66, 68
Wittgenstein, Ludwig, 190, 252
Woman, 183–84
Women, writings of, 8
Women's movement, 5, 8
Wordsworth, William, 102–3
Worringer, Wilhelm, 32

Yeats, William Butler, 29, 31, 45, 104

Zukofsky, Louis, 63, 64, 66

Library of Congress Cataloging-in-Publication Data

Early postmodernism : foundational essays / Paul A. Bové,
editor.

p. cm.

"This is a boundary 2 book, consisting of essays
previously published in that journal in the early 70s and
80s."

"A boundary 2 book."

Includes index.

ISBN 0-8223-1635-8 (cloth : alk. paper). — ISBN
0-8223-1649-8 (pbk. : alk. paper)

1. Postmodernism.   2. Postmodernism (Literature)

I. Bové, Paul A.   II. Boundary 2.

B831.2.E19   1995

149—dc20   95-6211   CIP